Chisungu

The girls kneeling in an attitude of humility

CHISUNGU

*A girl's initiation ceremony among the
Bemba of Zambia*

AUDREY I. RICHARDS

Introduction by
JEAN LA FONTAINE

London and New York

First published in 1956
by Faber and Faber Ltd

First published as a Social Science
Paperback in 1982 by Tavistock Publications Ltd

Published in the USA by Tavistock Publications
in association with Methuen, Inc.

Reprinted 1988, 1992, 1995 by Routledge
11 New Fetter Lane, London EC4P 4EE
29 West 35th Street, New York, NY 10001

Printed and bound in Great Britain by
Clays Ltd, St Ives PLC

British Library Cataloguing in Publication Data
A catalogue record for this book is available from the British Library

Library of Congress Cataloguing in Publication Data
A catalogue record for this book is available from the Library of Congress

ISBN 0-415-03695-X

In memoriam

BRONISLAW MALINOWSKI

Contents

Illustrations

Author's Preface to the Second Edition

I watched the ceremony described in this book in 1931, while I was doing field-work among the Bemba, the dominant people in the north-east of what was then Northern Rhodesia, and is now Zambia. I returned in 1933 for a year, but though I collected a number of additional comments on the rites known as chisungu (*cisungu*), I never witnessed another ceremony of the same kind. Twenty years later, when I published my account, such ceremonies seemed to be dying out in Africa; this book is therefore a record of what may now be quite extinct. Chisungu ceremonies were evidently held in the Bemba country when Cullen Gouldsbury and Hubert Sheane, then district officers in the area, took the excellent photograph of the interior of an initiation hut reproduced in this book, but though they gave an interesting analysis of the relation between the ceremony and Bemba marriage as then practised,[1] they gave no account of the ceremony itself, saying that they were not able to tell what went on inside the hut, and indeed, from our observation, it would have been hard for a man to secure access there. Twenty years later, there were already signs that the ceremony was dying out, although it must be admitted that when I did some work on the Copper Belt of Northern Rhodesia in 1934 I was asked to stay at Nkana mine in order to organize a chisungu ceremony there because the girls in urban areas were so very badly behaved—an invitation I did not feel capable of accepting. In this book, the present tense refers to practices current between the years 1930 and 1934; while such phrases as 'in the old days' and 'formerly' refer to customs which were then no longer evident.

[1] C. Gouldsbury and H. Sheane, *The Great Plateau of Northern Rhodesia* (1911).

Author's Preface to the Second Edition

The book first appeared shortly after *African Figurines* by Hans Cory, which describes the pottery figurines used in initiation ceremonies which resemble the chisungu. His book indicates their wide distribution in East, Central and South Africa, and their use as one of the teaching methods of the initiation rites. Figurines are also used in the Bemba chisungu: consequently Mr. Cory's fine set of photographs provide a valuable addition to this book. I am grateful for the opportunities he gave me to look at his collection, and for many talks I have had with him on the subject. My collection of the figurines I saw used in 1931 is now in the Ethnographic Museum of the University of Witwatersrand, Johannesburg.

Part of my account of Bemba marriage is derived from a paper entitled Bemba Marriage and Modern Economic Conditions.[2] Since this paper was out of print in 1956, I included some extracts from it in this book.

Songs and comments that I recorded during this chisungu ceremony have been reproduced here in Cibemba, the language of the Babemba. My spelling of the words reproduced is open to criticism. In fact Mr Patrick Mumba has already sent me forty or fifty small corrections, which are available to readers. But it must be remembered that spoken Cibemba is evidently changing rapidly, and may well differ from that used in 1931. It must be remembered also that my texts were recorded with pencil and notebook. The efficient recording apparatus now used by ethnographers was not available to me. Nevertheless, I thought it valuable to record the songs as actually sung during the ceremony as these are likely to be forgotten before very long. Cibemba is one of the many Bantu languages which have a complicated system of noun classes with different prefixes to verbs, nouns, and adjectives which involve a number of vowel changes. It therefore allows for many possible vowel changes and elisions. Terms in Cibemba are written here in the current orthography, in which the letter 'c' is used for the hard 'c' which resembles 'ch' in English. Since English readers would be in doubt about the pronunciation of the word *cisungu*,

[2] A. I. Richards, *Bemba Marriage and Modern Economic Conditions* (1940). Rhodes-Livingstone Papers No. 4.

Author's Preface to the Second Edition

I have rendered this throughout as chisungu. Initial vowels of nouns have been omitted, following dictionary practice.

A generous grant from the Wenner-Gren Foundation enabled me to write up this part of my field material, and the hospitality and secretarial help provided by Nuffield College allowed me to complete it. I am, like every ethnographer, grateful for the patient help of tribal informants to whom I refer in the text.

The book is dedicated to Bronislaw Malinowski, because it was his teaching that first led me to the study of primitive religion and magic. Some of his lectures on the mortuary ritual of the Trobriand Islanders are still vivid in my mind. They showed me how fruitful the careful analysis of a single rite could be.

A. I. R.
Cambridge

Introduction

J. S. La Fontaine

This book is a study of girls' initiation ritual from the woman's point of view. When it was published in 1956 there were few accounts of single rituals and fewer still of women's rites. In the twenty-five years since its publication there have been important developments in anthropological thinking about ritual but *Chisungu* has not been superseded. Most of the detailed studies of initiation have been of male rites; those that deal with the initiation of girls are either brief or unpublished. *Chisungu* itself has been out of print for several years, though the stimulus of Richards's ideas has been acknowledged by more than one author.[1] It seemed appropriate to introduce this welcome new edition with a brief survey of the interpretations of ritual that have appeared since the first publication. Today, religion is once more a focal issue in anthropology and the interpretation of ritual the centre of theoretical controversy. It will become apparent that many of these subsequent works develop ideas which appear in this pioneer book. Yet the topic of girls' initiation remains curiously neglected; to provide fresh stimulus for new work in the field is yet another reason for publishing a new edition.

The analysis of religion and in particular religious action, or ritual, raises central issues for anthropology. In 1956, British social anthropology had for some decades been focused on the study of social organization, to which the understanding of religion had been subordinated. As Richards herself noted in the Introduction to the first edition, anthropologists had long accepted Van Gennep's thesis that rituals such as *chisungu* were Rites of Passage that served to transfer individuals from

[1] See *The Interpretation of Ritual*, essays in honour of A. I. Richards and particularly Leach, The Structure of Symbolism, p. 273 in that work.

one status to another. However, they used an impoverished version of his ideas, shorn of the original concern with the details of ritual (see La Fontaine 1978). By contrast Richards emphasizes these elements and the cultural values they evoke. Chisungu is shown to involve human concerns with sex and reproduction, the birth and health of children involving, also, ideas about the continuity between past, present and future.

To Richards, such ideas are 'social' in origin, inculcated in the individual, however 'emotionally tinged' they may be.[1] Even though she writes of the 'function of religious rites in relation to the individual's needs and emotions' (p. 116) and insists on the necessity to record the 'feeling-tone of the actors engaged in ritual' (p. 56) she is referring to generalized sentiments in the Durkheimian sense, rather than the raw feelings of individual human beings. They relate to common and practical concerns, such as, for example, Bemba women's anxiety for the health of their children in an area where infant mortality is very high. Ritual, she argues, reflects these concerns, and 'It is for this reason that an analysis of the *chisungu* ritual should take into account facts and relationships that were omitted in the more straightforward institutional descriptions' (Introduction to first edition, p. 22).

As a pupil of Malinowski Audrey Richards is working from a basic concept of culture as a tradition that distinguishes a people and which includes the norms and values that constitute the framework of group organization and interpersonal relations. It also includes all that which is described in this book under the heading 'Ideology and Dogma'. The majority of anthropologists at that time, using the concept of structure derived from the work of Durkheim and Radcliffe-Brown, labelled such material cosmology and ignored it. Their interpretations of ritual do not take into account details of ritual costumes, objects and behaviour since a sociological approach concerns a different range of data. Gough's article on girls' initiation rites among the Nayar of Malabar (Gough 1955) is concerned with the nature of marriage and its connection with descent and affinity; it concentrates on those

[1] Introduction to first edition, p. 19.

details that relate to the structure of Nayar society. Gluck-man's discussion of ritual as a means of expressing social conflict [1] disregards much of the detail he sets out in his description. Part III of this book discusses sociological approaches to ritual and offers acute criticism of their deficiencies.

Richards's own study is intended to display the social context within which *chisungu* is set. She introduced the first edition of the book with a brief discussion of the force of blood, in particular menstrual blood, as a symbolic complex, but went on to write:

'Political and economic values are also 'taught' at puberty ceremonies and for this reason it is necessary, in order to understand their meaning, to have a background of knowledge of the social structure of the tribe concerned and of its dominant social values. This is particularly the case with regard to the Bemba chisungu, which is one of the tribe's two major sequences of ritual, and expresses many fundamental beliefs and values . . .'

Unlike her teacher, Malinowski, she makes use of the concept of social structure, introduced into British anthropology by Radcliffe-Brown. A section of Part I is devoted to it and concludes with the hypothesis: '. . . the chisungu . . . might be regarded as an extreme expression of the dilemma of a matrilineal society in which men are dominant but the line goes through the woman' (p. 51).[2] Nevertheless, this sociological aspect is subordinated to the cultural interpretation of *chisungu*. It was the original contribution of this book to relate the meaning of symbols to the structure of society.

The definition of symbols offered here has clear antecedents in Malinowski's description of myth as charter for institutions, but it goes much further than a mere analogy with myth and implies a theory of ritual. She writes: 'It is in the nature of symbols, whether they occur in dreams, speech or action to

---

[1] Discussed by Richards in connection with two articles published earlier than his better known *Rituals of Rebellion*, 1954.

[2] Compare Turner's conclusions on Ndembu initiation (Turner 1962).

become the centre of a cluster of different associations. The efficacy of ritual as a social mechanism depends on this very phenomenon of central and peripheral meanings and on their allusive and evocative powers' (p. 164), for 'All symbolic objects make it possible to combine fixity of form with multiple meanings, of which some are standardized and some highly individual' (p. 165). Turner writing on the Ndembu, another, similar, Central African people, uses a very similar approach to symbolism in the work that began to appear shortly after *Chisungu* was published. He defines a symbol as the basic constituent unit of ritual and presents it as unifying two poles of meaning: social and bio/psychological. Public structural meanings such as the identity of the Ndembu people or matriliny lie at one pole; at the other are such emotive concepts as mother's milk and the suckling of children, while in the middle can be found concepts of motherhood and womanhood. This 'fan' of meanings can be seen to underlie one of the central symbols Turner discusses, the *mudyi* tree whose sap is white latex. The similarity with the analysis in *Chisungu* is striking.

Yet the differences between the approaches of Richards and Turner are equally clear. Both Turner and Monica Wilson, who published her accounts of yet another Central African people, the Nyakyusa, in 1957 and 1959, make direct use of psychoanalytic insights. Wilson explicitly borrows from Freudian psychology while Turner's view is less specific, merely stating that the 'sensory pole' of symbolic meaning refers to the 'gross emotions' (Turner 1964). He and Wilson build individual emotions directly into symbolism, drawing on another discipline for meanings where these are not available to sociological analysis. Part of their interpretation of symbolism thus stands or falls on the assumption of the appropriate emotions in their informants and the actors. These assumptions are unverified; indeed the procedure by which public acts are interpreted in terms of the observer's attribution of emotional significance to the actors has long been regarded by anthropologists as unsound (see p. 119).

While Audrey Richards acknowledges her use of psychological assumptions and points to emotions such as those aroused by human blood or the uncertainties of 'growing up', she uses an approach in which the interpretation does not depend directly on these assumptions. Her description of the ritual gives an account of behaviour that indicates emotional states, a record of how the people looked, danced and spoke, 'which parts of the ceremony seemed to fill them with fear, excitement, boredom or a feeling of awe' (p. 56). She uses this material to indicate the critical moments of the ritual (see p. 138) but also to offer as data for the analysis that is the province of other specialists. She writes, 'Puberty ritual is of interest to different types of scientists . . . The psychologist studying symbolic behaviour, or the linguist interested in the ritual use of language, needs to know the whole system of symbols used if he is to draw deductions from the material' (p. 55). It is clear that the full interpretation of ritual requires the co-operation of several disciplines, and she argues, 'Single explanations of ritual behaviour, however satisfying to the observer, seem to me to deny the nature of symbolism itself . . .' (p. 169). As a result we have a wonderfully rich description, which includes the feelings, desires, and wishes of the actors, however ambivalent and confused they might be, but which segregates them from the aspect with which the anthropologist is concerned.

Conclusions about the social significance of the ritual and the objects used in it draw on the interpretations of informants, some of whom are specialists; the interpretations are not always consistent or clear. These variations are recorded, so that the observer's deductions may be distinguished from the actors' own interpretations. From the latter the anthropologist obtains understanding of the actors' intentions or expressed purposes, while the functions, or practical effects of the ritual, may be clear only to the observer. She thus avoids the methodological pitfalls that result in the circular explanations she criticizes.

Richards demonstrates the falsity of some earlier ideas about initiation. As she remarks, it was common to find anthropologists describing rites of initiation in terms of education; a common feature of such rites was the seclusion of candidates for a period under the authority of seniors. Such groups were often described as initiation 'schools'. Richards states that 'Most of the accounts of girls' puberty ceremonies in Central Africa contain such phrases as "the girls are then given *instruction* in sex and motherhood".' (pp. 125–6 italics in the original). Bemba women described *chisungu* in terms that make such an interpretation plausible: they emphasized, with repetition, that the rites 'teach' the girl, using the same verb *ukufunda* that they employed for teaching in European schools. Richards's own observation led her to the conclusion that 'the chisungu neither gives additional knowledge nor the right to use it' (p. 126). What the girls learn, in fact, are songs, with their associated moral referents and secret meanings, and some secret terms. Some of these will not be fully learned until they have witnessed the *chisungu* of other girls, when as newly initiated women they fulfil their duties to their mistress of ceremonies by helping her in subsequent rituals. The *chisungu* gives them access to secret knowledge that defines them as women.

A further expressed purpose of the *chisungu* is that it makes the girl 'grow'. Detailed consideration of the meaning of this phrase leads Richards to the conclusion that

'The women in charge of this ceremony were convinced that they were causing supernatural changes to take place in the girls under their care, as well as marking those changes . . . securing the transition from a calm but unproductive girlhood to a potentially dangerous but fertile womanhood' (p. 125).

She calls this the 'magic' aspects of the rite, following Malinowski's definition of magic, which is based, she states, on a distinction between magic and religion in terms of short- and long-term objectives (p. 112 fn.). Her interpretation of the statements by Bemba women brings out the complexity of the cultural associations that lie behind their words, and supports her argument that ritual is multidimensional and admits of no single explanation.

Introduction

A major part of what is revealed to the candidates consists
of the *mbusa*, which Richards calls 'sacred emblems'. The word
is glossed as 'things handed down'; they are 'referred to
directly in this way and this is said to be their value' (p. 146).
The mistress of ceremonies is *nacimbusa*, mistress of the
matters of *mbusa*, or of tradition. The emblems are objects
or drawings that embody tradition; great care and labour
are expended on their construction but they are ephemeral,
symbolic objects, which are destroyed soon after. They seem to
act as mnemonics for the moral 'lessons' of *chisungu* but they
are more than this, they are an integral part of the ritual, for
their names, and the songs associated with them, are part of
the secret lore of womanhood. They and the songs, dances, and
mimes range widely over the important values of Bemba
culture. Richards sets out these values in synoptic form
(pp. 140–5) to examine 'how far the values and beliefs [the
anthropologist] believes to govern the activities and relations
of a particular group are actually expressed or symbolized in
their rites'. The chart shows that *chisungu* is the pivot of the
ritual system and is the foundation for both the rituals of
chiefship and the cycle of agriculture ritual which was one of
the most important tasks of the chiefs.

Yet Richards indicates a difficulty in this kind of interpretation of ritual. She states: 'anthropologists are still
without a useful method of classifying tribal values in a way
which would make systematic examination easy' (p. 117).
This theoretical problem has still not found a solution. Both
'culture' and 'social structure' are insufficient as basic concepts
from which to approach the analysis of ritual. As I have
indicated, the concept of culture permits the anthropologist to
comprehend within a single framework a range of different
values; this allows for the interpretation of ritual details.
Thus a single perspective can include: the roles of men and
women and the value of children, ideals of marriage and chiefship, fertility and the respect owed to authority, whose
interrelations and representation in ritual can be set out. The
chisungu ritual can be shown to be linked to the institutions
of matriliny and chiefship, through the central ideas of the

dangerous power of fire, sex and blood. Yet these values cannot be ordered in a logical system, whereby certain values entail others in a logical hierarchy. The association between the ideals of marriage and those of hereditary chiefship can be shown to lie in the concern with the powers of the sacred trilogy, but logical priority cannot be given to any item in the cluster. Nor, and this is a particular weakness, can it be related directly to the observed everyday behaviour of members of any society except in terms of ideals which are adhered to or broken.

In discussing this new edition of her work, Audrey Richards remarked that she would wish now to emphasise the structural significance of *chisungu* more than she originally did. It is a question of emphasis, for the section entitled 'Social Structure' in Part I, and her discussion of 'The Chisungu in Relation to Tribal Dogma and Values' provides material organized by a concept of social structure. This concept of the constitution of groups and social relationships can relate ritual behaviour to secular behaviour and the 'realities' of economic and political power. The Bemba village has a core of related women, whose relationships are hierarchically arranged in terms of relative seniority. This principle pervades everyday life, even children display it in their games. In *chisungu*, as Richards herself notes (p. 191), 'more rites express the hierarchy of rank than any other form of symbolic behaviour'. The ritual that marks their emergence as women is a ceremonious and submissive greeting to their seniors in the village, in order of precedence. The *chisungu* constantly reiterates this theme in the song 'The armpit is not higher than the shoulder', which represents the ineluctable nature of such a hierarchy, condensing into a bodily metaphor the subordination of women to men, and of both to inherited authority and the seniority of experience that is acquired by age.

An awareness of Bemba social structure enables Richards to link the dramatization of subordination to recognized authority with the political economy of the Bemba. The key is her remark: 'the lack of any permanent form of possession makes rights over labour—here rights over the labour of the younger generation—of particular importance' (pp. 147–8).[1] The mistress of ceremonies interprets the rite of obeisance as 'They show they are willing to work for us' (p. 109). The power of senior Bemba women lies in their control of the labour of their daughters and, through them, their sons-in-law. What is underlined in the ritual, however, is not the mother-daughter link, but the generalized authority of older women: 'sex grouping cuts across those based on lines of descent'. The *nacimbusa* is a midwife, for the term has this meaning as well, and is expected to deliver the first child of each girl she initiates; she will become the girl's adviser throughout her married life, instructing her in all the practical and magical details of care of her spouse and children. The mother's role in rearing her daughter to physical maturity ends when she 'gives her daughter to the nacimbusa' who tests the girl's fitness for motherhood and admits her to the community of married women.

The association of girls' initiation ritual with matriliny is stressed at several points by Richards; Appendix A describes the distribution of such rites in Central Africa and their association with this type of descent system. The ritual itself seems not to stress descent, contrary to what would be predicted by a sociological theory. Moreover, the overwhelming ritual emphasis on marriage, on the subordination of a girl to her husband, found in the area as a whole, does not seem consistent with the observed realities that marriages were, and are, fragile, and that women have a great deal of freedom, after their first marriage, in deciding where they are to live. Such an emphasis is, however, consistent with the fact that villages must be built up by their headmen who persuade their kinsmen to join them. The basic relationships on which such a following is constructed consist of ties with, and through, women: wives, sisters and daughters (see Figure 1). Agriculture, though depending on men for the initial heavy labour, is the work of women. A man with a well organized labour force can produce food in unusual quantities,

[1] This insight has been developed by Bloch in respect of both kinship organisation and ritual (see 1974 and 1975).

Introduction

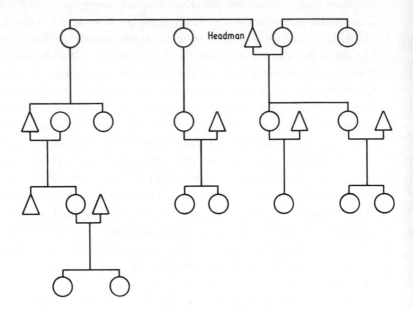

Fig. 1. Part of a Bemba Village.
(adapted from Richards 1950 p.b. edition p. 230)

and generosity with food is the mark of a leader. An enduring
marriage will bring to both spouses the control of others'
labour. In addition, for a man to qualify to approach his
ancestors he must have begotten a child in marriage; marriage
is thus a qualification for leadership. The emphasis on marriage is thus intelligible, though the lack of a similar stress on
matrilineal descent remains puzzling. It is not sufficient to
explain it, as Evans-Pritchard explains a lack of emphasis on
agnation in Nuer society, as 'taken for granted' and thus not
expressed.

In order to set out the social structural referents of *chisungu*
it is only necessary to identify the categories and roles
represented by the actors. Much of the ritual action, the
objects used, and the symbolic idiom are not relevant to this
purpose, as an inspection of the chart already referred to will
show. The work of anthropologists such as Fortes or Gluckman

shows this even more clearly.[1] Richards draws on Radcliffè-Brown's early work on the Andaman Islanders to show the social meaning of key symbols, relating them both to other rituals in which they occur and to central cosmological concepts. The book marks the beginning of a period in which concern with the meaning of symbols is a dominant theme. She suggests at several points that the analysis of symbolism, like the interpretation of dreams, is the task of the psychoanalyst. As I have already indicated, some anthropologists of the period drew directly on psychoanalysis in order to solve the problem of incorporating ritual with a theory of society.

Since *Chisungu* was first published, the impact of the French anthropologist Levi-Strauss has radically changed the approach to the analysis of symbolism. His work seems to provide a solution to this central problem. In his book on kinship and the early articles on myth, Levi-Strauss set out fundamental structures which, he claimed, lay beneath the surface of social life, producing both the structure of social life and organizing the symbolism of a culture. The essay 'The Myth of Asdiwal' demonstrates a method of relating environment to economic structures, kinship organization, myth, and symbolism in a single logical structure, built up out of simple pairs of concepts. (These concepts, it is implied, are universals of human experience.) A single myth is decoded for the underlying message, which cannot be 'read' from the narrative itself; it is generated by the combination of dyads into structures, which combine and recombine in multiple transformations. Myths communicate by repetition.

Levi-Strauss has concentrated on myth rather than ritual, although he has paid some attention to the latter. In his articles [2] ritual appears as the transformation of the myths of

[1] See also the consecutive analyses by Kuper (1944, 1947, 1973), Gluckman (1954), and Beidelman (1966) of the Swazi royal ritual, the *ncwala*. The last is influenced by the work of Levi-Strauss, which I discuss next.

[2] The Sorcerer and his Magic, The Efficacy of Symbols, both in *Structural Anthropology I* (1963). In *Structural Anthropology II* (1977) see Comparative Religions of Non-literate Peoples and Relations of Symmetry between Myths and Rituals of Neighbouring Peoples.

others, an inversion that occurs across space and defines differences between peoples. In *L'Homme Nu* (1971), the last volume of his great work on myth, he elaborates a general theory of ritual as the counterpoint of myth, recombining where myth fragments. It is too soon to see the effect of this exposition in anthropology generally, but his work on myth has already encouraged many attempts to transfer the method to ritual. Leach has interpreted a Tongan myth by a structuralist analysis of its charter myth and others have transferred a version of structuralist analysis direct to the symbols of ritual. As far as I know, no-one has yet related the symbolic structures of ritual to Levi-Strauss's elementary structures of kinship which have been so influential in studies of kinship.[1]

An underlying structure of kinship in the *chisungu* ritual links descent with the ritual's other major themes, and also with secular life, the 'realities' of economic and political power. It is as if several structures are superimposed so that each element in a pattern has multiple significance, linking different layers of meaning. If we start with the kinship structure we find matrilineal descent defined in opposition to the affinal links, which must be created, given the rule of exogamy. The main kinship roles in the ritual are those of the girl's mother, father, and mother's sister. The mother takes the role of a spectator and support to her daughter—it is she who is blamed if the girl fails her 'test' and the father's part is a small one although he may be providing for the ritual. The main kinship role is played by the father's sister. Another important role is played by the girl's bridegroom, who may also be represented by his sister or a cross-cousin. Both of the

[1] See the articles by Southall and Leach in *The Interpretation of Ritual* (1971), ed. J. S. La Fontaine. The Appendix (Leach) represents the outcome of a discussion between myself and Leach of the symmetry between the structure of the ritual and the fundamentals of Tongan kinship. What follows here is the view I was presenting him with then; he cannot be held responsible for it. For structuralist interpretations see also Rosaldo and others in Rosaldo and Lamphere (1974), Beidelman (1966), Needham (1973), though in the latter connection compare Beattie (1976). These are only a few of what could be a very large bibliography of recent work.

main roles are affinal ones, for the girl's father's sister is her mother's sister-in-law; she may also be her mother-in-law, for matrilateral cross-cousin marriage is the preferred Bemba form. Two lineages are thus represented in the ritual: the girl's own and her father's to which her father's sister and husband belong. It is an elementary structure in the Levi-Straussian sense (see Figure 2).

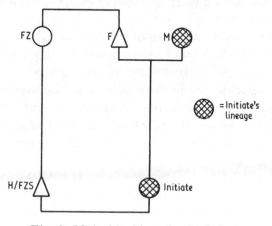

Fig. 2. Main kinship roles in Chisungu.

While the substance of a child is believed to come entirely from its mother, animated by her ancestral spirits, the Bemba regard impregnation as vital to the process of child-bearing. A husband initiates conception and is honoured for the gift of children he brings. The two lineages are thus in the position of givers and receivers of children. In addition a man must demonstrate his power to beget children in marriage before he may approach his own ancestors, so that in return for bestowing children on his wife, he is enabled to undertake responsibility for ensuring the continuity of his own lineage in ritual ways. Marriage is thus also an exchange between spouses; each has full adult capacity bestowed on him or herself by a member of an affinally linked lineage.

Mothers are barred from initiating their own daughters; women may, and commonly do, initiate their brothers' daughters, over whom they also exert the sanction of a curse which may destroy a girl's fertility. The *nacimbusa* gives an initiate protection for herself and hands over the marriage pot with which a wife purifies herself and her husband, preventing their mystically contaminating each other and harming their children. It is thus appropriate that she should be a father's sister, representative of the lineage that brought the initiate into being by a marriage in the preceding generation, and that initiates the girl's own child-bearing career, acting as midwife to her child.

The elementary structure of kinship is thus paralleled by a theory of marriage and child-bearing in which potency and ritual knowledge are bestowed by one lineage on another in order to activate the in-born powers of the members of the receiving group. The ritual knowledge is the property of women as a whole; it transforms a physically mature girl into a potential wife and mother. In this sense the father's sister/*nacimbusa* represents the community of women; she may also be the senior kinswoman in the village, outside her family, to whom a girl owes obedience and services. As *nacimbusa* she can expect help in subsequent rituals from her initiates; as father's sister she can command assistance in domestic tasks. The ritual thus removes the girl from her mother's sole control and gives her responsibilities in the community. It is in the light of this that we should understand Bemba women when they say they 'give their daughters to the *nacimbusa*'; they give up exclusive control of her labour. In exchange they will receive the deferential services of sons-in-law, who, in fathering children, 'found houses' in the lineage of their mothers-in-law.

The ritual role of the bridegroom is a dual one: he is represented as a chief, warrior, a lion. Elsewhere in the ritual he or his representative appear to burlesque the role of husband and raise laughter among the participants. (p. 73–5, p. 99). In the former sense there is a clear reference to chiefship, since the lion is the chief's symbol and bridegrooms are described and referred to as lions. A chief's mystical power is male potency in quintessence. Men are the initiators of action: husbands clear the bush for their wives' gardens; they sleep with their wives in order that children shall be conceived. A chief is responsible for the fertility and well-being of his people and country; he 'warms' the country and intercedes with his ancestors to ensure its well-being. The powers of a chief, like that of ordinary men, must be protected from pollution by similar taboos and all men, including the chief, depend on the knowledge of conjugal ritual in their wives. Wives are responsible for food, for the birth and rearing of children; a garden mound is the symbol of a wife, 'cultivated' by her husband. Yet it is knowledge of 'things handed down' that maintains the powers of husbands and chiefs, the knowledge of women. Innate (ascribed) power, or potency is dangerous; it must be kept pure by traditional ritual knowledge.

The chief's role is particularly fraught with danger; he alone can sleep with his wife on the site in the bush chosen for the future village to 'warm the country'. He is protected from the dangers of his office and installed in it by rituals which are 'owned' and performed by representatives of non-royal clans, who limit his powers but protect his potency (Richards 1960).[1] Chiefship, male potency and powers of reproduction all depend on outsiders, defined as being of opposite sex, different descent, or affines, not kin.

The *chisungu* uses all these abstract elements but it also emphasizes another: the authority of age. The subordination of the initiate to older women is an overt theme in the ritual. The very similar deference Bemba men owe to seniors receives only oblique expression but it is there. As a newly married man, a Bemba husband is a stranger in his wife's village, bound to work for his father-in-law and others of the village to whom he must defer in terms of utmost respect. Only when they are satisfied with him will they perform the final marriage ritual which will allow him to remove his bride from her village. It is as the father of daughters, mother's brother to younger kinsmen, that he has authority. The burlesque that is

---

[1] He is protected from the danger of first intercourse with his bride after her *chisungu* however. Another man 'eats the *chisungu* of the chief' (see p. 33).

performed by his sister may represent his subordinate role as son-in-law while the role of male representative of the affinal lineage and conferrer of child-bearing powers are represented in the final ritual, which he must perform himself. In the ritual observed by Richards, one of the bridegrooms was absent; significantly the role was taken by a male, his cross-cousin, not a female, his sister.

This last interpretation is somewhat speculative. We are on firmer ground in asserting the significance in the ritual of opposed male/female dyads: husband/wife and brother/sister. As Richards and others have shown, matriliny depends on the brother–sister relationship, the latter's children being the former's heirs. Brother/sister pairs appear in the *chisungu*, whose surface message concerns husband and wife. The role of the father's sister has already been set out, but there are other examples: sisters impersonate the bridegrooms, cross-cousins (children of a brother and sister) may substitute for one another, and there is an important rite (ninth day, pp. 82–3) which directly represents the relation of brother and sister. Two figures, male and female, represent brother and sister. They were interpreted as a brother comforting a sister whose father had died. The sister is described as depending on her brother; the reference to a dead father seems to emphasize that her marriage removes her role as child in a nuclear family under parental authority and associates her with the authority of her lineage, who arrange her marriage and protect her interests. Brother and sister represent male and female aspects of a lineage,[1] just as husband and wife represent distinct lineages. Each spouse thus stands for a brother/sister pair, linked in marriage.

Ultimately, the concepts of male and female form the foundation of the whole structure. The authority of age is stressed in the ritual but so is the solidarity of women and their power over reproduction. This theme is brought out by Richards as expressing the submission of wives to their husbands, and in her introduction she underlines the Bemba

---

[1] The mother and sister of the Paramount Chief, the Citimukulu, are also chiefs.

ideal of male authority and female submissiveness. However, she makes clear that age gives a woman not only greater authority, but power in the sense of control over others. The *nacimbusa* has both authority and power; she is, in many respects, the female counterpart of the chief and the parallel is symbolized in the right of great *nacimbusa* to wear the regalia of chiefs and be addressed with chiefly praise songs. The initiates are made submissive not only to their husbands but to senior women. Bemba women are regarded as independent by the men of neighbouring peoples and Richards tells us why this is so. Yet the *chisungu* appears to be a ritual expressing the dominance of men in Bemba society.

Under the influence of the structural approach of Levi-Strauss the definition of male and female has been the focus of much anthropological writing (Rosaldo and Lamphere 1974). While I have dealt with it directly elsewhere (La Fontaine 1981), its genesis is interesting and relevant here. Levi-Strauss has argued that all societies define themselves by marking the line between culture and the environment it transforms, defined as 'nature'. In Levi-Strauss's work the term 'nature' refers to the environment, including other human beings, which is the raw material *of* thought, ordered by the human mind through the binary structures of which culture is constructed. In this sense 'nature' is 'good to think with' but 'nature' also refers to a category *in* thought, a cultural concept which is contrasted to human society and culture. In the former sense it is a universal, for human beings think about the world they live in, and organize their perceptions in ways that define the world and their own society and that shape their behaviour. In the latter sense 'nature' is a concept in cultural repertoires, though it does not follow logically that it has the same content in all cultures where it is found. Failure to distinguish the two senses of the word has led to some confused 'structuralist' writing.

What is undeniable is that cultures represent their own social order as if it were natural and hence unalterable. The Bemba sing 'The armpit is not higher than the shoulder' and interpret this as saying that authority is given, an attribute of age and masculinity. Contributors to the volume edited by Rosaldo and Lamphere which I have just cited, and others writing in the same vein, have used a structuralist analysis, of culture in general and ritual in particular, to argue that in all societies the physical attributes of femaleness have been used to represent women as 'natural' beings and hence 'naturally' dominated by men, who represent 'culture' to women's 'nature'.

The Bemba data might also be interpreted in this way. A woman is represented as a garden, 'cultivated' by her husband; her bodily processes of menstruation and childbirth are dangerously polluting and must be controlled. However, it would be misleading, in my opinion, to accept this without question, for it is women's magical knowledge, owned and used by women, that transforms the girls into women. Moreover, what the *chisungu* makes clear is that successful womanhood is something that is taught and learned; it is not a 'natural' attribute, for a girl who has not had her *chisungu* performed is 'an unfired pot', 'rubbish' (p. 120). Richards's own discussion makes this point, although it is perhaps couched in terms which are less familiar now than they were at the time she wrote, and which therefore need some exposition.

In the Introduction to the first edition Richards wrote:

'In most societies there is some association in people's minds between the notion of sex maturity and that of social maturity, but in those cultures in which puberty ritual is most developed, the coincidence of the two is considered quite specific and the puberty ritual is either made the occasion of the assumption of adult roles in the political, legal and economic sense, or regarded as the first step in the gradual assumption of such roles.' (p. 18)

She continues: 'This two-fold aspect of puberty ceremonies is, to my mind, of great importance, for it gives rise to the variety in the types of ritual which mark this physical event.'

She goes on to argue that where the ritual concerns sets of boys or girls who acquire social maturity together, then the connection with sexual maturity is minimal, as Van Gennep had pointed out. By contrast, where sexual maturity is the main focus of ritual, individual ritual is performed. Later in Part II of the present work she discusses variations in the two variables of individual/group and sexual/social maturity by constructing a typology of such rites, in order to classify the *chisungu* ritual. Classifying *chisungu* as a nubility rite (although the book's title also describes it as an initiation) indicates that it does not emphasize physical but social maturity. Bemba girls go through an individual puberty rite at the time of their first menstruation; this is distinct from the *chisungu* and protects them and the community from the dangers implied in the pollution of menstruation (cf. La Fontaine 1971). Even the puberty ritual implies that the 'natural' attributes of physical womanhood must be culturally transformed. The *chisungu* itself may be performed for more than one girl; it precedes marriage and includes roles for the bridegroom. The label 'initiation ritual' clearly demonstrates that Richards considers the ritual as concerned with social roles. To use the terminology developed later, wifehood and motherhood are part of 'culture' not aspects of 'nature'. If one follows the line of thought indicated by Richards, who associates girls' initiation with the institutions of matriliny and hereditary chiefship, one is led to the recognition that women's roles are crucial to the structure of Bemba society and the distribution within it of rights to exercise authority.

Levi-Strauss, and those who have made use of his work, are, however, still limited by the concept of culture. For it is hard to see how the link between opposed concepts such as male and female, nature and culture, can be ordered in such a way as to demonstrate more than a mere association of ideas. Ortner (1964) argues that the association tells us that the terms nature and culture describe women and men; it could be said, and in my opinion more plausibly, that where such an association is made, nature and culture are symbolized by female and male. What is being asserted is not the dominance of men over women but the control of nature by culture.

Recently Bloch (1974) has criticized anthropological theories of symbolism for their assumption that ritual is

Introduction

merely a vehicle for the expression of meaning, neglecting the context in which symbols are embedded. Symbols are then discussed in isolation from the ritual sequence. By contrast, this book makes clear that ritual is, above all, purposive action. Richards's discussion of the expressed purposes of the *chisungu* (Part III) exemplifies her view that 'rites are invariably an effort to "do"—to change the undesirable or to maintain the desirable' (p. 113). Her description of the candidates presenting themselves at her door at the end of the ritual is given significance by the comment: 'In fact, the phrase "rite of transition" began to have a new meaning for me when I remembered the dirty frightened exhausted creatures who had been badgered and pushed through the *chisungu* weeks, and compared them with these demure and shy young brides' (p. 109). The *chisungu* aims to transform girls into responsible young women. As Richards states, 'It is a rite designed to change the course of nature by supernatural means and to test whether these changes have been brought about' (p. 121).

These insights make possible an understanding of initiation ritual as a whole (see La Fontaine 1977). The *chisungu* ritual includes ordeals, the successful outcome of which establish that the girls have indeed been changed by their experiences. These experiences are produced by the *nacimbusa*, using her knowledge of Bemba tradition which is represented in material form by the 'things handed down'. Such knowledge is the property of women, acquired and deepened over time. The success of the ritual demonstrates both the validity of the tradition, its power to transform, and the legitimacy of authority based on experience. The girls are material that is shaped, as the pottery models are shaped, by the experts; they are the occasion for the ritual but not its subject, which is the transformation of human nature into responsible social beings and the validation of Bemba traditional culture.

This rite described here was more elaborate than most of the *chisungu* rituals that were performed at that time. Even then some girls were married without being 'danced' and tradition was being steadily eroded by the economic and political changes that were the consequence of British colonial rule. However, as I have tried to indicate, this book contains more than a classic description of ritual no longer performed, although it does provide us with that, set in its social and cultural context. It also presents a plethora of ideas, which stimulate our thinking about ritual and social life.

References

Beidelman, T. (1966) Swazi Royal Ritual. *Africa* Vol. 36, No. 4: 372–405.

Bloch, M. E. F. (1974) Symbols, Song, Dance and Features of Articulation. *European Journal of Sociology* 15: 55–81.

—— (1975) Property and the End of Affinity. In M. Bloch (ed.) *Marxist Analyses and Social Anthropology*. ASA Studies. London: Dent.

Gluckman, M. (1954) *Rituals of Rebellion in South-East Africa*. Manchester: Manchester University Press.

—— (1962) (ed.) *Essays on the Ritual of Social Relations*. Manchester: Manchester University Press.

Gough, E. K. (1955) Female Initiation Rites on the Malabar Coast. *J.R.A.I.* 85: 45–80.

Kuper, H. (1944) A Ritual of Kingship among the Swazi. *Africa* Vol. 14: 230–56.

—— (1947) *An African Aristocracy*. London: Oxford University Press.

—— (1973) Costume and Cosmology: The Animal Symbolism of the Ncwala. *Man* (n.s.) Vol. 8, No. 4: 613–30.

La Fontaine, J. S. (1977) Ritualization of Women's Life Crises in Bugisu. In J. S. La Fontaine (ed.) *The Interpretation of Ritual*. London: Tavistock.

—— (1978) The Power of Rights. *Man* (n.s.) Vol. 12: 421–37.

—— (1981) The Domestication of the Savage Male. *Man* (n.s.) Vol. 16: 333–49.

Levi-Strauss, C. (1963) *Structural Anthropology I* (English edition). New York/London: Basic Books.

—— (1977) *Structural Anthropology II* (English edition). London: Allen Lane.

Ortner, S. (1974) Is Female to Male as Nature is to Culture? In Rosaldo and Lamphere (eds) *Woman, Culture, and*

References

Society. Stanford, California: Stanford University Press.

Richards, A. I. (1960) Social Mechanisms for the Transfer of Political Rights in Some African Tribes. *J.R.A.I.* Vol. 9: 175–90.

Rosaldo, M. Z. and Lamphere, L. (eds) *Woman, Culture and Society*. Stanford, California: Stanford University Press.

Turner, V. W. (1962) Three Symbols of Passage in Ndembu Circumcision Ritual. In M. Gluckman (ed.) *Essays on the Ritual of Social Relations*. Manchester: Manchester University Press.

—— (1964) Symbols in Ndembu Ritual. In M. Gluckman (ed.) *Closed Systems and Open Minds*. Edinburgh and London: Oliver & Boyd.

Wilson, M. (1957) *Rituals of Kinship among the Nyakyusa*. London: Oxford University Press for IAI.

—— (1959) *Communal Rituals among the Nyakyusa*. London: Oxford University Press for IAI.

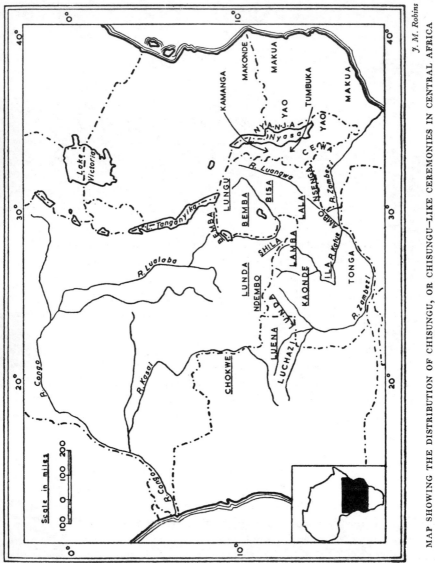

MAP SHOWING THE DISTRIBUTION OF CHISUNGU, OR CHISUNGU-LIKE CEREMONIES IN CENTRAL AFRICA

Territorial boundaries are marked thus: — · — · —

Tribes practising rites called Chisungu are underlined.

J. M. Robins

PART I

The Cultural Setting

☆

ENVIRONMENT AND ACTIVITIES

The Bemba were the dominant tribe on the North-eastern plateau of Northern Rhodesia. They have a centralized government with a paramount chief, the Citimukulu, whose empire formerly consisted of the territory between the four lakes, Bangweulu, Mweru, Tanganyika and Nyasa. The Citimukulus were the most powerful monarchs in this part of Central Africa and at one time they were able to exact tribute from as far north as Tabora in Tanganyika. The Bemba are still proud of their former position as a ruling tribe and feel that their traditions should be kept alive. Women as well as men are conscious of their superiority over the surrounding peoples.

The Bemba are a small tribe. At the time when these observations were made they numbered about 150,000. But they live widely dispersed over the plateau at a density of some 3·67 per square mile, in villages of 30–50 huts built at anything from five to twenty miles apart. Their territory is therefore larger than their numbers might suggest. The Bemba practise shifting cultivation of the slash-and-burn type. Their staple food is finger millet but they grow sorghum, maize, beans, peas and cucurbits. The growing of cassava is a modern introduction which does not feature, as does the cultivation of the other staple foods, in the chisungu rites.

The women are responsible for most of the food supply. To make a garden the men lop branches from the trees and the women pile them in the centre of a cleared patch so that they may be burned to form an ash bed on which the seeds are sown. The

25

dragging together of the branches is heavy work of which the women seem proud. It is their task also to select the seeds and sow them. They reap the main millet crop and dig and sow the garden mounds round the villages on which vegetables are sown.

The land of the Bemba is well watered but its soil is poor and it has a low yield per acre. There is an annual shortage of food which approaches famine in the worst years. This food shortage is probably greater now than it was formerly, owing to the constant emigration of able-bodied men looking for work in the mines. Yet hungry months seem to have been a feature in pre-European days, to judge from folk tales and the stories old men tell. For this reason, perhaps, great emphasis is placed on a woman's importance in controlling and husbanding the food supplies. Many forms of Bemba ritual centre round the production of food. There are, for instance, rites for sowing and reaping, first fruits ceremonies and prayers which precede the slashing of the trees before clearing new garden sites.

The Bemba live on high plateau land standing at a height of four to five thousand feet and this is covered with bush, scrub and low trees. It is typical savannah forest with few breaks in the vegetation except for the clearings formed by small river beds. The Bemba can be described as typical forest people. They depend on trees for the fertility of their millet gardens since they believe they can only sow their staple crop in the ash beds formed of burnt branches lopped off high trees. Bemba men are great hunters, and though game is not now plentiful, hunting, a forest pursuit, is considered the most pleasurable and exciting of activities. One of the most important forms of ordeal they perform is divination by hunting.

The bush also provides much of the people's food in the form of wild vegetables, mushrooms, honey and caterpillars. A Bemba woman must study and know the resources of the bush round her village since without such knowledge she and her family could not survive during the hungry months. A Bemba girl of about ten or eleven is able to distinguish carefully among the thirty or forty different kinds of mushrooms used and can tell which are edible and which are poisonous. Wood is also used for housing, the making of furniture and cooking utensils and for fire wood. The trees of the bush are believed to have magic properties as well as economic uses and even the most casual collection of 'medicines' will reveal as many as forty to fifty different trees with well-known magic properties.

The Bemba divide their world into village (*mushi*) and bush (*mpanga*). The village represents the civilized, orderly way of life and the bush a more mysterious, dangerous environment which must be cajoled to yield its resources for man's benefit. Spirits move about in the bush and trees can be used for their magic properties. As in other Bantu languages, the word for tree (*muti*) is also the word for 'medicine'. This distinction between the forest and the village, between the untamed and uncultivated sphere of life and the domestic and cultivated is constantly reflected in the chisungu and other rites.

There is little specialization in Bemba economy. Crafts are ill-developed. Men make clothing, baskets, mats, furniture, drums and other woodwork while pottery is the only craft in women's hands. As will be seen, the making of pottery images is an important part of the chisungu ceremony.

The Bemba had no form of storable wealth until the arrival of the Europeans. Houses were, and are, impermanent structures and subject to the ravages of white ants. They are constantly rebuilt and whole villages are moved every four or five years. Land is only cultivated for from four to eight years before it is returned to the bush, and garden sites are, therefore, not inherited. Cattle, the most common form of wealth accumulated by East African peoples, cannot be kept since the tsetse fly infests most of the area. Indeed a man had little to leave to his heir except his hereditary bow. The wealth of the Bemba consisted of the right to demand services from kinsmen and protégés and formerly from slaves, rather than of the accumulation of goods. The storing of food and its distribution to her household was one of the woman's most responsible obligations, since on its success depended the building up of a large family unit and ultimately a village. There was, however, little surplus food to be traded. Barter was ill-developed and markets non-existent. A certain amount of food was distributed from village to village in fulfilment of kinship obligations.

No cash crop had been introduced in the area at the time I studied it. In order to get a cash income Bemba men left the territory to look for work in the mining areas to the south. Between 40 and 60 per cent of males were absent from the area in 1931. Although this phenomenon probably only dates from the nineteen twenties it has already had such marked effects on the marriage system of the Bemba that it is reflected in the chisungu rite.

The environment of the Bemba is also responsible for those health conditions which are the source of many of their anxieties. Malaria is endemic and the figures for pulmonary disease were very high during my visit. The mortality of children of under three years of age was very severe. This was thought by medical experts to be due to the fact that children had no milk at all after they were weaned, usually between their second and third year; also to infections resulting in dysentery. Death in childbirth was not uncommon. Girls seemed to bear their first child immediately after puberty, at about 15 or 16 years. They received little skilled care either before or after childbirth, and the wide dispersal of the villages made it difficult for the Government to provide European medical facilities. The traditional processes of delivery were exhausting in the extreme to the mother and it was almost impossible for a Bemba midwife to secure conditions that her European counterpart would consider clean.

Bemba women seemed to accept the period of food shortage to which they had become accustomed but they were obsessed with the risks that their children ran and their magic was very largely concerned with rites designed to save their babies' health. The chisungu ceremony is a case in point.

IDEOLOGY AND DOGMA

The Bemba attribute their blessings and misfortunes to supernatural agencies, which are set in motion either by persons, dead or living, or by impersonal magic forces, good or evil. They do not believe in the dogma of chance.[1]

(*a*) The Personal beings include: (i) *the spirits of ancestors*

[1] I owe this term to Godfrey and Monica Wilson, *The Analysis of Social Change*, 1945.

(*mipashi*) mainly of the matrilineal line, which can be addressed at spirit shrines, the burial places of dead chiefs or in the huts of their individual descendants. They can also be born again with each new child, who acquires a *mupashi* as a guardian spirit, either from his mother's or his father's line, or from the royal dynasty of the territory in which he is born. These guardian spirits can also be inherited, and each dead man or woman is succeeded by a close relative of the same sex who acquires his or her name and guardian spirit.

(ii) *Malignant spirits*, (*fiwa*) who are the spirits of those who died with a feeling of injury because of some violent death, or who left the world with a sense of grievance. *Fiwa* return to strike their descendants with illness or misfortune.

(iii) *Living persons* who can produce good fortune by blessing (*ukupala amate*), which they do chiefly by calling on the ancestral spirits to which they have special right of address; or cursing, which they do through some less specified evil force. The blessings of a chief or a man in authority are particularly potent because of the great spirits such powerful persons have access to. The head of a matrilineage, or an important member of it can also bless in this way. A great social personage who has been injured or not given his due, is feared because he may withhold the blessings of the spirits, or actually pronounce curses (*ukutipa* or *ukulapishya*). The curse is specially important in relation to procreation and childbirth, since the malevolent wishes of the father's sister can produce barrenness in the woman, or impotence in the man. This is described as 'the great curse'. There are, however, a number of curses which can be used by injured people, who 'throw lightning' or are said to be able to 'throw lions', or who can threaten to curse, if their property is stolen, or when specially distressed by the treatment they have received.

(*b*) Impersonal forces include (i) *Magic* in general (*bwanga*), which is the force contained in the leaves, roots or barks of various trees or shrubs and a number of activating agencies (*fishimba*), such as parts of animals or human beings, which can be used by the specialist magician (*ŋanga*) for beneficent purposes (health, the production of crops, fertility and success) or for harmful purposes (illness, death or crop failure). *Buloshi* is evil magic or witchcraft, handled by people believed to have supernatural powers.

(ii) *The magic influence of sex, blood and fire* which, when brought into wrongful contact with each other, are thought to be highly dangerous to every Bemba, but particularly to babies and young children, who are believed to be vulnerable to so many dangers; and to chiefs, on whom the prosperity of the land is held to depend. This system of beliefs is extremely complex, and yet it is necessary to try to understand it, if the meaning of the chisungu is to be grasped. The dogma relating sex and fire is the *idée maîtresse* behind most of the ritual behaviour of the Bemba.

Briefly speaking, sex relations according to Bemba dogma make a couple 'hot'. In this state it is dangerous for them to approach the ancestral spirits in any rite of prayer or sacrifice; and any chief or headman who attempted to perform such a ceremony without purification would run the risk of bringing disaster on his district.

he chief's shrines are guarded by old women or hereditary priests who keep sex taboos. For the chief to be casual in keeping sex taboos, or to approach his ancestors without purification is 'to spoil the land' (*ukuonaula icalo*).

All persons of sex maturity are in fact distinguished by a special term (*wa kuboko*) and are excluded from a number of rites on the ground that they are 'hot', or are likely to be 'hot'. Such people can pollute the fireplace of a hut by touching it, and then a baby fed with gruel cooked on this fire might sicken and die. Parents who do not purify themselves after intercourse run the risk of killing their children by accidentally touching the family hearth. Adulterers are more dangerous still, as they cannot purify themselves since the necessary rite can only be carried out by husband and wife. Small babies and their mothers are therefore kept away from beer drinks where 'bad' people congregate drinking round the fire without care. The baby's gruel is often cooked on a separate hearth and in a separate pot. The art of Bemba motherhood in fact consists very largely in guarding children from danger from fire. A newly born baby is 'unripe' (*mubishi*) and is in a specially precarious position until it has been 'taken' by its parents (*ukupoka umwana*) by an act of intercourse and the lighting of new fire, when it is a few months old. To save the baby, it must be 'brought to the fire' by being held over the flames of a doctored fire when it is first placed to the breast, or when the cord falls off (*ukumwalawila*). If its father is away and the ceremony of 'taking the child' cannot take place, the baby is given medicine (*umuti wa lueshya*). The mother and the midwife extinguish the old fire, mud the hut and light a new fire. Then they carry the baby to the men's shelter where there are presumably many youths 'with heat' or 'with bad things', or to a kitchen where the people have been known not to have done the purification ceremony. In this dangerous company, they give the baby gruel cooked on the new fire to make it immune. The rite of *ukumukokotola* is a ceremonial spitting of raw food on the baby by a menstruating woman so that the baby can be safely touched by a woman who is in this condition. All these methods are believed to secure immunity on homoeopathic principles.

The chief's sacred fire, the fire of the land, must be protected with even greater care. It is placed in a separate hut and watched by a senior wife, past child bearing. The chief's food is usually cooked by a man and not a woman.

To remove the dangers due to sex intercourse a special ceremony is required and this is one which can only be performed by a legally married couple. Hence the close links between the rules of ritual and those governing marriage ties, and the great importance of magic belief in determining the strength of the marital relationship. At marriage each girl is presented by her paternal aunt with a miniature pot about $2\frac{1}{2}$ inches in diameter which must be guarded with the utmost secrecy. With this the purification rite is carried out. It is filled with water and placed on the fire, man and wife each holding the rim. Water from the pot is then poured by the wife on to her husband's hands, and some say on to the wife's as well. New 'pure' fire is then relit either by means of fire-sticks, or, as is usual nowadays, with matches. This apparently simple rite is the essential act which removes the condition of hotness from the body of man and wife and renders them free to touch a hearth with impunity or to approach the ancestral spirits. Some say that it used to be performed after each sex act and others that it was merely done before some ceremony of special undertaking such as harvesting. It is still spoken of with the utmost secrecy and shyness and still survives even in the face of strong opposition from missionaries. In the ritual life of a chief the pot ceremony is of particular importance.[1]

The ritual links uniting a married couple are thus particularly strong in this society. It is husband and wife who perpetually carry out the dangerous act of sex together, who thereby put themselves in each other's power, and who depend on each other for the ceremonial purification which neither can carry out alone.[2] The marriage relationship is ritualized from the start.

On important ritual occasions, such as the 'warming' of a new village site, the installation of a chief, a marriage, a death, or the protection rites for a young child, the old fire must be extinguished and a new fire lit with fire-sticks or matches, and the floor of the hut freshly mudded over. These are signs that the pollution is definitely removed. The fire is also harmed by objects or persons that are 'cold'. Contact with a dead body makes a fire cold, or contact with a menstruating woman, who is described in polite speech as 'being in a state of coldness' (*Akuba na mpepo*) or as 'fearing fire' (*atina umulilo*). People who eat food cooked on the fire by such women are liable to illness.

The most constant danger to the family fire is in fact the touch of the housewife herself, when she is passing through her periods. Then she must be careful not to touch the family fire that her husband or her children use. She has her own small fire separate from the main fire, and if it goes out, she can only borrow from a woman past child-bearing or a girl who has not reached puberty. Intercourse with her husband would be almost unthinkable for her during these days and there are heavy penalties attached to the showing of the menstrual blood by accident. A girl who allowed a drop of blood to fall on her husband's bed or who washed in the stream where others washed is thought to threaten illness to those near her. I was told she would be punished by her fellows by being made to sit over a fireplace till her flesh was scorched.

At the end of a period the old fire is extinguished; a ritual act of intercourse takes place and a new fire lit (*ukusangulula*), the word used for the similar purification performed after a village has been polluted by death.

[1] Cf. my *Land, Labour and Diet in Northern Rhodesia*, 1939, p. 365.

[2] Only the head wife of a polygamist can perform the pot cermoney for him. Hence the legal and ritual difference in status between her and her co-wives.

A murderer or a lion-killer can also harm a fire by being 'hot'. They have done something fierce and must not eat cooked food without purification. The clue to the solution of a murder case trial during my stay in the country was discovered by a Bemba detective who overheard the statement that on such and such a night, *X* and *Y* did not eat with the other men. 'They were eating their food cold'. In other words they had not yet been purified, and could not come near the common fire and hence could be presumed to be murderers.

It is difficult to exaggerate the strength of these beliefs, or the extent to which they affect daily life. In a village at cooking-time young children are sent here and there to fetch 'new fire' from neighbours who are ritually pure. Women in their periods call their sisters to cook for them. Young married women are seen sitting outside beer parties, and explain 'I have a young baby'. All the medicines have been taken and the protective rites done, but there is always the possibility that an adulterer might touch the fire when he is drunk and the beer might be polluted thereby.

There are other sources of danger. The first intercourse with a girl after her initiation ceremony has been performed is considered to be a perilous act. It is carried out with special ritual precautions and in the case of a chief, it must be undertaken by a special court official, (*kaulu*), who takes the risk on himself. This man must 'eat the chisungu' of the girl before she is taken to the chief. Yet, in spite of this danger, it is this act above all others which initiates the ritual relationship between husband and wife and it is valued on this account, so that a young man can claim damages if his betrothed has been seduced after her initiation ceremony, but before the marriage, for it is said that the chisungu of the girl has been stolen from him in this case.

One of the most fatal acts of all was for a girl to bear a child before she had been initiated or before one of the more abbreviated rites now performed at puberty was carried out. Her child would then be a creature of ill-omen—*wa mputula*—who would bring misfortune on any village in which it lived. The child would be a portent of evil. It would stop rain falling. It would make the granaries empty quickly. It might bring dissension. The father and mother of such a child should therefore be driven out into the bush with their baby to save the community from danger.

The penalties which fall on those who come in contact with polluted fire are always envisaged as illnesses, mainly of the chest (*cifuba*) and such complaints are very common in Lubemba as we saw. It is important to notice too that the punishment falls on the innocent and not the guilty. The adulterous woman who touches her hearth-stone causes her husband to fall ill 'of the chest' if he accidentally comes near the fire. The father who is 'impure' through illicit intercourse 'kills his child with fire' (*ukumuipaya umulilo*) so that the baby starts to waste away and then to die.

The reader will have gathered that strong mystic links are thought to exist between husband and wife. Though marriage appears unstable in Lubemba compared with the unions contracted by some of the patrilineal Bantu in South Africa, yet the destinies of husband and wife are mysteriously joined. If one partner dies, the other must sleep with some social equivalent of the dead—a brother or uterine nephew or a maternal grandson in the case of a dead man, or a sister or granddaughter in the case of a dead woman. This is to 'take the death off' the living partner. A member of the dead man or woman's matrilineage has to fetch back his or her spirit from the living spouse and makes him or her free to remarry.

But this is only one example of the belief that the guardian spirit (*mupashi*) and the blood of man and woman mix in sex relationships. Women of loose morals in Northern Rhodesian towns are said to bear few children because they 'mix the blood' of Bemba and men of other tribes. Again, a man who sleeps with two women unites the three in a relationship that is magically perilous. The blood is mixed (*mulopa uasakanya*). If woman *A* commits adultery with *B* and the legitimate wife of *B* sees the blood of *A* from a scratch, a tattooed mark or during menstruation, then she, the guiltless partner, will die at once unless saved by the right medicine. So also if *X*, a man, sleeps with the wife of *Y*, and *Y* sees the blood of *X* by misadventure, then *Y*, the guiltless partner, will die.

For mother and daughter to sleep with the same man, albeit unknowingly, is a terrible thing. For an adulterer to pass the dead body of his mistress's husband, or any other man who has slept with her, is also a danger to all the men concerned. These triple relationships are constantly mentioned in court cases and are made the subject of claims by the injured family of a dead man or woman who declare that 'their child' has been killed in that way. They recur in narratives of the rather lurid sex lives of Bemba princesses who are expected to take many lovers, but must not bring trouble on the land by simultaneous relations of this kind.

Lastly, in common with many Bantu peoples, Bemba believe that, if a man commits adultery while his wife is pregnant, the baby is born dead. He has taken the spirit of the child (*asendo umupashi wa umwana*). If the woman is unfaithful while she is pregnant, then she herself dies in childbirth unless she confesses and gets medicine in time.[1]

I have dilated on this system of attitudes and beliefs because I think it fundamental to the understanding of Bemba puberty ritual and also because it cannot fail, I think, to strike the field-worker in this area as one of the basic elements of tribal dogma. It would be impossible to live long in a Bemba village without running constantly across instances of the effects of these beliefs whether in terms of ritual or in the most practical problems of cooking, catering and entertaining. If the Bemba can be said to have an ideological obsession in the sense that they are constantly pre-occupied with one set of fears, it is this belief in the magical potency of sex, fire and blood. Such emotional attitudes set us puzzling problems. In this chapter I shall confine myself to stating them. Later in the book I hope at least to suggest some hypotheses which may stimulate comparative research in other tribes holding similar beliefs.

To recapitulate, Bemba dogma stresses the role of the ancestors in determining human fortunes as well as the power of injured spirits, who revenge the injustices they suffered on earth on the

[1] It will be seen from the above that the causes of barrenness or death in childbirth are numerous among the Bemba. Barrenness may be due to the special curse of the father's sister; to an injured spirit returning to punish a descendant at random; to allowing the umbilical cord of a baby to fall to the ground; to adultery; or to witchcraft. Miscarriage is thought to be due to an injured spirit shaking the womb of the pregnant woman so that the baby falls out; when it occurs all the women of the matrilineage must be treated with medicine. Death in childbirth is due to the adultery of the mother herself.

living. It also emphasizes the magical powers associated with sex which is linked with feelings of guilt and anxiety expressed in the taboos clustered round marriage, childbirth and the rearing of children. This feeling of guilt is so widely diffused that innocent people are thought to suffer from the magical results of a sex mis-demeanour committed by someone else.

These beliefs support the institution of marriage since safety from magical danger is acquired by means of a ceremony which can only be carried out by a man's head wife. No Bemba supposes that a husband will be kept from adultery by this means, but the legal wife is the only person who can secure him and those near him from the resultant punishment.

The reader is asked to bear in mind, without attempting further analysis, the association that exists in Bemba ideology between chieftainship, fire, sex and power to influence the fertility of the land and its people, and to remember that these powers are hurt by blood, intercourse out of marriage, death, murder, lion-killing and all cold, terrible or 'bad things' (*fibi*). Fertility which is so much desired is produced by conduct pleasing to the ancestors, and to senior and especially paternal relatives, the blessings of persons in authority and the carrying out of the ritual of marriage. Illness is inflicted usually on the innocent party, by sex relations out of marriage without ritual purification, by bad conduct, and because of injury to people who, since they have died in a state of righteous indignation, will 'come back' to haunt the family which did them wrong.

SOCIAL STRUCTURE

The most characteristic features of the Bemba social structure are its hierarchical and authoritarian type of government, of which the apex is a paramount chief believed to have supernatural powers; and its system of matrilineal descent with uxorilocal marriage.

The political structure of the Bemba is a centralized one. Its unity under a single head, the *Citimukulu*, was achieved, in 1931 at any rate, because of a belief in the spiritual powers the king was thought to control rather than to any very efficient executive machinery.

This political structure has been described by me elsewhere.[1] It is sufficient for my present purpose to explain that all the chieftainships in Lubemba were held by members of the royal clan (*bena ŋandu*). The paramount chief, the Citimukulu, traced descent through some thirty-one generations. He was chief in his own particular territory, but paramount over the whole country over which he was believed to exert supernatural powers. He also commanded the army in the old days and was head of a supreme court of appeal. He enforced his powers by inflicting brutal punishments, such as mutilation, selling into slavery, and death. He also had the right to preside over the poison ordeal which was administered to suspected witches. He was supported but also controlled by hereditary counsellors who were in charge of the chiefly ritual such as the ceremonies at the burial of all kings, princes and princesses, the rites performed at the ancestral shrines of the tribe, the care of the king's fire and decisions over succession cases.

Below the king were a series of territorial chiefs or princes.[2] These were his own brothers or parallel cousins. These were arranged in order of precedence. On the death of a chief the prince next in genealogical succession succeeded him. The king and the chiefs each had power to exact tribute and labour from his own territory. Each had his own court for his own territory. Chiefs were also in charge of shrines to the royal ancestors of their particular territory. They performed their own series of agricultural rites and kept their own sacred fire. These prince-chiefs had sub-chiefs under them in some cases and these were nearly always also princes of the royal blood. Below these sub-chiefs were headmen of villages. A man obtained the right from his chief to inherit a village from a dead headman by matrilineal succession or to build a new one if he had persuaded others to follow him to form a new community. Villages frequently moved as has been explained.

---

[1] 'The Political System of the Bemba of North-Eastern Rhodesia', in *African Political Systems*, edited by M. Fortes and E. E. Evans-Pritchard, 1940.

[2] All members of the royal crocodile clan (*bena ŋandu*) are princes, but all are not appointed to chieftainships. For this reason the term 'chief' will be used for princes holding these offices and 'sub-chief' for the lesser princes under them.

There was no permanent property to bind a man to one area rather than another and men moved easily to live with one relative or another. The headman's prime difficulty was in fact to persuade relatives to join him or if they had already done so to persuade these kinsmen not to leave him!

The headman could command small gifts in tribute and a little service. He also had a shrine to his own personal ancestors and performed ceremonies for the good of the village. He purified the village by an act of ritual intercourse with his chief wife and his fire was regarded as the fire of the village.

Princesses had an important part to play in the political system. The mother of the Citimukulu was known as the Candamukulu and she ruled over a small territory in the king's district and was thus in the position of sub-chief to him. The same was true of another royal princess, the Mukukamfumu who also had a sub-chieftain-ship in her own right. Both these princesses had important ritual functions to perform in tribal ceremonies.

The Bemba are organized in matrilineal clans distinguished by totemic observances, stereotyped forms of greeting between clan members, joking relationships with paired and opposite clans,[1] and honorific titles. Clan members reckon descent from a common ancestress and her brother, and they tell the legendary tale of the first arrival of these forebears in the country. They remember the villages where their ancestors first settled, although neither the clan nor any of its subdivisions can be regarded as localized groups at the present day. Clans are ranked in some kind of precedence, according to the order in which their ancestors are thought to have arrived in the country from the west.

Within the clan great emphasis is laid on the principle of matrilineal descent. Ancestors are remembered in prayers before the shrine of a head of a family. Here a man will pray to the spirit of his maternal grandfather or maternal uncle, if the latter is already dead. The spirit of a maternal ancestor is thought to quicken the child in its mother's womb and to protect it all its life. The name of this ancestor or ancestress is discovered by divination, and given to the child. When a man dies his name, his

[1] See my 'Reciprocal clan relationships among the Bemba of North-Eastern Rhodesia', in *Man*, vol. XXXVII, 1937.

kinship duties and his hereditary bow are passed on to his sister's son or to her grandson through a daughter. The heir actually becomes the dead man in a social sense: he adopts the kinship terms the latter used, calling, for instance, 'maternal nephew' the person he would previously have called 'brother'. The same positional succession takes place in the matrilineal line for women, and a dead woman will be replaced by her sister or a maternal granddaughter. In this system women are honoured as the bearers of many children and such a woman is said to found a house.

In the case of the royal crocodile clan the maintenance of descent is even more important. All senior chieftainships in Lubemba, the country of the Bemba, are held by members of the royal lineage.

A successor to such a chieftainship has access to 'great spirits', those of his dead predecessors, and he not only prays to them at the sacred shrines in his capital, but he acquires supernatural powers in his own person, so that he can bless and curse. His good health and vitality bring blessings to the community, and his ill-health or death, the reverse.

Princesses have the special duty to bear fine children in order to provide the country with chiefs, and they are honoured for doing so. The spirits of royal women are mentioned in prayer in tender and grateful terms as 'those who carried us in skins on their backs and gave us suck'. The first ancestress, Bwalya Cabala, is buried in a grove which is one of the most sacred places in Lubemba.[1]

Bemba clans are not segmentary. The effective kinship group within the clan is a three or four generation group, the men and women who trace their descent to a common great-grandmother and who remember a village of origin (*cifulo*). These are not corporate matrilineages in any territorial sense. The kinship system makes for a great deal of movement from village to village during a man's or a woman's life. The villages themselves change in composition and move from place to place following the shifting cultivation.

There appear to be no fixed leaders of the matrilineage, except in the case of the royal dynasty, but this group is the unit of succession to the offices and the names of dead men and women and to their ancestral spirits.

[1] Cf. *Land, Labour and Diet in Northern Rhodesia*, p. 357.

With this system of matrilineal descent the ties between a woman and her brother are very close. The woman produces children who are the heirs of her brothers. The man is the natural guardian of his sisters' children, and he must be consulted about his uterine niece's marriage and could claim the right to marry her where he pleased. He could protect her after her marriage if he wished to do so. The mother's brother could generally claim possession of his sister's children if her marriage broke down. In the old days he could give one of the children as a slave or a blood-wite to the head of a family to whom he or one of the lineage group owed reparation. He could command the services of his sister's son and bid him follow him to war. The woman in her turn could command the services of her brother's daughter and was thought to be able to bless or curse the fertility of the latter's marriage. Brother and sister can take each other's property and behave in a free and easy way with each other.

Marriage is uxorilocal among the Bemba and among kindred tribes such as the Bisa, Lala, Lamba, Cewa, and Kaonde which also perform a kind of chisungu ceremony. A young man who marries goes to live in his wife's village where he builds himself a hut and becomes a member of her extended family. This is a domestic and economic unit. The sons-in-law work together under the father-in-law and the daughters with their mother. The man gives service to his father-in-law rather than cattle or other goods as in most other Bantu societies. A young couple has no cooking fire of its own to begin with. The girl cooks with her mother and sends food to her husband at the man's shelter, where he sits with his friends. At first the couple have no granary of their own and no gardens and when they acquire the latter, later in their married life, the gardens are cleared near those of the rest of the extended family group.

As a family group of this kind grows in size, its head often chooses to separate from the old village and to start a new one of his own. Hence the desire of a Bemba to have many daughters in order to be able 'to found a house'.

After the marriage has been established, and children have been born to the union, it remains a question for individual decision whether the husband is given permission to remove his wife to the village of his own matrilineal relatives or whether he will remain for ever with his wife's relatives. In the old days, when conditions of life were more precarious, there is evidence that fathers were unwilling to let their daughters go away from home during times of war and raiding. When I was in Lubemba a man was allowed to remove his wife to his own village if he had produced children by her and shown himself to be a steady fellow. The decision seemed to depend on the relative personality and status of father-in-law and son-in-law. As I have shown elsewhere,[1] a chief was above the tribal rule and could marry virilocally, as could a polygamist in the case of a second wife. A man of rank or of good behaviour could certainly remove his wife within a few years, as could a man called to succeed to his maternal uncle's position, but during the year of my visit there were still men who had remained as 'strangers' in their wife's villages all their married life.

It will be seen at once that the pivotal relationships of the extended family, which is the basic residential unit in Bemba society, are the ties between a mother and her daughters. It is the women who attract the husbands who increase the community and it is they who usually remain in charge of the children when the young fathers go away to work in the mines. In fact a group of sisters living with their mother become so attached to each other and their joint way of life that one of them will sometimes refuse to follow her husband to the latter's village when he wants to move, and her marriage may then break up.

It will be seen, too, that there are several sources of tension in this type of kinship system. First the ties of loyalty which bind a man to his matrilineal descent group clash to a certain extent with the obligations he owes to his local group, his wife's extended family. At marriage he is separated from the very relatives with whom he is legally identified, and from the mother's brother to whose position he will ultimately succeed. He is in a galling position in many ways. He lives in a community based on kinship traced through women and he is economically dependent on his wife's people and working under their orders. Sometimes the bride-

---

[1] 'Some Types of Family Structure among the Central Bantu', in *African Systems of Kinship and Marriage*, edited by A. R. Radcliffe-Brown, 1950.

groom finds the early years of married life so irksome that the union breaks up and he returns to his own home. Bemba recognize the difficult situation of the son-in-law and make jokes at the expense of the young bridegroom alone in his wife's village without kinsmen to support him. On the other hand, if the husband can live through these first years and the marriage proves itself stable, he can himself acquire status and prestige as head of his own extended family with sons-in-law working for him, whether he moves to one of his own relative's villages or stays where he is.

The second source of conflict is, of course, that between the father and the mother's brother for the control of the former's children and this is a tension inherent in the matrilineal system. The Bemba father is head of his own extended family and is the chief authority in his children's lives during their early years. He has rights over his daughters' marriage payments, and over the labour of his sons-in-law; his sons may decide to live with him, if he is a man of rank and popularity. Nevertheless the mother's brother is the legal guardian of the children, as we have seen, and can command his uterine nephews' services and can control the marriages of his uterine nieces if he pleases.

The Bemba girl is also in a position of conflict when she marries. She is happy with her mother and sisters in a village to which she belongs, but her husband may demand to take her, after a few years of married life, to some other village where his own relatives live. These difficulties are overcome if the husband marries within the village and there are various forms of preferential marriage, with the daughter of the father's sister for instance, which do not involve the moving of the girl from her mother's home.

In the case of a successful marriage which has endured for a number of years and has resulted in the birth of several daughters both the man and the woman reach an advantageous position. The father is head of an extended family and whether he lives in his wife's village, in his mother's brother's village, or has managed to start a small community of his own, he is in a position of power and authority. The woman in her turn, wherever she lives, has a group of closely related households co-operating with her. If she remains in her own village her married sisters will be near her; if she moves to her husband's village her own married daughters will probably follow her there. Thus, though the difficulties of achieving a stable marriage in Lubemba are great the rewards for achieving such a union are high.

THE MARRIAGE CONTRACT

A traditional Bemba marriage was contracted by gradual steps, a series of stages, generally marked by ritual, by which a young man became incorporated in his wife's family by dint of joint residence and by exchange of his services for food and general support from his relatives-in-law. To reach a stable Bemba marriage the relationship between the two groups had to reach a fine equilibrium based on sentiment, shared economic tasks and an accepted division of rights over the children of the union. It had always something of the trial and error nature about it, during the first years of married life, and it still had these characteristics in 1931.

To contract a marriage a Bemba bridegroom makes a series of small payments to his relatives-in-law and does several years' work for his wife's father or mother. In return his wife's parents feed him entirely for a year or two, and give him substantial support for a larger period. To European eyes the husband gets the worst of the bargain since the labour he gives his father-in-law can never be returned in case of divorce; but Bemba consider the hospitality of the bride's family and the many presents of 'respect' they offer the bridegroom as a substantial contribution. I have seen a young man leave his tribe because he thought his mother-in-law was 'stingy' and lacking in respect. It is the women of the family who are responsible for honouring the son-in-law in this way. The husband gives a betrothal present (*nsalamo*), which is a token such as a copper bangle or, nowadays, a small coin. The main payment is the *mpango* which consisted formerly of two or three barkcloths but is now a sum of money, which averaged 8/- on 72 marriages I recorded in 1934. The *mpango* is given to the parents during the preliminary negotiations, or later, to legitimize a union not contracted formally. The bridegroom also used to pay money to his father or mother-in-law for organizing his bride's chisungu ceremony and gave a bark-cloth or money to the mistress of the ceremonies for 'dancing his bride'.

The characteristic feature of the old Bemba marriage was the small size of the payments in comparison with those made in the cattle marriages of the Southern and Eastern Bantu. The *mpango* gave the father those limited rights he secured over his children, although it did not, in this matrilineal society, give him complete control over his son or daughter, and never gave him, or his lineage, control over his wife's reproductive powers as does the cattle *lobola* among the Southern Bantu.[1]

The stages by which the marriage relationship is gradually developed in the case of a girl's first union are as follows:

(*a*) *The betrothal (ukukobeka)*—literally 'to hook yourself down a branch from a tree'. Boys and girls meet at dances during the harvest season, or when visiting from village to village. The young man then proposes to the girl and sends his betrothal present (*nsalamo*). The boy's family should give approval but this did not seem essential in 1931. The consent of the girl's parents and her mother's brother and father's sister was, however, a necessary step in marriage negotiations.

The betrothal ceremony was usually accompanied by an exchange of beer and cooked food between the families. The *ukukobeka* was not however considered a very serious or binding step, but merely one stage in the trial and error process of contracting marriage. It often took place during the childhood of the boy and girl.

(*b*) *The courtship visits (ukwishisha)*. The bride and her friends then visit the bridegroom in his village. The girl friends may laugh and talk with the boys they visit, but the bride, if she is nearing puberty, or has reached it, must sit with downcast eyes and will only be tempted to enter her future husband's hut by a little present and will only talk to him if he gives her another small gift.

(*c*) *The boy's move to his bride's village*. If the bridegroom has reached puberty, he then moves to his father-in-law's village and builds himself a hut and starts to work for his wife's family.

[1] The extent to which the introduction of money payments has altered the old Bemba marriage system is fully discussed in my *Bemba Marriage and Modern Economic Conditions*, Rhodes-Livingstone Institute Paper, No. 4, 1940.

The Marriage Contract

The ceremonial admission of the son-in-law to the wife's village takes place in stages throughout the next few months or even years. These include:

(d) *The food offerings.* The ceremonial offering of cooked food to the bridegroom is considered exceedingly important by the Bemba and both parties to the marriage watch eagerly to see if the presents have been made with due respect. When first betrothed the young man may not eat the gifts of food sent him by his mother-in-law as he is still keeping food taboos. He divides the food among his friends. Then one of his supporters is bound to say casually 'The stranger's child (i.e. the outsider) is wasting with hunger'. This is a hint that the big feast of admission of the son-in-law should take place. All the bride's family are asked to bring beer, meat or porridge and each dish must be covered carefully with a basket and a small gift, such as a bangle, laid on top. Bemba delight to describe this feast in great detail and it is represented in mime in the chisungu ceremony. The bride's family then says to the mother of the bridegroom 'We have shown the son-in-law the fire, now he will eat food with us'. The boy nevertheless has to be made free to eat each different food used by the tribe. He is given a small dish of porridge one day, then beans, then meat, then fish. This is known as the formal presentation. Similar ceremonial removal of taboos takes place with regard to the bride entering her husband's village among some of the Southern Bantu.

(e) *The handing over of the bride.* The giving of the bride to her husband also takes place in a number of stages. At first the young man asks for someone to sweep his hut and to fetch him water and his betrothed may be allowed to do this for him. Having gradually won the right to her domestic services, payment gives him the privilege of taking his young bride to sleep with him. This stage of the marriage continues until the young girl is about to reach puberty when her mother will take her away for fear she bears a child before her chisungu ceremony.

(f) After this comes the chisungu ceremony which is the subject of this book and this is followed by the consummation of the marriage. The bride must be tempted by gifts to enter her husband's hut. Ritual surrounds the first act of intercourse, and when the marriage is consummated the bridegroom throws a burning log out of his hut to the crowd of waiting relatives outside. This is proof of his virility: the women shrill their plaudits and the men shout. The bride is given her marriage pot at dawn by her father's sister, and then follows the presentation of the bride and bridegroom to the community. Later comes the setting up of the fire-place for the girl and still later, perhaps after a year or two, the giving to the son-in-law of his granary and his garden.

The form of social structure I have described exists in a culture in which there is no permanent form of property, such as land or cattle, which could bind the members of a kinship group together or link one generation with the next. Consequently, social relations in Bemba society consist very largely of the giving and receiving of services.

Wealth consists of the power to command service such as a chief calls for from his subjects, a headman from his villagers, a father-in-law from his son-in-law, or a mother's brother from his maternal nephews. Service could also be demanded in the old days from surrounding tribes which were raided for slaves.

Service makes it possible for a man to put big fields under cultivation, to build a big granary and hence to be able to feed more workers in another year.

Service was given to the chief in return for food provided at the capital and also the supernatural powers on which the people believed they depended. Service was given to the headmen from some of these motives also, but the headman was also usually a relative and he received these dues in his capacity as head of a kinship group. Those not so closely related he had to attract by a nice mixture of authority and the formal expression of courtesy.

In such a society the ceremonial expression of respect by kneeling to a superior, clapping hands before him, offering him food in a specially formal fashion, or even rolling on the back is characteristic. Men should creep into the presence of their chief, throw themselves over on their backs and roll from side to side clapping their hands; the abject humility of the gesture is striking to the European observer. In such circumstances it will be readily understood that the father-in-law attracts his son-in-law not only by the economic support he provides but by much formal giving of food for which the women in the household are almost entirely responsible. The son-in-law in his turn behaves respectfully towards the elder members of his wife's family. The tensions which I have described as inherent in a matrilocal marriage system of this kind make these presentations very significant in maintaining a family and village structure which, as I have explained, is one of rather precarious balance.

Accepted sex roles. Social structure, as I have used the term here, consists of a series of social roles which are associated with membership of the different social groups of which the tribe is composed, or with different status positions in it or with formalized relationships, such as that of subject to chief. In the present connection the roles which are of special interest are those based on sex and age and the social behaviour expected of husband and wife.

The ideal of a Bemba in the old days was military success and with it the exaction of tribute and slaves from conquered peoples. This is arrogantly expressed in the phrase 'We Bemba cultivate with the spear and not the hoe'. Patient industry in agriculture was not as much admired as the power to command service from others. The ability to attract followers by generosity, the elegant exchange of courtesies, and by personal popularity was highly rated. The organizing powers and judgement which are essential to the achievement of either of these aims are admired in themselves.

Thrift and the slow accumulation of property are not admired since they cannot be achieved in terms of Bemba economy. Children are brought up to share everything they have with the group they are with and easy and even reckless giving is praised. Bemba also admire display of all kinds, but here, as may be imagined, the display is not so much of personal possession but of followers and adherents, who walk about with a man of note and praise him.

Bemba admire ceremonious behaviour in personal relations, exact forms of address, the recognition of social precedence and rights to respect, and the avoidance of quarrels, unpleasantness and 'scenes' which might disturb the delicate balance of village relations. They praise suavity and self-control in personal relations. They delight in circumlocutions and allusive speech, and seem sophisticated in social contacts, as compared with their neighbours, the Bisa.

47

The Cultural Setting

Bemba ideal behaviour is that of the *mwina umusumba* or man living at the court, as distinct from the *mwina impanga* or inhabitant of the bush; the country bumpkin.

A commoner is expected to be loyal to the death to his chief, and to accept the fact that his rulers have the right to all his time and all his possessions. He must be silent and respectful. Members of the crocodile clan are expected to be arrogant and even ruthless, but they must be generous in feeding their adherents.

Extreme deference is paid to age. Each child knows his exact position of seniority in a group of village children and is given precedence in games. Each group of men sitting in the village shelter does the same. A younger child is scolded for putting itself forward before its elders.

Bemba women share many of these ideals. They work for their chief in his gardens and make the same abject obeisance to him. They have a lively interest in the ritual centred in the court. They play an important part in attracting followers and kinsmen to a village. A headman's following or 'crowd' (*bumba*) is attracted by means of beer, good entertainment and company, and these depend both on the successful organization of labour, which is largely a man's job, and on the wise and tactful distribution of food, and happy personal relations, which are mainly in the women's sphere.

Women, unlike men, are admired for industry and for resource in finding food in the bush. They are honoured for bearing and rearing many children and for courage in childbirth which is often, under Bemba conditions, a terrible ordeal. They are expected to be loyal to their own sex and to accept the domination of older women.

In the sphere of tribal life women have an important part to play, or rather one that is thought to be important. As we saw, two senior princesses have districts of their own; and junior princesses often act as village 'headmen'. In all these cases they wield political authority but are regarded as chiefs with feminine attributes, that is to say, with more gentleness and hospitality to the needy. They are not expected to be ruthless in discipline. They have male counsellors to advise and support them. Besides these real political functions the senior women have important ritual duties since, like their 'brothers', they are in charge of

A young mother's pride in her first baby

Nangoshye, the mistress of ceremonies

Chisungu solo dance outside a hut

ancestral shrines. They are also the potential mothers of future chiefs and provide their brothers' heirs. Senior princesses stride in and out of their brothers' royal enclosures, advise them, hector them and borrow their things. The senior wives of chiefs are also honoured highly since they hold in their charge the royal fire and they can, by their conduct, destroy or maintain the supernatural powers of the chief. They are thus able at any time to 'spoil the land'.

In courts of law women can plead their own cases; this is most unusual in the patrilineal societies to the south. When contracting their first marriage they are under the control of their fathers' and their mothers' brothers, but they are fairly free to contract second marriages at their own wish. They are certainly able to break a marriage contract with much greater ease than women in patrilineal Bantu societies who pass under the control of their husband's patrilineage on the transfer of cattle at marriage, and divorce is rather frequent in this society. Bemba women have the reputation on the copper belt of Northern Rhodesia for being quite unmanageable by men of other tribes. Such men shrug their shoulders, raise their eyes to heaven and say 'These Bemba women! My word! They are fierceness itself'.

Compared to many patrilineal tribes, the Bemba women seem to have a high status. Parents welcome the birth of girls since they bring husbands into their village and build up its strength. Daughters become founders of new lines since the succession passes through them. When they first marry they are under the very definite authority of their relatives, but they are 'at home' whereas their husbands are outsiders from other villages. They have the support of their parents and may form part of a solid phalanx of married sisters, and they are therefore in an extremely strong position. As they become mothers and grandmothers their authority increases. Teknonymy is practised and women are called by the names of their sons or daughters with the female prefix 'na' On the birth of the first grandchild their name is changed to grandmother of so-and-so—this is a title of respect.[1] The Bemba woman is shy and submissive as a girl, but once a grandmother she

---

[1] E.g. Na-Kampamba = the mother of Kampamba;
Nakulu-Canda = the grandmother of the Canda.

often becomes imperious and managing and obviously enjoys her position as she sits on the verandah of a large hut, directing operations and dividing food. This is the position a woman achieves by a stable marriage, and one which she longs to achieve.

Sex relations are openly desired by Bemba and celibacy for men or women is not admired. A girl who rejects men is criticized as having 'pride of the womb' (*cilumba ca munda*). Abstinence is only practised for ritual reasons, by a woman nursing a child, for instance. Adultery in women was, however, savagely punished in the old days and is a cause of divorce. It is still thought to cause death in childbirth. Men are not very seriously criticized for adultery although it is thought a terrible crime for them to 'kill' their children by not submitting to the purification rites.

The two sexes are divided in everyday life as regards their work and recreations. Men sit in their own shelter at night and eat together there. Women, on the other hand, are grouped round their own house verandahs. Men have their own economic tasks and women theirs. Girls do not enter marriage with any ideal of companionship with their husband. A young couple is not expected to show affection in public and a bridegroom tends to be despised for spending time with his wife. But affection grows over the years in the case of a stable marriage.

There are certain obvious contradictions in the husband's position. Menfolk are dominant in Bemba society. Women used to greet men kneeling, and they still do so on formal occasions today. Men receive the best of the food and take precedence at beer drinks and on other social occasions. They speak first in family matters. Men are expected to take the initiative in sex affairs. Women are married (*ukuupwa*—the passive form) while men marry (*ukuupa*—the active form). Girls are taught to please their husbands and are considered responsible for giving them pleasure in sex relations. Women calmly accept the fact that their husbands will beat them 'when they are young and their hearts get hot quickly'.

The contradiction between the masterful male and the submissive son-in-law, between the secure young married woman backed by her own relatives and the submissive kneeling wife, is one which first struck me forcibly in the course of the chisungu

ceremony. This contradiction, I think, finds expression and perhaps resolution in the chisungu which might be regarded as an
extreme expression of the dilemma of a matrilineal society in
which men are dominant but the line goes through the woman.

PART II

The Ceremony

☆

THE RITUAL TYPE

Puberty ritual among the Bantu peoples can be divided into the following types:

(a) *Puberty ritual proper*, that is to say, ritual acts which take place immediately after the first signs of physical puberty have appeared and which are directly concerned with this physical event. They appear to be designed to give magic protection to both the adolescent and his or her family, from the magic danger associated with the physiological change. Rites of this kind concern the individual rather than the group and they are rarely elaborate since there is not time for the collection of food and drink for a big ceremony. In fact such ritual acts commonly occur in cultures in which the fear of puberty is most pronounced, and it is thought dangerous even to wait for a few days before securing the necessary protection for the boy or girl. They often precede a more elaborate initiation ceremony.

In the case of boys, individual puberty ritual takes place among the Natal Nguni, the Nyasaland Ngoni, the Shangana Thonga and some of the Northern Sotho. The ritual is not elaborate or prolonged.

In the case of girls the ritual marking of physiological puberty occurs among most of the Nguni and Shangana Thonga; among the Northern Sotho it precedes the girls' initiation schools such as the *byale* of the Pedi or Lovedu. Among the Venda it precedes the *domba*, a fertility rite for boys and girls.

(b) *Nubility ritual and fertility cults.* Most puberty ritual is, in some sense, nubility ritual since it is a preface to marriage; but

52

some such rites directly precede the marriage ceremony and are considered so much a part of the nuptials that it may be difficult to distinguish between the two. Such ceremonies seem to be limited to girls. They are sometimes only concerned with the first marriage of a girl, and are believed to provide protection against the magic dangers associated with the first act of intercourse in legal wedlock.

Nubility rites invariably include fertility magic of one sort or another, but Bantu societies also provide examples of group rites for adolescent girls and boys which follow puberty, or are associated with it. These appear to be fertility cults carried out for the whole tribe, as well as a preparation for individual marriage. The *domba* of the Venda which culminates in the famous python dance is described, for instance, as a means of preparing boys and girls for marriage and securing fertility for the community. The *Boxwera* schools for boys of the Northern Sotho and Tswana and the corresponding *byale* for girls follow a circumcision ceremony and are described as closely associated with fertility. The Lovedu of the Northern Transvaal practise individual puberty rites for boys, followed by a circumcision ceremony, a *boxwera* ceremony and finally a *komana* ceremony, which is a form of rain ritual. For girls there are individual puberty rites, followed by a long *byale* ceremony.

(c) *Puberty ritual associated with initiation into age grades.* These are mainly group rites for boys or girls and vary between ceremonies designed to initiate boys into an adult status, and those which mark the entry to the lowest rank of an elaborate system of age sets, such as are characteristic of the Nilo-Hamitic and some of the Nilotic peoples. Such ceremonies may be limited to boys alone or they may provide for parallel initiation for boys and girls. Where groups of adolescents are initiated together it is obvious that the ceremony may have to be postponed for years or months after a particular individual has reached puberty; the individual's social maturation becomes a far more important element in it than the sexual.

(d) *Puberty ritual linked with the joining of special associations.* Here the adolescent joins, not only an age grade, but a secret society with special magical functions and social privileges. Admission to the society is usually limited to certain sections of the community and entry is often purchased as a privilege rather than required as a duty. The *butwa* society of the Western Congo is a case in point.

(*e*) *Maturation rites dissociated with puberty.* The complete separation of puberty rites proper from those of social maturation is seen in those societies where the one is followed by the other. Among the Akamba of Kenya for instance there were triple ceremonies for boys and girls; these included simple puberty ceremonies for individuals followed by the 'small initiation ceremonies' at which circumcision took place, and the 'great initiation ceremonies', only performed occasionally, for adult men who had reached special wealth and honour in the tribe.

The Bemba chisungu is an individual nubility rite practised for each girl, or for two or three girls together and it is preceded by a short puberty ceremony proper. When a girl knows that her first period has come she tells older women and they must 'bring her to the hearth' again (*ukumufishyo peshiko*), or 'show her the fire' (*ukumulanga umulilo*) since her condition has made her 'cold'. This is done by rites which vary slightly from locality to locality. The *ukusolwela* ceremony is one in which doctored seeds are cooked on a fire and the girl must pull them out and eat them burning hot. In another rite she is washed with medicine cooked in a special pot and she drinks this medicine too. She is then isolated indoors for a day or more and fed with a small ball of millet porridge cooked in new fire so that she may be made free to eat again without harming herself or others. This is the usual Bemba way of returning to the community a person who has passed through an unusual or dangerous state.

The girl then waits till it is convenient for her chisungu ceremony to be danced. I call this latter a nubility rite since it is clearly considered as a preliminary to the marriage ceremony; indeed, Bemba accounts frequently confuse the two. Formerly the girl came to her chisungu already betrothed, and this is usually the case today. The bridegroom plays a part in the rite in his own person, or is represented by his sister. He contributes to the cost of the rite by paying the mistress of the ceremonies. The chisungu protects the young couple against the magic dangers of first intercourse and gives the bridegroom the right to perform this act, which is thought to be entirely different from all that follow it, in or out of marriage. Anyone who takes this right from him is said to steal or spoil the chisungu.

The actual ceremony I witnessed will now be described.

The presentation of this type of ritual material raises difficulties. The chisungu ceremony I attended in 1931 lasted continuously for over a month. (I was told that in the old days the rites would have spread over six months or more.) During this time I saw over eighteen separate ceremonies in the initiation hut and surrounding bush; each of these can be split into a number of simpler ritual acts the symbolism of which was as obscure to some of the observers as it was to me. Over forty different pottery emblems were made and handled during the ceremony and a number of others have come to my notice since that date. The walls of the hut were painted with nine different designs on the occasion in question.[1] I recorded over fifty special chisungu songs during the rite and I should estimate that those I was able to take down formed a little over half the total sung.

The rites include dramatic episodes which could not fail to strike the imagination of any onlooker, but these were interspersed with days and nights of incessant dancing, which were wearying even to watch. They are likely to be even more tedious to read about.

It would, of course, be possible to make the material more readable by rigid selection, and the Bemba themselves eliminate detail in the most ruthless fashion when providing outline accounts of the chisungu to European enquirers. (See page 135.) But if an account of a series of rites is to be given at all, it must surely be complete. Omission merely reflects the anthropologist's own threshold of boredom. Puberty ritual is of interest to different types of scientists. There is, for instance, no full account of the nubility ceremonial from this area and, to the ethnologist interested in mapping out the affinities of different cultural groups of the area, the presence or absence of a particular detail of ritual may be of the utmost significance.

The psychologist studying symbolic behaviour, or the linguist interested in the ritual use of language, needs to know the whole system of symbols used if he is to draw deductions from the material. I have, therefore, given all the song and mime data I

[1] Vernon Brelsford has published line drawings of sixteen others, cf. 'Some reflections on Bemba geometric art', *Bantu Studies*, vol. XI, 1937.

have. Moreover, I have thought it necessary to add to the straight-forward description an eye-witness account of the behaviour of the people concerned. How did the people look, dance and speak? Which parts of the ceremony seemed to fill them with fear, excitement, boredom or a feeling of awe? What were the comments made and the views held? This is an addition to detail already wearisomely full, but I believe it adds rather than subtracts from its interest. In spite of the mass of literature on primitive ritual that exists, it is extraordinary how few of the accounts we have give a clear idea of the feeling-tone of the actors engaged. This places a duty on those who have had the fortune to witness a long ceremony to record their impressions of it fully. Without such detail, it is impossible to study the function of a ceremony in a particular culture or of ritual as a whole.

I have endeavoured to lighten the reading by page headings. These should make it possible for the reader to pick out elements of particular interest and to separate the eye-witness account of the ceremony from the interpretation. I have also relegated the chisungu songs to an appendix at the end of the book.

THE ACTORS IN THE CEREMONY

The owner of the ceremony (mwine). Plans for a chisungu ceremony are initiated by the parents of a single girl or by two or three sets of parents whose daughters reach puberty at roughly the same time. These parents provide beer and food for the ceremony with the aid of the parents of the girls' betrothed. The father and mother of the girl engage a mistress of the ceremonies (*nacimbusa*) to organize the rite. In the old days they had to provide bark-cloth for her payment. Nowadays she seems to receive between five and ten shillings as well as an additional present from the bride-groom. This formerly consisted of a bark-cloth but is now more often a blanket or a few shillings.

The man or woman who provides for a ceremony is known as the owner or *mwine*. The owner is not necessarily a parent. A chief will commonly provide for the chisungu of a young wife betrothed to him before puberty, or for his maternal nieces or sisters. Men of rank will also provide for ceremonies carried out for their sisters, daughters or grand-daughters as well as for their own daughters. In fact, it increases the reputation of a man of substance to be able to hold such a ceremony. He is said to 'dance the chisungu' of so-and-so (*ukumucindila icisungu*).

The mistress of the ceremonies (*nacimbusa*).[1] The *nacimbusa* organizes the rites, leads the dances and songs, and arranges for the making of the pottery and other emblems required. She is considered to perform a very important service. It is work that demands a detailed knowledge of ritual, industry in carrying through long and even arduous tasks, organizing ability, tact and personality. A successful *nacimbusa* probably has unusual intellectual ability as well as leadership and the power to attract women from surrounding villages to attend a ceremony and to keep a body of helpers alert and interested for some weeks. The *nacimbusa* is usually an elderly woman who has proved herself to be a successful midwife. The same terms are used for both roles. She is commonly, though not by means always, a member of the royal clan, and there is a tendency for the office to be hereditary. A *nacimbusa* will teach the secrets of the chisungu to her brother's daughter, to whom she owes special obligations, and from whom she can demand service, and she may also teach them to her own daughter. But mere heredity is not enough. A young woman must build up a reputation sufficient to win the confidence of parents so that they will call her in to 'dance their daughters' for them. To do this she must show assiduity in attending local ceremonies and attach herself as a special helper to the *nacimbusa*. She must show capacity and personality, and make a name for herself as a successful midwife. I heard from one old woman that a form of initiation of young *banacimbusa* took place in the old days, and that they were rubbed with medicine and paid an initiation fee, but this account was not substantiated.

The *banacimbusa* are treated with great consideration by other women in the community. In the old days they were allowed to wear a feather head-dress (*ngala*), which was reserved for certain chiefs and hereditary counsellors. They were given respect at a chief's court and have to report the carrying out of each chisungu ceremony to the chief. I am not sure whether this is still done at

[1] The plural prefix for nouns describing persons is 'ba'. Hence *banacimbusa*, or *banacisungu*.

present, but *banacimbusa* are rather wealthier than their fellows owing to the payments they receive, and they carry themselves with considerable dignity and circumstance.

The *nacimbusa* stands in a special relationship to the girl she has initiated throughout her life. She will probably deliver the girl's first child and act as *mbosua*, or special guardian, to the baby.

The messenger. In the old days when the exchange of feasts formed a more important part of the ceremony than they do now, the *nacimbusa* was assisted by a woman known as the *nakalamba*, who was employed to invite the guests to the ceremony by rolling on the ground in front of their houses—the Bemba form of obeisance to a chief. They also fetched clay for the pottery and supervised the ritual cooking of the food.

The candidates and their bridegrooms. The initiation candidate is known as the *nacisungu*. As I have said, these girls were usually betrothed before the ceremony, but it was possible to carry out rites in the case of a girl who was not yet affianced. The bridegroom of a betrothed girl takes part in certain of the ceremonies under the title of *shibwinga*, and this term is also extended to the sister or cross-cousin who may replace him in certain parts of the ceremony.

The relatives. Other relatives include the girl's parents and her father's sister. The girl's mother is responsible for providing food and beer, and her father's sister is believed to have a special influence over the fertility of her paternal niece and to stand in a special relationship to her. But the ring of relatives is comparatively small. The uxorilocal family is the chief unit involved.

The character of the rite. The chisungu is a popular ceremony involving much dancing and singing. There is a special drum-beat characteristic of chisungu ceremonies which is frequently used at ordinary beer feasts and always used throughout the rite. Drums are beaten inside the initiation hut, and on the dancing space outside, but they are also carried wherever the women go, some miles out into the bush and back again. The singing is accompanied, as always among the Bemba, by the beat of the drums and by the clapping of hands. Some songs are peculiar to the ceremony and are necessary parts of the rite, but some can be sung at other times. All the chisungu dances are of a characteristic type. They are solo performances with a definitely dramatic character, and are not round dances of the kind usually seen on the village ground of an evening.

Dancing among the Bemba is done for amusement, but it may be also done 'for respect'. Commoners will dance for their chief: a young man will dance for an older woman or man; a senior man may dance for a senior woman of his wife's family. In such dances of respect it is common for the soloist to dance in front of the person he wants to honour, and to sing definitely to him or her. It is particularly respectful to dance with vitality and dash. I have frequently heard headmen rebuking a crowd of bedraggled young women brought out to dance for me in the rain. The phrase was always the same: 'Rejoice, can't you? Do you want people to think we have no respect? Go on, there! Try to rejoice.' In the chisungu ceremony this type of dance of respect is as important a way of carrying out obligations as the provision of food and beer. It is no mere accident that the chisungu is described as 'dancing the girl'.

The mimes representing domestic and agricultural life are usually more serious performances. They sometimes involve real play-acting and the exact imitation of the animal or the behaviour of the person concerned. In most cases, however, what I have described as mimes are formalized representations of an action, such as pounding grain or sowing seeds, and they tend to resemble the rather stereotyped movements of a kindergarten singing game in this country.

The term 'sacred emblem' is used throughout this account. I have selected this word to translate a Bemba word, *mbusa*, which means 'things handed down'. The *mbusa* are of various types, but they may all be considered as secret in the sense that they either have a secret name or a secret meaning. They are of three types. The first of these are the pottery emblems. These are a series of models of common objects made of fired clay, usually painted with white, black and red. Some of them represent domestic objects (a water pot, a hoe or a pipe), some animals or birds (a crocodile or an egret), some are fertility symbols, and some represent historical characters. Many of them are realistically modelled and easily recognizable, while others are conventional pot designs each with a name. A certain number of designs are common over the whole district although there is individual variation in their modelling, while others seem to be of local distribution. I made a collection of about forty-three myself, but think there are likely to be twice that number either made or still remembered in the Bemba country. Each of the pottery emblems has its name and its song.[1]

Larger models of unfired clay decorated with beans, soot, chalk and red dye, are also made in the chisungu hut during the ceremony, and destroyed the same evening. They include, for instance, an enormous snake the coils of which cover the whole floor, a figure of a man and a woman, and lion made of logs covered with clay and with a head of hair. These are also described as *mbusa*.

The second type of *mbusa* are the wall designs. These are rough designs painted on the inside of the initiation hut at a certain stage in the ceremony. Most of them are conventional patterns with names and secret interpretations. Nine of these designs were used in the ceremony I saw, but Brelsford has recorded twenty others.

The third type of emblem consists of small bundles of objects representing the domestic life of the Bemba, that is to say, essential food of the tribe, such as millet, sorghum, meat, dried fish and salt, as well as fire wood, snuff and the red camwood dye known as *nkula*. Certain groups of trees used in the ceremony are also known as *mbusa*.

THE CEREMONY

The chisungu ceremony that I attended started at Cisonde village near Chinsali on June 1st, 1931. Chinsali is a Government station. It consisted at the time of two European officials' houses,

---

[1] H. Cory has collected many hundreds of these figurines from Tanganyika tribes. His book, shortly to be published, gives an account of their distribution, together with a number of illustrations. See also his 'Figurines used in the initiation ceremonies of the Nguu of Tanganyika', *Africa*, vol. XIV, No. 8, 1944. The Venda, Lovedu, and Vandau of Portuguese East Africa also use figurines. Schofield considers the Bemba figures similar to the pottery images found at Zimbabwe, cf. 'Pottery images or mbusa used at the chisungu of the Bemba people of North-Eastern Rhodesia', *South African Journal of Science*, vol. XLI, Feb. 1945.

The Ceremony

Government messengers' quarters, and some stores. The big Church of Scotland mission of Lubwa, with its teachers' training school, lay a few miles away. It was therefore a matter of some surprise to me to hear that the ceremony was to be carried out in a village so much in contact with European civilization. The reason was, I think, that the mistress of the ceremonies (*nacimbusa*), Nangoshye, was a sister of the head Government messenger and living under his protection. She was a woman of some position in the neighbourhood and reckoned herself as of royal rank although she was only a member of a junior branch of the royal clan. She had an unusual personality, great organizing power, and a sharp tongue that sent her fellows scampering to carry out her commands. She was extremely anxious to keep alive the days of her past glory and to teach and interest the girls of the neighbourhood. I estimated her age as between 50 and 60, and she had an unusually good memory. She was well known to me as she had travelled with me through the neighbourhood for a period of at least four months, and had been one of my chief informants. She was anxious that I should see a ceremony correctly carried out, and the fact that one of her paternal nieces was due to be initiated gave her a suitable opportunity to arrange this. It was also a time of great food shortage, and she realized that it would have been difficult to get sufficient beer for the ceremony unless I had been able to procure the necessary millet for her.

I think the chisungu ceremony would have been performed for this particular girl, and a companion from a neighbouring village, if I had not been there, but it would probably have taken place at a later date and on a smaller scale and possibly the scene would have been shifted to a more remote village. It is certainly true that my presence attracted more women from the surrounding village than would otherwise have attended and that an effort was made to carry out the rites as nearly according to tradition as possible. The younger women spoke of the ceremony as an unusually important one for the neighbourhood, chiefly, I think, owing to their admiration and respect for Nangoshye. The rites were, therefore, more elaborate than were usual in that area in 1931 but much less long and complex than would have been the case in pre-European days. The whole ceremony was complete in just under a month, whereas, in the past, it would have lasted six months to a year.

Nangoshye was supported by an extremely old woman, Nacitembo, reckoned as 'father's sister' to one of the girls initiated. Her memory must have been longer than that of the *nacimbusa*, but she was no longer very articulate. Five or six other *nacimbusas* from surrounding villages attended for the most important rites. The headman of the village was himself the maternal grandfather of one of the girls to be initiated, and showed interest in the ceremony. There were only two candidates for initiation. Both had reached maturity a few months earlier; one was already betrothed to a young man who was away at the mines, but the other was not yet affianced.

In some ways conditions were favourable for observing a ceremony of this kind. I had been in the country for over a year and could speak the language fairly fluently, although I did not find it possible to follow all the archaic phraseology used in some of the ritual. I knew the *nacimbusa* personally very well. As the provider of the beer, I was described as the owner (*mwine*) of the ceremony and had the right to attend any part of it. I had a tent in the village opposite the chisungu hut and could, therefore, hear and see everything that was going on. On the other hand, it is hardly possible for one field worker to get all the relevant material in a ceremony of this kind. There is the difficulty of taking photographs and simultaneously writing notes during rites that take place in bush and village and on the road between the two. There is also the factor of exhaustion. Songs and dances often went on until two and three in the morning. On such occasions the company is usually elated by beer and accustomed to the heat of a small hut about eight feet in diameter filled with twenty or thirty people and an enormous fire. The observer is dead sober, nearly stifled, with eyes running from the smoke, and straining all the time to catch the words from the songs screeched around her, and to transcribe them by the firelight that penetrates occasionally through the mass of human limbs.

I realize, therefore, that there are many blanks in my material which were probably unavoidable. I was also obliged to leave before the follow-up of the ceremony, i.e. the actual marriage of the girls in question, and I had little time to get subsequent comment from other sections of the community such as the men of the village as distinct from the women, or from one or two of the Christians living in the neighbourhood. A striking gap in my material is the absence of any comments made by the girls themselves. This is, I think, significant. These girls, who are obliged to remain silent, often covered with blankets, seem to lose all personality for the observer as the rites follow one after the other. They are both the centres of the ceremony, and yet the least interesting of the actors in it. However, I consider my failure to arrange for longer conversations and more intimate contacts with the two girls to have been a serious omission. It leaves an element of uncertainty in my interpretation of the educational function of the rites.

In the following account, I try to give a straightforward description of what I actually saw and heard with comments made by informants during the ceremony or in answer to questions afterwards. I was able to check up much of the data during a visit to other areas in 1933–4, and with specialist students of Cibemba, Paul Mushindo, A. Chileshye, I. A. Nkonde and Kasonde.

Comments made to me during the course of the rites are given in brackets. Unless otherwise stated, the comments were made by any woman present. Interpretations made subsequently, either by one of the *nacimbusas* or by one of these Bemba experts are given in footnotes.[1] N.G. stands for Nangoshye, P.B.M. for Paul Mushindo and A.C. for A. Chileshye.

FIRST DAY

The blessing of the girls (*ukupala amate*)

The first rite of the ceremony took place on May 31st. I was told that the headman of the village called the blessing of his ancestral spirits in the early morning. This he did by spitting into the air and calling on the names of his ancestors. I did not see this rite but it is the common Bemba practice in ceremonies of the kind.

The entry into the hut (*ukuingishya abanacisungu*)

At about four in the afternoon, the village drums began to go with the characteristic chisungu rhythm. I was called to the hut

---

[1] A free translation of songs is given. The full interpretation follows in Appendix B. The song numbers refer to this appendix.

which had been provided by the father of one of the girls and which was hence known as the chisungu hut. It had been cleared of all furniture and had in it nothing but a fire and the enormous water pots kept bubbling when there is any chance of their being needed for beer. The women crowded round the entrance of the hut with an air of bustle and importance. Nangoshye was shouting imperiously to all and sundry. Young girls and children were eliminated by indignant shrieks from the older women. The rest of us were pushed into the hut and crowded against the walls, leaving a rectangular space down the centre for dancing. Everyone shouted for the *banacisungu*. The two girls finally appeared covered with blankets and crawling laboriously on all fours backwards under the guidance of some of the younger helpers. The women broke into one of the first of the chisungu songs (No. 1 of Appendix B):

> '*How are we going in?*'
> '*We are going in as through a tunnel into a secret place.*'

('They are crawling as though they were monkeys.' 'What are they doing it for?' 'Oh! just to make the girls look stupid, just to make us laugh.')[1]

The hierarchy of the elders. The ceremony opened with a ritual representation of the hierarchy of rank among the women present. It was the first of one of the series of such acts that took place over and over again throughout the ceremony. Nangoshye squatted on her toes with her knees bent and jogged up and down to the drums. She picked up in her mouth two small enamel bowls that covered baskets of seeds. Picking up one of the baskets in her mouth, she offered it to the oldest woman present and the latter, in turn, started jogging up and down and offering the basket to the women below her in rank and so on in exact order of age.

('We are honouring the great ones, these are the big *banacimbusa* from the district.' 'Why?' 'We just have to honour them' (*Tule bacindikafye*) said with an impatient shrug at my stupidity.)

---

[1] *Subsequent Bemba interpretation.* The girls are crawling in backwards, i.e. they are forsaking their old way of life. They are made to look ridiculous and to do unusual things. They are crawling stealthily like monkeys who go out to steal something. They are crawling under blankets, i.e. concealed from others (P.B.M.). They are passing through a tunnel, a dark place into the initiation hut, i.e. into the heart of the mysteries, the knowledge of how to build up their future homes (A.C.).

Nangoshye has modelled the crocodile

Going out to the first woodland ceremony. The girl is hobbled to make her look ridiculous: she hides her face in shame as she is made to walk half-naked

On the way to the bush. The girls with their cloths round their waists, their heads hung down

The Ceremony

There followed a series of solo dances done by the old women. The rhythm of the drums was definitely of the chisunga type, but some of the songs did not seem to be connected with the ceremony. The tone of the company was serious throughout. The two girls themselves hardly ever ventured to peep out from under their blanket coverings. When they did, they looked frightened and shy.

The enclosure of the girls (ukusakila banacisungu)

After about an hour spent in this way, the company rushed out with a good deal of laughter and talking to a small *mufungo* tree that stood on the village garden mounds. The two girls trailed behind, still covered by blankets, pushed and shoved along by the younger helpers. There were no men present and young children were warned off by excited screams. Nangoshye sat down by the *mufungo* tree and began pulling out leaves with her mouth. Then she made the girls crouch against the stem of the tree while the women built a sort of windscreen of branches round them. This was described as 'hiding the girls'.

('They are hiding them from the young girls and children.')[1]

Making fish-traps for the girls (ukuteela banacisungu)

Quite suddenly, Nangoshye shouted new directions. With screams of merriment, each women began to snatch at a *mufungo* bush for leaves. These pear-shaped leaves they folded into cones to resemble the small conical fish traps used by the Bemba. They sang a song about setting fish traps (No. 2) and ran round laughing as they pretended to catch each others' fingers in the leaf traps.

('It is a parable.' (*Ni milumbe*) 'The fish has many children and so will the girl.' 'It represents the organ of the man.')[2]

The girls' first jump (ukuciluka banacisungu)

More shouted orders from Nangoshye and the piled-up branches were snatched away from round the girls as they cowered at the foot of the tree. The boughs were stacked on their backs and

---

[1] *Subsequent Bemba interpretation.* All informants agreed that the girls were to be hidden from the community by this act.

[2] *Subsequent Bemba interpretation* (A.C.). The mother says she has given the girl all the teaching she can. She hands her over to the *nacimbusa* now.

roughly tied, and they were made to crawl a few yards in this position. Then the branches were pulled off again and piled into a heap about two feet high. The girls were told to jump over it. Both scuttled across the open space like frightened rabbits to the accompaniment of screams of encouragement and threats from all around. ('Don't tremble!' 'Don't be frightened, you silly girls.' 'Jump now! Jump high.') The girls were evidently nervous to a degree, and one failed to manage the moderate jump expected and had to try again and again. When both the girls were over, there was an outburst of congratulation. Nangoshye rubbed red cam wood (*nkula*) on the faces and shoulders of all the older women present and on me as the giver of the chisungu. This red powder used to be rubbed on returning warriors and men who had passed successfully through the poison ordeal; and it is still daubed on lion-killers.

Nangoshye picked up her paternal niece and carried her across her back, and the other girl was shouldered by her own father's sister. The two old women led the procession back to the village carrying the girls shoulder high as chiefs or brides are carried as a sign of honour.

> '*We have dragged a heavy stone down from the hills*
> *We have brought it in.*'
> '*The skin of the leopard which makes you cry,*
> *We have dragged it and dragged it;*
> *We have brought it in.*' (No. 3.)

('The chisungu has fallen off.' 'Yes like a stone.' 'The red powder is the blood.')[1]

Arriving at the village, we crowded into the chisungu hut again. The girl helpers picked up the big drums and the characteristic chisungu rhythm rang out. As the initiation candidates were hustled into the hut, the women broke into another song calling on the people to look at what had been brought in. (No. 4) 'I have

---

[1] *Subsequent Bemba interpretation.* The heavy stone is the weight of the chisungu. (A.C.). It means the difficulty and hardship she will have to go through before reaching maturity. They have passed through danger. Therefore they are marked with red powder like the lion-killers. The leopard skin makes the girls cry. (The leopard skin was worn by *banacimbusa* in old days and therefore represents authority.) The leopard signifies the hardship the girls will have to face.

been given to my lion husband. Come and look! Come everyone and look! We are taking them to where they were left at the *mukolobondo* tree.'[1]

The rite ended with a ceremonial obeisance by the three senior *banacimbusa*. The three wrinkled old women rolled flat on their backs in the centre of the hut in the salute usually given to a chief. A definite episode seemed to have ended.

('They did it for respect, (*mucinsh*)—to give honour, (*uku-cindika*)'.)

Some of the visiting women broke away from the crowd at the door of the hut and rushed into the open. They began to vie with other women in solo dances. The performance went on far into the night. Beer was being served in front of the huge fire in the centre of the hut and the dancing went on in the moonlight outside.

The teasing of the girls (ukubacushya)

At about nine in the evening, Nangoshye suddenly shouted out, 'Now let's start to tease the girls.' She and her helpers pushed into the hut and picked up the two girls by their arms and legs and swung them to and fro in front of the fire singing (No. 5):

> '*Let us shake her, shake her,*
> *The enemy has made himself hard.*'[2]

('It is just done to give them knowledge of the world.')

SECOND DAY

The next day passed without special rites. The *banacisungu* were sent out of the village to visit relatives elsewhere. The beer was exhausted, but dancing sprung up in the evening at about five o'clock outside the chisungu hut and went on until half-past ten at night. A number of visitors had already assembled from other villages, and this seemed to stimulate further solo dances. Most of these dances were of the play-acting type. They represented little

---

[1] *Subsequent Bemba interpretation*. We are bringing the girls to the place of life, i.e. the *mukolobondo* tree. The girl is given to her husband who is strong as a lion. She calls on the women to see what kind of man her husband is. (A.C.).

[2] A reference to the women's punishment of the girls for the faults of their youth.

scenes of everyday life, extravagantly burlesqued and done with great character and abandon. Some of the dances belonged specific-ally to the chisungu ceremonies and were done to the chisungu rhythm, but others were dances that might be done at any beer drink of a rather formal character.

Most of the dances were comic. For instance, two or three women did dances imitating the hop of a frog to an accompanying song by the whole company. One gave a rendering of a woman gathering potatoes, and another of a woman grinding maize. Then a young man suddenly leaped into the centre with a light springing step from side to side. He snatched up a maize cob from the floor and tied it on his back to represent a baby, amid roars of laughter from the clapping crowd. A woman got up to join him and they threw the baby from one to the other in a way that was evidently considered comic in the extreme. The dance was described as 'just dancing', (*ukucindafye*). Then came a special chisungu dance. A young man who was not only the brother of the affianced bridegroom, but the son of a *nacimbusa*, sprang into the middle of the circle to do a typical dance of respect. He danced to each of the older women in order of seniority, calling them out to dance opposite him and singing one of the songs of respect that belong to such occasions. (No. 6.) He evidently knew the etiquette, and was determined to make the party go with a swing. He was described as 'a very respectful young man', (*wa mucinshi*).

Other dances of respect followed. Men of the girl's family did solo dances in honour of the women of the bridegroom's family. The younger women saluted the older *banacimbusa* in this way. One or two of the dances were modern, imitating the drill of the local Protestant Mission school.

THIRD DAY—SIXTH DAY

The making of the small pottery emblems
The third day opened with the carrying of a small pot of beer to Nangoshye and her helpers. It was presented by the mother of the bridegroom as part of her required payments.

68

The Ceremony

At about twelve o'clock, ten to fifteen women went out into the bush round the village and started to make pottery emblems from clay which had been piled there by the younger helpers. It seemed to be a compulsory task as one of the women who was kept away sent a bracelet as a fine. Nangoshye gave instructions to each woman and allotted them their work, but it was clear that they were all experienced potters. She herself modelled the most important figures using pieces of bark as stands for her work. (She is seen modelling the crocodile p. 64.) The women gossiped but they worked quickly with marked concentration. The atmosphere was that of a sewing bee or Women's Institute meeting in this country, although the women occasionally broke out into rather racy jokes about the fertility emblems (see p. 211). There was no sacred tone about the occasion at all although Nangoshye was decidedly severe in manner, and once told the party they ought not to laugh while making the *mbusa*. A passing man was driven away with mock abuse.

At about two or three, the mother of one of the girls brought food. The women fell on it with their hands covered in clay. It was evidently a snack, a reward, and not a full meal. Later, a dish was sent by the mother of the second girl and was sent back with a peremptory demand for more. Such a small dish showed no respect to the ceremony, Nangoshye declared.

The fourth, fifth and sixth days passed quietly, with further work on the pottery emblems in the morning and more dancing in the hut in the evening. The *banacisungu* were remarkable for their absence. They once appeared with their cloths folded in the ordinary way, but were immediately shouted at. 'Pull down your cloths, you! Good heavens! Are you walking about just like us people of quality? Are you trying to hide your breasts as we do?'[1]

Nangoshye complained constantly that she did not get enough food. It was her pride that was hurt. It was true that people called her to eat with them, she admitted, but they called her from pity only. There was no formal presentation of food, no 'respect'.

[1] Women wear their cloths round their waists when working but above their breasts when at leisure. Princesses always wear them in the latter way.

The Ceremony

The first woodland ceremony

Taking them out to the bush (*ukufumisha banacisungu mumpanga*). On the seventh day we were all summoned to the hut at about nine in the morning. The *banacisungu* were bundled in under rugs as before. Each was then hobbled by having one foot strapped with bark rope to her thigh, so she could only hop on the remaining leg, and had to be supported by an older woman.[1] Both girls looked embarrassed, and hid their faces as they came out to the public gaze.

('We are doing that just to tease the girls. That is what they did to us when we were initiated.' With evident relish, another added, 'We always do that to tease the girls.')

Outside the village, the girls' legs were untied but they still had to walk naked except for a cloth around the waist. They strode in front with heads hanging in acute shame. Behind them came a swarm of gesticulating women, running, shouting and scrambling. Two or three ran off into the bush to look for some of the emblems that would be needed for the rest of the ceremony—a special creeper used to tie up other emblems, and supple branches to be used to make mock bows. The young girls of the village followed behind carrying drums on their heads.

The gardening mimes

We stopped at a large *musuku* tree,[2] about an hour's walk away from the village. The base of the tree was quickly cleared of undergrowth with a hoe, and Nangoshye and her younger helpers began hopping round the trunk of the tree like frogs followed by the *banacisungu*. They sang 'O, you wild pig, come and hoe up the rough grass.' (Song No. 7.)

'Because the pigs root up the ground.' 'It is to train the girl to hoe.' 'It is to teach her to work hard now she is married.'[3]

[1] Van Warmelo reports a similar 'hobbling' of girls in the *domba* ceremony of the Venda.

[2] The tree of fertility, as is the *mukolobondo* tree.

[3] *Subsequent interpretation* (P.B.M.). The women imitate the wild pig because the pig digs up food in difficult places. So the young wife must break up the ground to get food out of it.

N.G. It is to teach the girl to get up early to help her husband, as the pigs are out in the bush before it is light.

A.C. 'You have to look for food to feed those about you and bring children up in the way we have brought you up.'

The Ceremony

After about ten minutes, the group broke up and formed up again into another dance representing the guinea-fowl. The women pretended to churn up the ground with their feet and sang calling on the birds to come (No. 8).'You guinea-fowl come here and wait!'

('That is the way we teach them. The guinea-fowl scratches up the soil. If a girl idles and they scold her, then she remembers the teaching of the chisungu, and she will say, "This is what they told me about the guinea-fowl"!' Cf. also p. 30.)

All the main actors then pretended to sow seeds they had brought with them in a basket—maize, ground nuts and beans. After 'sowing' them, they scraped the seeds up with their hands, singing (No. 9):

> '*The small garden,*
> *The garden of the ground-nuts.*'

('It is just to teach the girl how to garden.')[1]

The heat was now intense. Sweat poured down Nangoshye's face and back, but she was indefatigable. She kept urging her helpers and the *banacisungu* to sing louder and to dance harder.

She then picked up the maize cob in her mouth and gave it to the girls to bite. Everyone sang over and over again (No. 10):'The tortoise never climbs, but today he is climbing the *mukolobondo* tree.'

(Subsequent interpretations were varied. P.B.M. 'You see, tortoises do not climb, but today they are climbing. The girl must learn to do impossible things. Even though she is not a man, she must climb trees to get firewood if it is needed.' An old *nacimbusa* 'They teach the girl to go and fetch firewood—if she does not know how to use an axe she must do it if her husband is away.' A younger *nacimbusa* 'It is just a story. If the husband commits adultery, she must say nothing about it. She has just to ignore it. We teach her this so that she can remember "This is the thing they taught me about the tortoise".')[2]

---

[1] *Subsequent Bemba interpretation* (A.C.). 'You do not use the word garden for land that has not been dug. You cannot expect to get ground-nuts, or anything else, unless you have worked on the land.'

[2] *Subsequent Bemba interpretation.* (A.C.) 'You say you never do a thing but when the testing time comes your resolve breaks down and you do a thing against your habit as the tortoise who suddenly climbs a tree. The young girl must be careful especially in time of hunger when she is tempted to break hospitality rules.'

The Ceremony

The maize cob was then tied with special creepers to a branch of the tree, and Nangoshye and the two elder women dodged to get it into their mouths. Then a girl climbed up and tied the maize cob to a high bough. The *banacisungu* had to try to climb up, leg first. They were finally helped on to the bough by the younger helpers.

('The girls are to imitate monkeys because the monkeys eat everything on the trees.' 'The monkey is always stealing. A good wife must try to find food for her family whenever she can. This song is to make the girls imitate the monkey.')[1]

> '*The monkey eats everything that bears freely*
> *That is why he climbs the mukolobondo tree.*' (*No.* 11)
> '*The monkey calls its mother.*' (*No.* 12)

The honouring of the musuku tree

The next rite was the blessing of the *musuku* tree which is one of the symbols of womanhood in this tribe. It was described as '*ukusapila mbusa*'. Two small rings of white beads were tied round twigs of the tree and the girls were made to bite them off in their mouths and give them to Nangoshye. Having taken the decorated twigs in her mouth, she began to jog up and down and to offer them in her mouth to the elder *banacimbusa* in order of seniority. Each one went down on her knees and reached out both hands to take the twigs covered with the saliva of the woman who offered them. As each woman took the emblem she made the *ulla ulla* sound of general congratulation.

('The girls are to get firewood always now.' 'It is to honour the *musuku* tree. If we did not do this there would be no parenthood for the girls.' 'Why?' 'Because the *musuku* is a tree that bears much fruit.' 'This is called "the blessing of the child's *mbusa* with spittle".' (*ukupalila imbusa shya umwana*).

Then came the first singing of the song, 'The arm-pit can never be higher than the shoulder' (No. 13) which was repeated so often during the subsequent rites. The song appears to represent the

---

[1] *Subsequent Bemba interpretation* (A.C.). 'The monkey steals. It is to frighten the girl from stealing. Hunger forces one to do the unusual, i.e. climb a tree upside down. It brings trouble.'

The Ceremony

unalterable prerogatives of age. As a man's arm-pit can never be higher than his shoulder so the younger can never be more important than the older.

Preparation of the emblem bundles

Bundles of domestic emblems were now made up. These consisted of things commonly used in daily life—firewood, salt, meat, tobacco, the various seeds used in cooking, red cam wood powder, twigs of trees with magic properties and particularly of the woman's trees (*mwenge, mufungu* and *musuku*).

There followed an interminable series of songs. The initiation candidates hung uncomfortably from the branches of the tree, while beneath the emblems were offered, taken in the mouth and honoured by each of the women in turn, the company singing over and over again:

> '*Let me pick it up*
> *Let me pick it up with my mouth.*
> *My mbusa.*' (*No.* 14)

At last, the girls were brought down from the tree and with five or six of the younger helpers they were told to lead a round dance. They were shy, tied and awkward, and the dance went lamely. It was evidently important, however, that an impression of jollity should be given for the older women sat round them screeching vehemently, 'Rejoice, can't you? You girls, why can't you manage to rejoice?' Asked why this was necessary, Nangoshye said shortly, 'They must do it for respect.'

The mock bridegrooms

It was now between one and two o'clock, and we turned to go back to the village. As we went, two women dashed across the front of the procession shouting. They had armed themselves with toy bows and arrows and had tied twigs round their heads. They had leaf cups similar to those of the fish trap ceremony hung all over them. They were shouldering a long sapling on which hung a piece of ant-hill to represent a load. They had stained themselves all over with the red powder.

These were the sisters of the bridegrooms and they were greeted with shrieks of delighted laughter, 'Here come the bridegrooms.' The two women imitated the swaggering gait of young gallants, and pretended to speak in bass voices. They carried male symbols —the bow and arrow, the red cam wood powder of the successful warrior and lion-killer, and the salt, which the husband had to fetch for the household in the old days. The twigs round their heads were said to represent the circlets worn formerly by magicians, and the leaf cups might well have been fertility symbols, though I did not ask.

We formed into a triumphant procession as we neared the village. Everyone carried branches or imitation bundles of firewood on their backs. Even the children who ran in front, shouting, had tiny faggots strapped on their backs. The mock bridegrooms followed and behind them came the *banacisungu* with the emblem bundles strapped on to their shoulders.

As we got near the first houses, the two girls were made to crawl single file with some of their companions, and then they were hidden by a couple of mats carried like a screen round them. The women waved their branches to and fro and began to surge first forward and then backward—four steps forward very slowly behind the crawling girls, and then four steps backward. They sang again and again (No. 15).

> '*Mark one step after the other*
> *Let us not turn back.*'

('The crawling backwards is to teach the girls obedience.')[1]

The mother-daughter rite

The procession wound interminably on, forward and back, forward and back, until we reached the house of one of the girl's mothers. Here the *banacisungu* were told to lie down and to put their heads first on a bunch of sorghum and then on some clusters of finger millet. These are the two most important cereal foods of the tribe. The seeds had been thrown there by the girl's mother.

(The mother says, 'I shall get every kind of seed and give it to my child.' This sentence was repeated by several women with great

---

[1] *Subsequent interpretation.* A *nacimbusa*: 'It is to teach the girls they have to go back if they have made a mistake. A.C. 'What you have gone through is over. You have entered a new world, but you mustn't forget and fall back.'

pleasure and confidence. It seemed to be the ritual acknowledge-
ment of the mother's duty to provide food and to cook for her
married daughter for some years after the wedding has taken
place.)

The mock bridegrooms suddenly reappeared, pretending this
time to be lame old men who could hardly walk. Again the same
delighted screams of, 'Here are the *shibwinga*' and the shouted
badinage with the mock old men, who came this time with horns
of leaves on their heads. The company started singing a song
about fetching salt.[1]

The whole procession danced three times round the girls who
stood in the centre with downcast eyes. Then the crowd moved off
to sing in front of the house of the bridegroom's (classificatory)
mother. His own mother lived in a village elsewhere.

The hidden emblems

We then turned back to the chisungu hut where another type of
mbusa had been hidden in the hut roof. Presents such as copper
bangles would have been used in the old days, but on this occasion
heads of millet were thought sufficient. The women all pretended
to look for the *mbusa* while singing a song. (No. 16)
    '*You look for a little snake for me on the roof*.'[2]

The test of maturity

We crowded into the hut in which the fire had been extinguished
preparatory to its ritual relighting later in the day. Two large
water pots were set on the floor and into each was put one of the

---

[1] *Subsequent interpretations.* The explanations were particularly contradictory
in this case, and they were instructively so. A youngish and knowledgeable
nacimbusa said the horns were to keep off witchcraft. They were to imitate the
horns of the witch-doctor. The mock bridegrooms pretended to be old to show that
the girls were to learn 'to grow up with their husbands and never to despise them'.
An old woman said, 'Yes, the women are imitating the witch-doctors, those who
know how to give parenthood (*bufyashi*)'. R.B.M. explained, 'It is to teach the
bridegroom that even though he is old and tired he must look after the girl. Also,
however ridiculous he is made to appear in the eyes of the world he must still do
his duty'. A young girl, obviously considering the question for the first time, said
'It is good for a husband to be old. It is nice to marry a young man, but then he
only goes off to the mines and leaves you alone. An old husband will stay behind
and make you a garden.'

[2] A.C. 'You must plan for dangers ahead, i.e. the snake unexpectedly in the
roof.'

little darting water insects known as *njelela*. The dancing and the drumming started up and Nangoshye alternately jogged up and down on bent knees and tried to catch the little insects in her mouth. It seemed an almost impossible task and she failed, after many efforts, and much encouragement. Then the two girls themselves set to work, this time with unwonted animation. Both succeeded in catching an *njelela* and spitting it into the hands of Nangoshye to the sound of much clapping and ululation.

This rite which was carried out with all the laughter and excitement of a game of snap-dragon at an English Christmas party was evidently considered of some importance. It seemed to be a test of the maturity of the girls in the sense of their acquisition of that important social attribute of every Bemba—*mano*, or social sense.

('They try to find out if the girls have grown up (*nga nabakula*).' 'If the girl doesn't catch the *njelela* the women all know "She has not yet acquired *mano*", and the mother has to pay a forfeit.')

The girls made free to offer food

Two large winnowing baskets were then brought in and filled with ground nuts, peas and beans. One had a small basin with a collection of miscellaneous objects in it—a bracelet, a maize cob, some salt, some snuff, etc. These again were described as *mbusa*. Both of the baskets were covered with lids as food is covered when it is carried as a token of respect. There followed more offerings of respect to the *nacimbusa*. Drums and singing went on incessantly, the company jogging up and down with bent knees as before and a younger woman uncovering the basket with her mouth, picking up seeds in her mouth and dropping them into Nangoshye's hands. They sang, among other songs (No. 17):

> '*You have uncovered it.*
> *You have eaten the whole nsomo.*'[1]

The *mbusa* were looked for, found, picked up with the mouth again and handed to and fro. Again came the song of the arm-pit not being higher than the shoulder. All this was described as, 'It is a way of honouring the senior people' (*ukucindika abakalamba*).

---

[1] A.C. comments: the *nsomo* was the bridegroom's gift. It tells the girl: 'You have uncovered it. This is your life. You have to look after others in need.'

The Ceremony

Then the girls were pulled to the front and told to invite the company to eat. They sang:

> '*The food from our gardens is finished.*
> *Help yourselves, mothers*' (No. 18)

('We older women say, "Now we have danced the child as a gardener. She must start to cultivate herself now".' (*Fwe abakalamba twacindila umwana wa umulimi. Nomba ali no kulimishva.*))

There followed an endless business of handling the seeds which were offered to everyone present in order of seniority and then handed back. It was a relief when the father of one of the girls danced into the hut and did a capering solo in honour of the *nacimbusa*, throwing a cheap bracelet into one of the baskets. He was criticized as being mean in his gift, but the dance was done with great dash and gaiety.

The ritual lighting of the girls' fire (namushimwa)

An important stage in the ceremony had now been reached—the lighting of the new fire. This might be described as the first of the rites of aggregation. The senior 'father's sister' of one of the girls, wrinkled and bent with rheumatism, danced to the company and then lay down on her back. Nangoshye picked up a fire stick and started twirling it round in the groove on the old woman's thigh, telling the two girls to copy her afterwards. Then the two old women set out to make fire in earnest. Women do not commonly make fire among the Bemba. The work needs skill and practice as well as considerable strength. The two old women rubbed the fire stick in turns, sweating and groaning with the effort. The company swayed to and fro moaning the chisungu fire songs:

> '*We have come to beg fire,*
> *Lion we beg it of you.*' (No. 19)

and

> '*Scratch, Scratch (The grating of the fire-sticks),*
> *How many children have you borne?*' (No. 20)

After half an hour of growing anxiety, I offered a box of matches which are commonly reckoned as 'new fire' in Bemba ceremonial.

This was received with shocked protest, 'No, this isn't just ordinary fire. Alas, Mother! We can't use matches.' It seemed an impasse.

At last, to the intense relief of everyone, the wood shaving set to catch the sparks began to smoke and a little flame flickered up. Clapping broke out and cries of 'ulla! ulla!' saluted the new fire. It was a curiously moving moment because of the tenseness of the women packed tight on the floor of the hut through the long wait.

The rite is described shortly as 'to beg for parenthood' (*ukulomba ubufyashi*). The father's sister plays the leading part in the ceremony and it is she who by tradition influences the fertility of the girl. 'The sticks must be rubbed on the back of the father's sister so that the girl will bear a child quickly.'

(As we have seen the lion is equated throughout this ceremony with the bridegroom, the chief, or the male principle. Two women when questioned about the song (No. 19) just said, 'The lion is a chief.' Fire is also equated with generation. The girl owes parenthood to the older women who have made fire for her, 'We say to the girl "We women have made your fire for you. We are in pain now. Our hands ache from the rubbing. You must take over now".')[1]

Twigs and sticks were deftly built round the young flame and a considerable fire began to crackle. Nangoshye crawled towards it on all fours with a water pot on her head. The two girls crawled behind her clasping their arms round her waist. All three lowered the water pot on to the fire with hands and teeth. I have no recorded comments on this part of the rite. I think it almost certainly symbolizes the heating of the marriage pot of the girl which is stood on the fire by an old woman with the bridegroom and bride clasping her waist. It may also signify the handing over of the fire from the old to the young as suggested in the comment above.

The seeds in the winnowing basket were now divided out so that each woman had a handful to cook. The remains were thrown into the big pot over the fire, the pot of the *namushimwa*. We all retired exhausted to our own quarters to eat for the first time since morning.

[1] A.C. adds: 'You cannot beg fire from a woman in a different sexual condition. The girl must have a new fire after her chisungu. She must not have intercourse during menstruation.'

The Ceremony

The teasing of the girls (ukubacushya)

About seven the same evening, the women gathered again in the hut. Young children were turned out and the *banacisungu* were fetched.

Nangoshye put a basket on her head covered with a white cloth. She knelt on the ground and danced up and down with it, finally offering it to the two *banacisungu* in turn. Everyone watched anxiously to see whether they would cry. One girl burst into tears at once and was greeted with roars of appreciative laughter. The other did not weep at all, and was immediately smacked by her relatives who shouted, 'You child you! Cry a bit! Cry a little bit!' The excitement rose as the women burst into a crooning song, 'I make you cry. . . .'

(All women had an explanation for the *ukucushya*. They used such phrases as 'If they cry we know that they have understood. Otherwise we say, "That is a *citontolo*! She doesn't hear. She doesn't respect authority".')

The rest of the evening was spent in similar efforts to make the *banacisungu* cry. I watched seven different singing games in which the girls were pulled about and tormented. Their legs were stretched out; the backs and faces were rubbed with dust ('to teach them to wash'). They were rolled on the ground; they were pummelled all over; they were stood against the wall and made to imitate a crying noise, which the shyer of the two completely failed to do. They were swung to and fro by fingers hooked inside their mouths. Their heads were bound with grass above the eyes so that the eye-balls stood out.

The two girls were strained and taut, under a constant fire of criticism, and apparently simply concentrated on following blindly the commands shouted at them. The company sometimes gave the impression of boisterous high spirits and sometimes seemed to be acting as though they were bravely carrying out a tedious duty. If the games flagged for an instant, Nangoshye shouted, peremptorily, 'Come on, friends. We must keep on tormenting the *banacisungu*' and the weary women started up another song. Most of the songs had some moral associated with them, such as in No. 21, which was said to tell the girl not to sit on the village square with idle friends who might teach her to abuse her husband, or No. 26,

79

which was to warn her not to finish up her granary at once like the hawk pouncing on food.

I left the hut at half past eleven at night but the dancing went on till half past three, and there was desultory singing till the cock crew.

The women then tasted the stew made of the seeds cooked in the *namushimwa* pot and drifted away to their homes. The *banacisungu* were told not to sleep, but to go out and fetch more clay for the modelling to be done during the day.

EIGHTH DAY

Painting the hut designs

The following day was given to painting the special chisungu designs on the walls of the huts. Nine separate panels were painted with crude designs in white, red, chrome and black washes applied with grass brushes. Two of the younger women did the work with great concentration and determination but no one referred to the designs in my hearing in the forthcoming days: nor did they seem to be discussed or admired. The majority of the designs are conventional patterns and only 'the bird' and 'the leopard' (neither of which is illustrated) can be reckoned as representational art in any sense of the word.[1] The names of the designs are as follows (the first five are shown opposite page 112):

'the butterflies' (*cipelebushya*) red and black star design.

'the guinea-fowls' (*amakanga*) a conventional design.

'the eyes' (*amenso*) a highly stylized design.

'the owl' (*cipululu*) a conventional geometric design of black and red.

'the bean' (*cilemba*) another geometrical design.

'the birds' (*fyuni*) which is roughly representational.

'the *cimbulumbulu*', wavy lines of alternate red and black.

'the whitewash' (*lota*) a criss-cross of black and red lines.

'the fool' (*cipuba*) alternate wavy lines of black and red.

A circular patch was painted on the top of two contiguous panels. Each was said to belong to one of the girls.[2]

[1] The designs illustrated by Mr. V. W. Brelsford, *op. cit.*, are also conventional in character.

[2] Brelsford suggests that the circular dot represents the vagina of the girl, and in view of the shooting ceremony described on p. 107 this seems likely.

The mime of the wild pig scratching up the grass round a tree
(Song No. 7)

The sisters of the girls' bridegrooms act as men, carrying bows and
arrows and a mock lump of salt

The father's sister on whose back the fire-stick is rubbed, together with the girl's mother

The Ceremony

I have no full comments recorded on these designs. The young women present were too junior to reveal the secret of the names on their own responsibility and I omitted to get a comprehensive interpretation from those in charge. One *nacimbusa*, when pressed, took me out to the bush, completely out of hearing of the village. She looked round nervously and said: 'People call whitewash "*pemba*" but we women call the design "*lota*".' It was an old word, she said, from very long ago. Throughout the ceremony, the whitewash represents the washing away of the menstrual blood. It was sent to chiefs in the old days to announce the end of the chisungu ceremony of an important Bemba princess. The bean design evidently had a sexual significance. Nangoshye said it was a parable (*mulumbe*) of manhood. The eye design was described as of teaching the girl submission. When her husband insults her and scolds her, she is to sit silent and merely raise her eyes at him. He will be ashamed and say, 'Indeed, you have done well,' (*mwawamya*). The wild guinea-fowl design has also apparently a sexual meaning. It was to teach the girl to hold on hard. The *cimbulumbulu* was another name for a great *nacimbusa* of the past, referred to in song (No. 41) as Cibale. The owl is a name used for a stupid person who suddenly becomes clever. The girl is taught at initiation so that she becomes clever or educated. The fool has presumably the same interpretation as the model with that name described below on page 88. Another woman described it as a design to teach concealment. The girl should hide everything in her heart, all the things taught her.

I believe that these designs and their names can be reckoned as the most esoteric part of the chisungu. I think that the meanings I give are very superficial ones. I regret I did not give more time to discussing them with the *nacimbusa*.

In the evening began the first rite of handing over the designs to the girls. Each of them was pulled into the hut by Nangoshye and stood up against the wall under her own wall design. The drums began and the company started singing 'Take the girl to the crocodile' (No. 22).[1] Women shouted at her, 'Look what you have been given! Look at the lovely clothes your mother's brother

---

[1] *Subsequent Bemba interpretation.* (A.C.). The crocodile represents wisdom and loyalty to the tribe. If a girl does not go through the ceremony she will not be loyal.

81

has given you.' The ceremonial from this moment begins to represent the handing over or giving of secrets to the girl, and it emphasizes her kinsmen's and husband's obligations to help her.

Modelling the large pottery emblems

The next morning's work began at about eleven o'clock. Great piles of clay had been collected outside the hut and Nangoshye and a few helpers set to work to model what looked like an enormous snake coiled to cover the whole of the hut floor. When it was finished, legs were added round the outer coil. The whole was decorated with white, red and black earth and stuck all over with marrow, castor-oil and bean seeds set carefully about two inches apart. The work was very heavy. The group of women slapped and smoothed the clay with the utmost concentration until about five in the evening, none of them pausing for a regular meal. The task seemed to me endless. As the evening wore on, I suggested sticking the marrow seeds further apart to get the work done quicker. The idea was evidently a shocking one. Nangoshye was indignant. 'Ala! Mother! We couldn't do a thing like that. We must do everything with elegance (*busaka*). We must do it as we always do it.' Here was evidently a part of the ceremony that could not be skimped.

The interpretations of this emblem were curious. The women were reluctant to talk about it. Nangoshye first called it rays of the sun (*amashindo eya itengo*) and said it was to teach the girl that the sun was high and she must get on with her work. Later, she admitted it was also a snake. It was manhood (*bwaume*).

The brother and sister

Meanwhile, some of the younger women had been modelling two small figures of a naked man and woman standing flat against the wall about two feet high. The man's arms were flung out wide, one hand on the shoulder of the woman who had her other hand folded across her face. The figures were described as 'the brother and sister'. They were the subject of eager delight throughout the day. Visitors kept pointing them out to me with evident pleasure. 'Look, the girl is crying because her father has died, but now the brother is looking after her.' 'There is the brother. He says, "Hush! don't cry! Follow me. I am going to look after you now." ' 'Yes, she must honour her brother now because her father is dead.' Over and over again details of the figures were criticized and admired. Most Bemba delight in describing the brother-sister relationship which is such a pivot of the matrilineal system. They refer to it in proverb and folk-tale, and adopt a specially sentimental tone in speaking of it in daily life. Most of the chisungu ritual stresses the husband's duty to feed and clothe his wife, but here the women seem to emphazise the brother's perpetual obligation to look after his sister before, during and after her marriage. Some obscene jokes made about the navel of the woman's figure made me wonder whether there was also some representation of brother-sister incest, but the navel itself is considered an amusing and obscene part of the body by the Bemba, so that I do not know if I am right.

The bed

A third model standing against the wall consisted of three hollow squares of clay. It was known as the bed or the 'blankets'. This model did not seem to attract much attention, although women began to sing a song about a great *nacimbusa* wearing a plumed head-dress. (No. 23)

(One woman said the model represented the girl's bed. Another that it was to teach the girl that even if her husband gave her no blankets or clothing yet she was to stay with him. Whatever he did she was just to look on (*ukutamba*) and not to speak of it to her friends. In the old days, she added, a girl could not get a divorce from a man who did not provide for her. If she went to complain, her grandmother would merely say, 'Well, you must sit naked, then. Stay with the fool you are with'. (*cipuba cobe.*))

Magic of attraction

After this hard day's work, I was surprised to find that the whole design was suddenly pulled to pieces two hours after it was finished and when it had only just been shown to the *banacisungu*. Every marrow seed was taken out carefully and whitened in sorghum flour for use the following day. The clay was stacked up outside the hut. Nangoshye remained behind to stick some magic leaves in the roof of the hut. 'It is magic (*bwanga*). We put it there so that there will be a lot of visitors and everyone will say the chisungu is a very good one indeed.'

The rest of the company had already returned exhausted to their homes.

The guinea-fowl

The next day was spent in the same laborious fashion. A stellate design covering the whole floor was modelled and covered with colour and seeds. It was described as the guinea-fowl design (*amakanga*) and appeared to be associated with agricultural fertility as in the case of the guinea-fowl dance described on page 71.

('It is to remind the girl not to forget her hoe, and that she is to go on giving the people food', said one of my best informants. The guinea-fowl is also a sexual symbol. (See page 81.))

Again the elaborate models were cleared away at night. Desultory drumming and dancing went on until late.

The festive porridge eating (bwali bwa ukuangala)

I was called in the middle of the morning to see an enormous cooking-pot full of water being set on the fire in the hut of the mother of one of the girls. Ordinary porridge was to be made, but the cooking itself was a ritual act. The flour was first stirred in by Nangoshye, who then handed over the spoon to one of the girl's maternal relatives. When the meal was cooked the girl's maternal grandmother was called to dish up the porridge and to hide *mbusa* in it. She filled a great enamel basin with porridge served in the usual way, and then stuck on top of it a small rounded lump of the cooked meal filled with the domestic *mbusa* (tobacco, salt, beads, meat, red dye and a small lump of whitewash). The whole was then decorated with marrow seeds and red dye and carried to the chisungu hut. Here a similar bowl had been prepared by the mother of the second girl and it stood waiting with the accompanying relish beside it.

It was a day of offering and receiving offerings—from the girls' mothers to the *banacimbusa*; from the younger *nacimbusa* to the older in order of seniority; from the initiated women to the girls. It was a display of ceremonial obligation, of precedence, of *mucinci*, to use the common Bemba term. The younger helpers danced with the porridge bowls on their heads while the *banacisungu* were pushed in backwards, again on all fours, to the singing of the entering-in song (No. 15). The porridge bowls were ceremonially uncovered and covered again with ululation. The girls' paternal relatives seized the dishes and offered them to all present in order of seniority. The bowls were then put on the girls' own heads and they were made to dance round with them to show their respect to the *banacimbusa* present.

Singing games followed. The two senior paternal relatives of the girls pretended to chase each other off a small stool with Nangoshye scolding them and the company singing, 'Don't sit on the stool.' (No. 26) This was said to represent the Bemba custom of chasing the Shimwalule, the official burier of the Citimukulu from office after he had performed the mortuary ritual required of him.[1]

The same two old women next pretended to hunt and spear fish under the porridge bowl. This was explained as, 'The girl tries to hide food from her mother-in-law and asks her friends to keep the matter dark.'

Nangoshye picked up a porridge bowl pretending it was too heavy to carry. The women sang about a bat (No. 25) who represents the woman who goes out to hunt for lovers in the dark. They also sang another song about the hawk who pounces down on food without ceremony—which no girl should do. (No. 26)[2]

The girls were then made to touch each bowl all over and each lid was again picked off in a woman's mouth and offered to each elder in order of precedence. The oldest paternal aunt, Nacitembo (see page 62) then gave each girl a small lump of porridge and took it back; she then hid some of the porridge on the roof.

The hidden *mbusa* were now to be shown to the company. Nacitembo, as the oldest woman present and the representative of the father's side of one girls' families, danced holding the small

[1] *Subsequent Bemba interpretation* (A.C.). A woman must not sit on a stool in the presence of her elders.

[2] A.C. interprets No. 25: 'Evening is the time for play but wait until the housework is over before chatting with friends.'

balls of porridge filled with the domestic emblems. The two girls were stood against the wall under their own wall marks. Paternal relatives stood one on each side of them and passed the balls with the hidden emblems from side to side across them. This was to make them free to eat all the foods. It was, in other words, the removal of the girls' food taboos.

The company burst into song which goes with the representation of the washing of the husband's hands, (see page 202) and the girls' hands were washed. The paternal aunt danced out in front and kept pretending to show the hidden *mbusa* to the girls and fighting with Nangoshye who pretended reluctance to let them be seen.

The endless giving and taking came suddenly to an end in one of those dramatic moments that move even the weariest onlooker. The women broke into a song of unusual melody (No. 41):

> *Cibale! Cibale!*
> *Come and wash your husband!*
> *You ignorant creature,*
> *Go and draw water,*
> *Cibale! Cibale!*

A younger *nacimbusa*, dancing with great vitality and charm, bent as though to pour water on the hands of every woman present in order of the assembled hierarchy. She pretended to whitewash the floor beneath each and bowed low to clap obeisance.

The company were roused to excitement immediately. To my questions they whispered: 'That is respect!' 'That is how the woman honours her husband. That is how he knows she has been taught. If a woman does not know how to wash her husband's hands, he will say, "That is not a woman. She is like someone who hasn't been danced!" ' (*Canakashi! Cabanga bashicindile!*)

The tension seemed to break. The ceremony was over. The porridge was divided up in a business-like way and each family took its portion. There was scrapping about the size of the bowls and a general return to normal life.

In the late afternoon, dancing began again and at night the teasing of the girls went on once more. One girl cried at once and was applauded. The other girl was throughout more stocky and reserved. A woman said to me: 'Well, we can't give her up! We must go on and on trying to teach her.'

This was a blank day. Nangoshye declared herself insulted and went off to reap her own fields. She had plenty to eat, as was clear to anyone sitting in a tent near her hut; but the relatives did not bring her enough 'dishes of respect'. 'They neglect me,' she went off grumbling.[1]

In the evening the pottery emblems were piled with branches, scattered with leaves of the magic *mufungu* tree, and fired.

This was another quiet day. In the morning, Nangoshye and her helpers went to inspect the pile of pottery emblems still covered with smouldering ashes.

The snake

In the afternoon a new pottery figure was made in the hut. It was an immense snake (*yongolo*). The clay was smoothed into coils that circled round the floor of the hut with a tail on the fire-stands against one wall and a head rearing up the opposite wall. Again the work was heavy and lasted two or three hours. There was the puddling of the clay outside the hut, the fetching of gourd and bean seeds and the meticulous arrangement of seeds along every coil of the snake's body. There was the same concentrated air about the women and the sense of a fight against time, but the same unwillingness to shorten the work at all.

(The women were reluctant to speak of the meaning of this emblem. 'It's just a snake' several said impatiently. Another added, 'It is to teach her not to deceive her husband.' On question, Nangoshye looked down with great embarrassment and said, 'Yes, it is a sign of manhood.'[2]

---

[1] "*Bansula*". *Ukusula* is to despise, neglect, or fail to acknowledge a person's rights.

[2] *Subsequent Bemba interpretation.* P. B. M. commented afterwards that it was not an ordinary snake. It was a *yongolo*, a very rare snake. It was to teach the girl that unexpected things might happen. She must support them all patiently.

The fool

Near the door of the hut two of the younger helpers modelled another human figure. It was a squat, round female form, highly stylized. It was at once recognized by visitors with shrieks of laughter as the fool (*cipuba*). This is a word that is difficult to translate. It means a person who is either naturally stupid, or else just obtuse, unconscious of the niceties of civilized life, and either unaware of her social obligations or just too lazy to bother to carry them out. In this context, I was told 'The *cipuba*? She is a woman who just sits about.' The speaker imitated someone sitting limp and collapsed on the floor. 'She just refuses to do what is asked of her—all kinds of work. She just says "No" to her husband. She refuses food to visitors. She doesn't fetch water or keep the house nice! This is what she looks like.' There followed another imitation of a woman sitting huddled up with rounded shoulders and head bent down. All this information was volunteered eagerly amid much amused comment on the figure itself. One of the *banacimbusa* said to me in an undertone, 'Besides it is a woman who doesn't understand how to do things. She hasn't been taught. She would let a man see the menstrual blood.' Her voice changed to one of real horror and disgust. 'She just doesn't bother about anything.' The figure represented both the uninitiated woman who has not been taught the patterns of female conduct, and the lazy wife who has forgotten the lessons she has learnt.

At about seven o'clock, the models were again completely destroyed and the clay put back outside the hut for further use next day.

FOURTEENTH DAY

The whitening magic (ukuya ku mpemba)

When the mid-day meal was over the drums began to beat and the village women gathered outside the chisungu hut. We went in straggling procession down to the river and stood by the soft black mud that lined the banks. Nangoshye took a mouthful of the dirty water and sprayed it in the air. Everyone clapped and ululated.

(The rite seemed significant in the sense that the performers were serious and interested, but I could not interpret it fully. I was told it was to teach the girl not to pretend to be thirsty when she had already drunk. The spraying of saliva in the air is the usual Bemba way of asking the blessing of the ancestors.)[1]

A small hollow was then cleared in the wet mud and Nangoshye balanced herself on both elbows over it, swinging herself to and fro above the muddy pool.

The women sang:

> '*Following the ways of God*
> *We imitate our mothers.*' (No. 27)

(The details of this ceremony are obscure to me. Nangoshye explained that she swung over the hole in the mud to 'imitate our mothers who bore us' and implied she was representing the act of birth. She also said she was teaching the girls how they were to bathe in the river during menstruation, that is to say, apart from others so as not to contaminate the stream. P.B.M. referred to the song sung at the same time as meaning 'Sometimes we do not follow Lesa (God) but follow our mothers.' This seemed to be an explanation of a Christian type, but the idea of the passing down of tradition and the passing down of the child from the womb seemed to be implicit. A.C. writes: 'It is our duty to follow God, to pass on knowledge as we had it passed on to us. We make you a mother as your mothers were to you.')

The *banacisungu* were then pulled forward. Their clothes were kilted round the waist and they were pushed into the muddy water and thoroughly splashed all over. Then they were washed, cleansed and covered over body and face with whitewash. The white clay was brushed on with meticulous care with a grass brush. A lump of black mud was put cross-shaped on the head of each girl and decorated with the usual pumpkin seeds and red dye. Their heads were then covered with a cloth and, still with down-cast eyes and apparent embarrassment, they led the procession back to the village. The women sang:

> '*We tracked a lion in our garden and reported it,*
> *The hunter has not forgotten.*' (No. 28)[2]

---

[1] *Wilaba cilaka nga amina menshi! awikasakaminawa!*

[2] *Subsequent Bemba interpretation.* (A.C.): The ceremony is like the spots of the leopard which never change or are forgotten.

They also sang again and again a song about the white egret (No. 48) as they surrounded the whitened forms of the girls and danced them back to the village.

As we came near the houses men sitting in the doorways of their huts lowered their eyes ostentatiously as we passed.

We assembled at the initiation hut and began again songs and offerings of respect to the *nacimbusa* in order of precedence. All the relatives in the hut were touched with white clay. The girls were then led to the house of the village headmen who 'spat the blessings of the spirits' on them, (*ukupala amate*).

(This ceremony, literally 'going to whitewash', seemed to be thought rather romantic and interesting by the women. They referred to the girls throughout in an almost sentimental way as English women speak of the beauty of brides on their wedding day. 'We make the girls white. We make them beautiful.' 'We make them white like egrets.' 'Yes, they are white now from the stain of the blood.' 'It is finished now, the thing that was red.')

The *ukuya kumpemba* seems to mark a definite stage in the ritual. It is a rite of purification from the menstrual blood and a form of beauty magic. It is followed by the second calling of the blessings of the ancestral spirits.

FIFTEENTH DAY

The shelter and the screen

Nangoshye and a few helpers went out in the middle of the morning to collect stout logs in the bush. By the early afternoon I found them hard at work setting a grass roof on five strong uprights to form a small shelter of the type commonly found in Bemba villages. The supports and roof were covered with clay and the whole stuck with the inevitable beans, pumpkin seeds, red cam wood and white flour. On top of the roof a stick was frayed out to form a plume, or *ngala*. The whole erection was described as an *nsaka*, or a man's shelter, or an *nchenje*, the special term used for the shelter built by the head army captain in a chief's village. This was a place of protection, a spot where the soldiers gathered together in the evening.

(The symbolism was rather obscure, not only to me, but also apparently to many of the women engaged in making the shelter.

The Ceremony

It was described as a place of safety, and again as a place to idle about in, (*ukuangala*), or to rest in. One woman said it was to teach the girl that she must no longer sit about in the village square. Her place, as a married woman, was inside the hut. Another referred vaguely to the crest on top of the roof and said it was like the feathered head-dress worn by a *nacimbusa* in the old days. It was a curious example of work done with a great expenditure of effort and apparently little interest in the meaning of the emblem produced.)

In the meantime, other women were at work making a screen about four feet high. It was covered with decorated clay. A small window was made in the wall and in the centre a round lump with a feather stuck in the middle of it.

(Here again, the symbolism was complex. The screen was called the *lubondo*. It was described as the wall of the house the man would build for his bride. The boss in the centre was called the navel and was referred to in a rather sly manner. The navel is always thought of as a rather amusing and slightly obscene part of the body by the Bemba and one woman said in a shamefaced yet slightly defiant manner, 'Yes, it is to teach her to yield herself to her husband—to let him sleep with her when he wants to.')

Whether or not the esoteric significance of these *mbusa* was realized by the company present, the atmosphere in the hut was that of a rather jolly children's Christmas party in England. The girls and their parents and close relatives crowded into the house in the evening and played uproarious games in and around the shelter and the screen. There was dodging behind the screen with a good deal of giggling and shouting, a ring dance round the shelter, and a ball game played with a rolled-up piece of cloth. The company enjoyed themselves and were most impatient of requests to 'explain' what they were doing. 'We are just honouring the past,' said one girl nonchalantly, smiling and poised to catch 'the ball' a fellow was aiming at her.

The games went on till about nine at night. After this, Nangoshye, the *banacisungu* and one or two helpers walked round and round the village beating the chisungu rhythm on the drums until late into the night. She said the drums would let people know how important a ceremony it was.

The Ceremony

This was a quiet day. The older women were away all morning collecting millet and flour for subsequent festivities in the neighbouring villages. In the afternoon, the fired pottery images were decorated with red, black and white and some of those kept permanently hidden away for use at chisungu ceremonies were brought out for re-painting. Dancing went on in the hut all night. The shelter and the screen had already been removed.

The second woodland ceremony

Bringing the girls out of doors (ukubafumya panse). The day opened with a good deal of discussion and coming and going. I was told this was the day for bringing the girls out of doors, and I definitely had the impression that a new and important stage in the proceedings had been reached. We were to go out into the bush to a *mwenge* tree,[1] and there was a hot altercation among the older women as to which tree would be most suitable. The rest of the company gathered at the initiation hut, the two candidates looking for once quite cheerful with their clothes tucked above their breasts as Bemba women usually wear them. Their serenity was, however, short-lived, for Nangoshye immediately spotted them on joining the group. 'Pull your clothes off your breasts,' she shouted imperiously. 'Who do you think you are? People of status?'

The women seemed to be tired and there was quarrelling over the *mbusa* to be carried into the bush—an enamel bowl with the domestic emblems, salt, tobacco, white chalk, red dye and beads; a winnowing basket full of ground-nuts; and two of the pottery emblems which resemble a pot and its cover but are known as the garden mound (*mputa*) and the garden (*amabala*) (Cf. p. 96). A small gourd of beer was also carried by one of the younger girls who kept eating the sludge on its side with one finger although constantly rebuked for doing so. We made one or two false starts owing to someone having forgotten axes or hoes which were to be needed. In fact, I had the general impression that morale was low.

[1] One of the female trees.

92

Either the company was exhausted or else they had the feeling that the ceremony was coming to an end or that this particular rite was not of great significance.

Honouring the mwenge tree

One of the older women had cut a supple branch of a *mwenge* tree *en route*, and we assembled at the base of a tree of this kind. There followed one of the rites of 'honouring the *mbusa*' repeated so often during the chisungu. The vessels in which the emblems were carried were covered and uncovered by the leading actors, and the *banacimbusa* present were offered the same objects ritually in order of precedence. It was characteristic of this particular ceremony that every object touched was handled with the mouth and not the hand. Nangoshye picked grass with her mouth from under the tree and spat it over the *mbusa*. She spat red cam wood powder over the roots of the *mwenge* tree. She took a hoe in her mouth and started to clear a space under the tree, only taking the implement in her hands to finish the clearing more completely. Throughout the rite the drums were going and the women sang, (No. 14):

> '*Pick up what you have,*
> *Pick up things with the mouth.*'[1]

As objects were offered in order to the older women they sang again the song of precedence:

> '*The arm-pit is not higher than the shoulder.*'

Everyone seemed rather bored and hot under the midday sun. Nangoshye had to exert all her authority to keep the party going. She scolded them for leaving behind one of the domestic emblems— the whitewash. 'It isn't a laughing matter to dance the chisungu' she said. She continued singing with the rest of the lack-lustre company, but in an exasperated sort of way as though anxious to get through with a tedious task, yet under compulsion not to skimp the work.

(This part of the ceremony was described as the honouring of the *mwenge* tree. It will be remembered that the *musuku* tree, the

[1] *Subsequent Bemba interpretation* (A.C.): What people say should not be taken for true. Do not gossip!

female tree representing fertility, was honoured in the same way during the first bush ceremony (p. 70). The *mwenge* is another female tree, representing apparently the pliancy of the woman, just as the *mulombwa*, the hard-wood tree which exudes a red juice, represents the male, the lion, and in some cases the chief.

The act of picking up objects with the mouth was described as a method of honouring the *mbusa* or the *mwenge* tree, with the complementary remark that things were picked up in the mouth because it was unusual. The girls must learn to do unusual things, said one woman.)

The drinking of the beer

Nangoshye then dug a small hole in the ground under the *mwenge* tree and poured the small gourd of beer into it. The earth seemed to hold the thick sludge of the beer and its foam frothed level with the surface of the ground. Nangoshye scattered red dye powder, small rings of white beads and lumps of white clay on top. She was still exasperated and paused to scold the helpers: 'Who has drunk some of the beer on the way down?' she asked. This was a serious matter and not just a time when you could snatch beer without ceremony just as you pleased. However, she addressed herself to the rite in hand without waiting to clear the matter up. She lay on her back beside the hole and supporting herself on her two elbows bobbed up and down to the drum beats until she got herself into position. Then she lowered her head on to the ground near the hole and lapped some of the beer with her tongue, first on the right side and then on the left. She was followed by the senior *banacimbusa* and finally by all the helpers in turn. Each had to make a formal obeisance to Nangoshye and to me. It was quite a difficult operation to carry out and each woman who managed to suck up a lot of beer was greeted with shouts of applause and song:

> '*I shall not answer you*
> *I shall not answer you, useless creature.*'[1]

The two girls themselves then had to drink from the hole with much advice and shouting. The company was by now very much

[1] *Subsequent Bemba interpretation* (A.C.): 'Do not talk when under the influence of drink.'

amused and interested, and the rings of beer foam round everyone's mouth were thought excruciatingly funny.

Finally, there was another rite of 'honouring the *mbusa*'. Nangoshye picked up the pottery emblems and hung beads on them. She
offered them ceremonially to the elders in order, singing as a solo
this time the precedence song, 'The arm-pit is not higher than the
shoulder.'

The women shouted in congratulation to her. They used one of
the old praise songs of the chief:

> *Mpuba musumba!*
> *Kwewa! Kwewa!*

and greeted her with the nick-name that had been given her
during the chisungu, '*Washishye*' 'You have been refused food'—
a reference to the stinginess of the girls' mothers during the
ceremony.

The symbolism of this rite is still obscure to me. The making
and distribution of beer is one of the married women's most
important duties and it is natural that this aspect of the girls'
future work should be mimed in the ceremony. Women told me
that the rite was to teach the bride to hide a gourd of beer in her
hut and to produce it for her husband when the guest had gone.
Another added that it was to teach the girls to submit themselves
to their husbands (*ukunakila*), the latter perhaps in conjunction
with the honouring of the pliant *mwenge* tree. The association of
beer-making with gardens is obvious in the day-to-day speech of
the Bemba and the offering of the pottery emblems known as the
'garden mound' could be interpreted as making the bride free to
cultivate her own garden and hence to brew the resultant beer.
The garden-mound also symbolizes the woman owned and 'cultivated' by her husband (No. 44).

The preparation of the jumping hoop (mupeto)

The two girls were then sent off with some of the younger
helpers to fetch a piece of the *mulombwa*, or male tree. They came
back carrying a branch on their shoulders and they were left to
kneel with it thus with down-cast eyes in the humble attitude (see
frontispiece) whilst the older women offered the different *mbusa* to
it ritually.

The branch was then stuck in the ground and bent over to form an arch while the *mwenge* branch was crossed over it at right angles to form a double hoop, known as the *mupeto*. Everyone was now animated and interested, even though it was about one o'clock and they had had no solid meal during the day. The *mulombwa* bough was brittle and broke, but the company waited for the best part of an hour for a new one to be found, and they waited in the best of spirits, laughing and talking of this and that. The hoop was apparently to be set up for a trial jump to see if the girls could clear it. This they finally did.

The return of the lion killers

In the meantime, Nangoshye and some helpers had been to look for a heavy log of a third tree—the *kabumba*—which represents a lion, and was throughout described as the lion. The two girls again knelt holding it on their shoulders, and again the older woman offered the *mbusa* to it one by one with endless singing, drumming and dancing. Finally, Nangoshye danced up to it brandishing an axe tied round with leaves as was done in the old days when a lion had been killed and purification of the lion-killers took place at a chief's court. The effect of this solo dance was electrical. The company shouted and danced and broke into the famous song:

Kakoshi sompa! Cilipi! Cilipi!

that used to be sung by lion-killers and also by a man who had had his eyes put out for some offence and was made to come and do obeisance to the chief who had given the order for his punishment.

The return to the village was uproarious. Each of the *banacisungu* carried one of the hoops of the *mupeto* with the two ends lashed together to form a hoop. The log lion was balanced and carried on their shoulders. Nangoshye and the older *banacimbusa* brandished axes and hoes, running and shouting all the way. At the entrance to the village the girls were covered with a black cloth and the rest formed into some sort of a procession. The older women and I were daubed with red dye and castor oil. The oil melted the red powder in the sun and a single spot spread to make a great crimson splash on the side of the face, so that we must have had an uncouth and eerie appearance. In fact, some of the younger girls, mission-trained, began to look embarrassed and to refuse to

The second woodland ceremony. Nangoshye puts beer and red camwood into a hole in the ground. (Note the garden mound *mbusa* (Songs 44 and 45) in front)

A girl about to try to drink the beer in the hole backwards over her shoulder

The girls carry a sapling of the male tree (*mulombwa*). It is decorated with white beads

The girls fetch a log of the *kabumba* tree to represent a lion

be daubed in the same way. The women circled the headman's hut three times singing the lion triumph song over and over again.

The headman's wife came out to offer the party ground-nuts and various members of the two girls' families gave some small bracelets and other token gifts. The excitement died down as quickly as it had sprung up. Everyone was tired and hungry and therefore dispirited, and the company melted away.

(The symbolism of this rite is complex. The lion represents the male and therefore the bridegroom. A woman said the honouring of the *kabumba* tree meant the honouring of the man. Men who kill a lion are congratulated, and rubbed with red dye. They are doctored and sing the lion-killers' song before the chief to prevent the spirit of the lion 'coming back'. The blinded man sings the same song to show he harbours no grievance and that his spirit will not 'come back'. The rite therefore seems to represent the bridegroom who comes as a lion, but there is also implicit the idea of the danger of the chisungu and the association of the red dye with the red blood. The women are congratulated because the danger is over. They circle round the headman's (chief's) hut to sing the song of those who have come through danger in triumph.)

The planting of the mbusa (ukushimpe mbusa) and the final jump

At about three, the older women went down to the river edge and set up the *mupeto*, that is to say, the crossed hoops of *mwenge* and *mulombwa*. They covered it with clay and stuck it with seeds and red dye. A small round ball of clay, about 4 inches in diameter, was stuck on top so that the whole structure was about 4 feet 5 inches high from the ground. The company assembled by the river bank for the final jump. Both girls cleared the hoop from one direction. They then had to return and make the jump from the other side. This time one of the girls failed twice. It was apparently a terrifying thing to have happened. Her mother looked really angry and distressed and beat her on the legs with a branch. She herself looked petrified with fear and had obviously lost her nerve. Everyone shouted advice, 'You lazy girl, you!' 'Look in the air, don't look at the *mupeto*.' 'You are going to bring shame on us.' 'Jump, you just jump.' The girl was by this time sobbing miserably, but with a final whack on her shins from her mother, she made a supreme effort and cleared the jump. The relief of the crowd was tremendous. Ululation broke out. Both girls were lifted on their mothers' backs with cries of triumph. The *nacimbusa* had to crawl under the hoop and the girls themselves were pushed under the hoop, first in one direction and then in the other. One of the girls' mothers gave a bracelet to hang on the *mupeto*, and then the two candidates uprooted the whole structure and carried it off to the river and threw it in. The scene was very animated. There was a hot discussion as to who should carry the girls, the maternal grandmother or the paternal. When this was settled the candidates were finally carried into the village.

(The jumping of the *mupeto* was described as a rite to make the girls grow (*ukubakushya*).)

The making of the lion

The helpers got no rest, but went immediately to the initiation hut where they started more potting work. The drums were going all the time, but everyone was tired. One young girl escaped to try and eat something, but was rebuked as being very insubordinate. Some of the older people managed to slip away.

The women worked hard at making a lion out of the log of *kabumba* which had been brought in from the bush. It was set up on four forked sticks and a most life-like head was then modelled in clay at one end, with the mouth reddened with *nkula*, and teeth made of pumpkin seeds. The clay head was then covered with grass arranged to look like hair, and the feet studded with beans. The whole effect was most impressive. It was by far the most realistic image that had been made.

Then the roof of the shelter made the previous day was used to make a new shelter against the wall, and again new beans were stuck up the supports of the shelter. The work went on at the utmost speed until about five o'clock when most of the women melted away and the *nacimbusa* was left by herself to repaint all the small pottery emblems for the final rite.

THE RITES OF THE LAST NIGHT

The blind bridegroom

We were called to the initiation hut at about eight o'clock in the evening. A big fire was lit on the hearth and water was already bubbling in three great pots ready to pour on the beer when the time came to serve the drink. The heat was already intense. Some twenty or thirty women were crowded on the floor of the hut with a small open space for dancing kept clear in the centre. Everyone seemed exhausted, with nerves on edge and a tendency to quarrel at the slightest provocation. But there was also a feeling of excitement in the air and I sensed that the climax of the ceremony had come.[1] Drums and singing went on right through the night into the early morning and accompanied every rite. Each of the songs I have mentioned was sung over and over again, so that there was rarely a moment of silence. The drums were played in relays, the younger women taking it in turns to play them.

The evening started with the entry of the mock bridegrooms once again. They came in shading their eyes and feeling along the edge of the door and the roof of the hut with their hands. They sang:

> '*I am groping about in the dark*
> *I am ill.*' (No. 30)[2]

The company burst out laughing. 'There they come, the blind men! The bridegrooms have come.'

(Women explained to me that the female bridegrooms were pretending that they were blind and could not see the *mbusa* that were to be shown the girls. 'It is because they have come to the house where the work has gone on.')

Swinging over the roof

The two girls were then lifted up and made to hang with their hands from rafters in the roof with their knees pulled up under their chins. They were swung to and fro so that they just cleared

[1] It was difficult to know this in advance since actors in a Bemba ceremony were never able to give me an exact programme of events beforehand. I think it likely that most of them knew the general sequence of the rites but that practical considerations determined the days which they fixed, and that there was considerable elasticity over timing.

[2] I did not get this point explained more fully. The bridegrooms may be blind because they are approaching the sacred emblems, the secret things of the women; or because they are being admitted to the initiation hut for the first time during the rite.

A.C. said: 'I am outwitted. I cannot see what I am doing. I am ready mishap.'

the 'shelter' with their buttocks. This would be a considerable gymnastic achievement for an ordinary English girl, but was evidently not thought difficult by Bemba girls with arm muscles developed by much grinding and pounding of food. The mock bridegrooms then repeated the performance and the rite was followed by a dance of respect to the older women by the father of one of the girls who came springing with a sort of chassis step into the hut, danced to acclamation and then disappeared as suddenly as he had come.

(The symbolism was again complicated and not described coherently by any of the women. I was told that this was the ceremony of 'the father of the roof' (*shintembo*). It meant that the bridegroom and bride were now to look after their relatives by marriage with kindness, i.e. not because of legal duty.

The triumph of the nacimbusa

Nangoshye then pushed her way into the dancing space and mimed a tired woman who yawned and stretched, but could find no place to sleep. A mock bridegroom ceremonially presented her with a sleeping mat and she lay down on it singing over and over again:

'Let us all lie down and sleep.'

Then the 'bridegroom' gave her a length of cloth and she wrapped herself in it singing:

'Spread the mat
So that we may sleep
The banacisungu *say*
You have wrapped us in cloth.' (No. 31)

(Women whispered that the bridegroom was paying the *nacimbusa* to hand over the secret things to the bride. The *nacimbusa*, in her turn, tells the bride that she must accept her husband, (*ukusumina umwaume*).)[1]

Nangoshye then went out of the hut and returned with the big baskets filled with the pottery models that had been made with so much labour for the rite. She stood triumphant at the door with

[1] *Subsequent Bemba interpretation.* A.C. added: 'When you have something to do, do it so that you will not be misunderstood.'

the pottery helmet known as the 'plumed head-dress' (*ngala*) on her head. A piece of bark-cloth was wrapped round her waist. The severe and rather domineering woman stood tense and excited at the doorway of the hut. Her great moment had come. She sang:

> '*The skin of the lion is worn*
> *At the court of* Mwamba.' (No. 32)

(The messenger of *Mwamba* (*musolo*) used to be clothed in lion skin in the old days. The *nacimbusa* is honoured as the messenger of a great chief. She is dressed in bark-cloth since this was the payment made to a *nacimbusa* at the end of a chisungu ceremony in the old days.)

The presentation of the mbusa. The pottery models were then pulled forward and the long rite of the giving of the *mbusa* began.

Each model has its associated song and the meanings of these songs are given in Appendix B. Each song was sung first by Nangoshye, then by some of the older women in turn, and then by each of the two girls. Each had its appropriate action to accompany the words. Some *mbusa* were merely offered ceremonially to different individuals present; others were handled with mimes suited to the associated song.

On the night in question forty-three different *mbusa* were presented to the girls. I have given interpretations for thirty in Appendix B and drawings of eighteen are given there. Here I try to group them somewhat arbitrarily under different headings. As each emblem may have several meanings this grouping is inevitably rather an artificial one.

A. DOMESTIC DUTIES

The mortar (Song 52, Fig. 15). The company mimed the stamping of grain and the song stressed the woman's duty to provide and prepare food.

The water-pot (Song 62). The imitation water-pot was put on the head of each girl in turn to the accompaniment of a song emphasizing the duty of the wife to get water for her husband.

The hearth-stone (Song 62). This was a conical-shaped model representing one of the pieces of ant-hill used to make the Bemba

101

fire-stands. The girl stood on the model and pretended to put a pot on the fire.

The pipe (Song 59). This was a rough imitation of a white man's pipe. It was used to teach the girl not to idle, smoking, all day.

B. AGRICULTURAL DUTIES

The garden mound (Song 44, Fig. 7). This model represents one of the women's gardening mounds. The song refers to industry in gardening and also, by a double meaning, to the husband's rights over his wife—the woman is a cultivated garden through which another man must not pass without trespassing.

The garden (Song 45, Fig. 8). This model, a helmet-like bowl, was handed to and fro by the actors during a song which urged the girl to put her energies into gardening and to take care to preserve the seeds so that she did not use up all the food in time of famine. This *mbusa* was also used in one of the woodland rites (see p. 95).

The hoe (Song 47, Fig. 10). Nangoshye took an imitation hoe, about 8 inches long, and pretended to hoe the ground and this the two girls did in turn after her, the other women miming the gesture of hoeing with their arms. The accompanying song urges the girl to cultivate her garden and, by a double meaning, likens the husband to a hoe which will open up the girl, who is thus compared to the garden.

C. OBLIGATIONS OF HUSBAND AND WIFE

The bracelet (Song 38, Fig. 1). This is a large clay bracelet, daubed with whitewash, which was put on each of the girls' arms in turn. It represents the *nsalamu* or initial instalment of the marriage payment and it stresses the husband's duty to provide clothes and other things for his wife.

The bead necklet (Song 39, Fig. 2). In some ceremonies this is a mushroom-shaped object representing the conus shell from which the triangular beads (*mpande*) worn by Bemba women are cut; in the ceremony that I witnessed the model was of the triangular bead itself, threaded with string and hung round the girl's neck or swung in one of the actors' hands. The song stated that 'My mpande bead has fallen in the chief's court' and referred to the fact that a wife, if ill-treated, would run back to her family. The husband would have to beg her back with as much humility as he would have to observe if he had dropped something precious in a chief's court.

The crocodile (Song 45). This was a realistic model of a crocodile with spines on its back and whitewash daubed all over. It was handed to and fro amongst the women. The reference was to the husband who is regarded as the crocodile which provides everything as does the chief. The crocodile lives in reeds which represent the secrecy guarding the house secrets. The husband may also behave like a crocodile and lie in wait for his wife if she deceives him.

The man who is a fool (Song 55). This was an inverted bowl put on the head of the actors like a helmet. The man is a fool if he doesn't look after and clothe his wife.

Cilume ca ciboa (Song 56, Fig. 18). This was a figure of a man with a large head and phallus and no arms. It represents the man who stays in the house all day finding fault with his wife and doing no work.

The young man walking smartly (Song 55b). This was a figure of a jaunty young man in European clothes with a hat on. He is the man who dresses himself up and does no work; or the man who goes to look for hoes for his marriage payment.

Ciboni musuma (Song 65). This is a conical-shaped model covered with small projections. It is said to represent a tree, and it is also the name of a beautiful head-wife of a legendary chief. The husband is to look upon his wife as the most beautiful of all women just as the chief preferred his head-wife to all others.

Sonsa nkalamo (Song 60). This is another conical-shaped model with small projections on it. The song tells the girl not to tell tales or to spread rumours or to gossip about her husband.

The porcupine (Song 49, Fig. 12). The porcupine model is a small round ball of clay stuck with spines and threaded on string. It is hung round the girl's neck and she is made to sway to and fro to the music so that the spines prick her breasts. This is said to be a punishment for her misdeeds before she reached the initiation ceremony. The song tells her that wrongs are never hidden but will come to light and be punished.

The star (Song 46, Fig. 3). This is a large round pot with a narrow mouth. It is perforated all over with small holes. A lighted taper is put inside to represent the starlight. The song urges the girl to show forgiveness even if her husband abuses her obscenely.

The husband with the plumes (Song 42, Fig. 5). This is a pine-apple-shaped vase with an irregular hole at the apex about eight inches high. It is covered with small projections and painted half white and half red. This is put on the *nacimbusa's* head. The company sings of the honour due to the husband who comes with plumed head-dress like the warrior or chief of old days. While she still wears this head-dress, the initiate takes the little spoon (Fig. 4) and pretends to pour water over the husband's hands with it and rubs the floor beneath with the other hand. This is a further representation of the wife's duty to wash her husband's hands with the water out of the ceremonial pot after intercourse (see p. 31).

D. OBLIGATIONS TO OTHER RELATIVES

The clan (Song 46, Fig. 9). This is a small basket with a handle. It is swung to and fro in the hand while the *mbusa* called the 'husband with the plumes' is worn on the head. The model illustrates the girl's duty to her relatives by marriage. She carries her marriage on her head, i.e. in the superior position: her clan is dangling in her head.

E. MOTHERHOOD

Coshi wa ŋoma (Song 53, Fig. 16). This is a figure about eight inches high representing a woman suckling two babies and carrying two on her back. The song describes the woman who weaned her child too soon so that it died.

Mwanakashi (Song 54, Fig. 17). This is a figure of a pregnant woman. The associated song says her days have come to give birth.

The house (Song 51, Fig. 14). This is a small model house with a tiny door made separately of sticks and clay. This is moved in and out by the singers. The child cries because the mother has gone out to a beer-drink and left it alone.

The Ceremony

The centipede (Song 64). This is a form of centipede like an enormous caterpillar which appears with the rains, with a black back and yellow legs. The model is coloured white. The song tells the girl that she must not have intercourse too often or she will produce twins which will die: multiple births like the many legs of the centipede. Or according to another account, she is warned to do purification after twins.

G. GENERAL ETHICS

The hyena (Song 64). A realistic figure with spines down its back. The girl is not to steal like the hyena.

The tortoise (Song 50, Fig. 13). For this model Nangoshye and her fellow *banacimbusa* squatted on their toes and jogged up and down to the music, pushing their heads alternately out and in with a curious change of expression from the eager and questing to the blank and uninterested as they sang:

> '*The tortoise when it is at home puts in its head*
> *Into its shell.*

The girl is not to be like a woman who, when she goes out visiting, peers into every basket and pot saying, 'Friend, what is here? Give me a taste of this. Let me share that.' Whereas when the friends come to visit her, she sits with lowered head and tries to divert attention from the food in her own house.

H. THE CHISUNGU CEREMONY

Some models refer to the rite itself.

The cardinal bird (Song 63) is a small bird painted white, with spots of red on its wings. The *kabangula* has a red crest and hence resembles the *nacimbusa* of old days who had a red feathered head-dress.

The egret (Song 48, Fig. 11). A bird on a twig. The song refers to the whitening and beautifying of the girl (see pp. 88–9).

The lion (Song 56, see p. 129). This is a large pot closed on top and with two open arms—it is called the lion because a noise resembling the roar of a lion can be made by blowing down one arm and blocking the other. The lion symbolism has been described before.

'Giving the child her *mbusa*' lasted far into the night and drumming and singing became somewhat languid as time went on.[1] 'Why doesn't the *nacimbusa* sing the song alone?' I asked a rather weary-looking woman. She looked startled at such a stupid question. 'But of course, each of the *banacisungu* must sing the words herself,' she said. It seemed to me a very significant remark to which I shall refer again.

The coming of the bridegroom

It was a relief when the hut-door opened and a shout went up, 'The bridegrooms have come!' Up till now the bridegrooms had been represented by female substitutes but at this culminating rite the *shicisungu* himself appears, or should appear. In fact, one of the girls was betrothed to a man away at the mines and he was represented by his sister, the mock bridegroom of the previous rites. The other girl was not betrothed, but one of her male cross-cousins took the part, since the cross-cousin is the preferential mate for a Bemba girl.

The bridegrooms came in gaily carrying bows and arrows. In front of them crawled two young girls, their sisters, carrying bundles of firewood strapped on their backs. They sang:

> '*You have not come back from fetching the firewood*
> *From where you went looking for faggots.*' (No. 33)

Meanwhile, each of the girls had been put to sit against the wall under the round spot representing her. The young brides were now dressed decorously with their cloths folded neatly over their breasts. They looked prettily demure rather than dazed and silent as heretofore. Neither looked up to watch the bridegrooms come in.

The bridegrooms then broke into a new song and took on a swaggering gait across the room, debonair, nonchalant, half-laughing. They danced, singing:

> '*I have tracked my game;*
> *Now I have speared my meat.*' (No. 34)

[1] The songs themselves are short but with a minimum of four singers, each repeating the couplet at least six times, the length of the 'giving the child her *mbusa*' can be imagined.

The Ceremony

Each aimed carefully at the round mark on the wall, above his bride. The arrows quivered in the soft whitewash of the wall and stuck there. Each bridegroom then put his foot ceremonially on the head of the girl posed there and then laid his bow against the wall above her. The two of them went swaggering out while the women made excited comments. 'See, he has shot her! He has wounded her! He has got the mark.' It was evidently considered a romantic moment by the company, and indeed seemed so to a mere stranger. It was the climax of the night's ceremony. The girls had been given their *mbusa*. The secrets had been given up. Their husbands had come to claim them in marriage.

The rite ended with the opening of the firewood bundles by the girls with their teeth. Inside was the usual packet of domestic *mbusa*, the meat, the beads and the red dye. These were ceremonially offered to the *banacisungu* present and to the grandfather of one of the girls, brought in for the occasion.

It was now about half-past one at night. The excitement had fizzled out. Bickering and shouting began and the beer was served out. The smoke in the hut was thick. Women were streaming with sweat and the two girls lay exhausted on the floor. Nevertheless the drums and the singing went on sporadically throughout the rest of the night. I slipped out of the hut at about half-past two, no longer able to write. The company stayed, still watching for the dawn.

EIGHTEENTH DAY

The cocks of the dawn (nkoko ya ncela)

I was called just after 4 a.m. The first cock had crowed. It was the signal for the final rite of the killing of the chickens. The two birds were tied up with their heads held on the ground. The drums were beating urgently and the two girls were jogging up and down to time, sitting and rising, sitting and rising, banging the heads of the chickens each time. This is considered an important rite. 'Why, if she can't kill the chicken we shall know that she isn't grown up yet. We shall call her a *citongo* (an uninitiated person).' It takes a long time to kill birds this way.

After their heads and necks had been bruised and the fluttering ceased, the birds had to be plucked by the girls and scorched and

107

then put to stew in water after the ordinary Bemba fashion of cooking chicken.

By now every cock in the village was crowing lustily and the women poured out of the hot smoky hut in to the bitter morning air of the cold season of the year. Everyone was drunk. Everyone was happy. Uncouth figures staggered round the village, like some satyr rout, laughing and singing:

> '*Mr. Cock*
> *When you come, have gone,*
> *Let us come and play.*' (No. 36)

The words had a catchy tune, and the drum beat went at the rear of the laughing crowd. A few men came to their hut doors blinking sleepily. They looked on acidly as people do when they have been woken from their beds by other people's merriment. At last the noise died down and only the oldest of the *banacimbusa* still ran round the village gardens alone singing in a cracked, drunken voice:

> '*You have slept with the chisungu child,*
> *You have slept with the lion.*' (No. 37)

The communal eating of the chickens

At about eleven, we were called again to the initiation hut. A big pot of porridge was being made to be eaten with the ceremonial chickens. The paternal grandmother of one of the girls was in charge. She pretended to hand a spoon of porridge to each and then took it back. Then came the common Bemba rite known as *ukulishya* by which those who have undergone a ceremony or kept taboos are made free to eat again with the rest of the community. Such people cannot touch food with their hands. They must be made free to do so. In this case, Nangoshye touched the girls' lips with the porridge and then made a big ball of it which each had to swallow whole. They were now free to eat with other people and join the ordinary life of the community again.

The porridge was then divided into three portions for the elders, the children and for the *banacimbusa*. Nangoshye carefully kept aside a wing of chicken for each girl and the rest of the stew was divided out as relish for the 25 or 30 women present.

108

The Ceremony

The bathing of the girls

The two girls were then taken down to the river to be ceremonially bathed—another rite which follows most Bemba ceremonies. A little beer must still have been hidden away in the village for some of the older women seemed happily drunk. They did intoxicated solo dances in the mud on the water's edge singing:

'*We have gone to fill the pot.*'

They put grass bracelets round the girls' arms saying that they were an earnest of the many things their husbands would give them later.

NINETEENTH DAY

At about five next morning, I was woken by soft clapping outside my tent. I lifted the flap and there knelt the *banacisungu*, washed and shaved and with shining new white handkerchiefs on their heads. They were still in the humble, submissive attitude with eyes on the ground but they answered me quickly with the shy smiles and the little courtesies expected of polite young Bemba girls, their faces for the first time alive and responsive. In fact, the phrase 'rite of transition' began to have a new meaning for me when I remembered the dirty frightened exhausted creatures who had been badgered and pushed through the chisungu weeks, and compared them with these demure and shy young brides. They begged for little presents. Later I watched them kneel and clap obeisance outside each hut in the village. 'They are submitting themselves to the elders' was Nangoshye's proud comment. 'They show they are willing to work for us.'

TWENTY-THIRD DAY

The congratulations (*ukushikula*)

Just as Bemba rites of transition are followed by the *kulishya* or the giving of the freedom to eat, so they are also usually followed by the *ukushikula* or presentation to the community. The chisungu candidate, the bride after her wedding ceremony, and the chief or headman who has succeeded to a new title are all submitted to the same rite. The person who has changed his status is brought out of his hut and placed on a new mat outside its door. He is bathed, oiled, usually shaved and dressed in new clothes and he sits in silence in front of the villagers. These come up in order of seniority and throw small presents on the mat and scold the person who has reached the new status for any faults he has been guilty of in his previous state. This is the *ukushikula*.

On this occasion each of the newly initiated girls sat on a mat with a real or potential husband at their sides. Their kinsmen came up shouting home truths at them as they dropped small bracelets or coins in a basket at their feet. The offerings were then gathered up by Nangoshye and distributed among her helpers. The chisungu rite was at an end.

The wedding ceremony

The wedding ceremony should have followed closely on the chisungu rite. It consists of the carrying of the bride to her husband's house, the consummation of the marriage when the bridegroom throws a burning faggot out of the door of the hut; and the ritual inauguration of the marriage pot of the young pair. There is a further *ukushikula* when the father of the girl gives the young bridegroom an arrow with which to protect her honour. The wedding ceremony was not performed for either of these two girls. One was not betrothed and the bridegroom of the other was at the mines.

CALENDAR OF EVENTS AT CHISUNGU PERFORMED AT CHINSALI, NORTH-EASTERN RHODESIA, IN 1931

1st Day *Entry into the hut (Ukuingishya)*
    The blessing of the girls.
    The hiding of the girls (*ukusakila*).
    The first jump.
    The first triumphant return to the village.
    The teasing of the girls.
7th Day *The first woodland ceremony.*
    The gardening mimes.
    Honouring the *musuku* tree.
    Preparation of the emblem bundles.

The Ceremony

First appearance of the mock bridegrooms.
Bringing the firewood back to the village.
The hut ceremonies.
   The first test of maturity (*njelele*).
   The girls made free to offer food.
   The ritual lighting of the girls' fire.
   The setting on of the girls' pot.
   The ritual cooking of the seeds. (*namushimwa*).

8th Day	*The painting of the wall designs.*
9th Day	*The modelling of the sun rays.*
	The modelling of the brother and sister and the bed.
10th Day	*The modelling of the guinea-fowl.*
11th Day	*The festive porridge eating.*
	The girls made free to eat food.
	The washing of the husband's hands.
13th Day	*The modelling of the snake.*
	The modelling of the fool.
14th Day	*The whitening magic.*
	Blessing of the ancestral spirits.
15th Day	*Modelling of the shelter.*
	Modelling of the screen.
17th Day	*The second woodland ceremony.*
	The honouring of the *mwenge* tree.
	The beer rite.
	The preparation of the jumping hoop.
	The triumphant return of the lion-killers.
	The final jump (ukushimpa umupeto).
	The modelling of the lion.
	Arrival of the blind bridegroom.
	The presentation of the pottery emblems.
	The bridegroom with the bow and arrow.
	The second test of maturity—killing of the chicken.
18th Day	*The communal eating of the chickens.*
	The bathing of the girls.
19th Day	*Obeisance of the bride to the village.*
23rd Day	*The congratulation ceremony (ukushikula).*

PART III

The Interpretation of the Ceremony

☆

METHODS OF INTERPRETATION

The anthropologist struggling to interpret a complex ceremony has to use a number of different approaches.

Expressed purposes (Primary)

His first step is obviously to ask the performers what they think they are achieving by their ritual behaviour and to summarize as accurately as possible the different views of the members of the community on these points. Such explanations may be called the *expressed* or *formulated* purposes of the rite, and it is important, to my mind, to distinguish very clearly from the outset what is said by the believers about a ritual act and what is deduced by the observer. There is certainly a good deal of variation in the extent to which people are able to formulate the objectives of their ritual. Some ceremonies are apparently performed with short-term ends which are clearly conceived and easily expressed. 'We do this to make childbirth easy' or 'to make the rain fall' for instance. Other symbolic acts may be performed with much more generalized objectives.[1] People will say they are carrying out a rite to ask for the blessings of the ancestors, to bring general good luck or happiness, or just 'to please the Gods'. They may believe that they can produce by their behaviour a desired condition of mind, or a harmonious system of relations. 'We do this to bring peace to the village' they may say; or 'to take anger from men's hearts'.

[1] Malinowski's distinction between magic and religious behaviour is mainly based on a distinction between short- and long-term objectives.

Painted designs on the walls of the hut showing (left to right)
1. 'Beans'; 2. 'The owl'; 3. 'The eyes'; 4. 'The wild goose'; 5. 'The butterflies'

Nangoshye putting white-wash on the girls

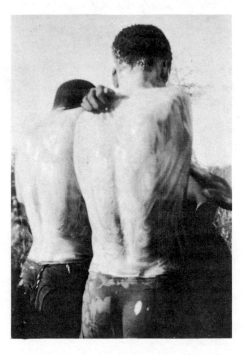

Girls covered with white-wash

Methods of Interpretation

It is obvious that a complete interpretation of every act in a ceremony is unlikely to be given by the whole community or even by the ritual experts in it. The nature of ritual, as I hope to show, demands that there should be multiple explanations for most of the forms of symbolic behaviour which compose it. But since rites are, to my mind, invariably an effort to 'do'—to change the undesirable, or to maintain the desirable, I believe that there is always some purpose, however general, behind a ceremony which the performers can, and will, express. In our society a man will tell us that he is going to church to marry Miss Brown although he may be quite unable to explain the symbolism of the different ritual acts which contribute to this end. In the cultures more usually studied by the anthropologist even the statement that 'We do this because our ancestors did it' may be an expression of some purpose or end.

Primary purposes of this kind may be single or multiple. For instance it may be quite clearly recognized by the performers that a rite has several objects. The *ncwala* ceremony of the Swazi is stated by the people to strengthen the king; to test the courage of a new regiment of young men; and to make the people free to eat the first fruits without harmful effects, besides producing many other results observed by the anthropologist and not by the performers themselves.[1] Such multiple purposes are characteristic of puberty ritual, as I have shown earlier.

Expressed or formulated purposes can be derived from an analysis of statements of dogma known to the whole community or to its ritual specialists; from comments and explanations heard in the course of inquiry, and perhaps from argument with informants; or from casual remarks which are made during the performance of the ceremony itself. There is obviously much individual variation within a given community as to the knowledge of the purposes of a ceremony, general or particular, which a man may possess. One purpose behind the rite may be known to the whole community, while another is esoteric knowledge, or information that is so detailed that only very intelligent members of the society, or ritual specialists, are able to verbalize it in answer to a question. The Archbishop of Canterbury does not give the same account of the meaning of the Holy Eucharist as

[1] Cf. Hilda Kuper, *An African Aristocracy, passim*, 1947.

the verger who watches at the church door, the worshipper in the Church or the young boy or girl who has just been confirmed. Again some ritual symbols are easily interpreted because they are formulated in a stereotyped way in that particular society; while others require thought and abstract generalization and the power to grasp the inquirer's point of view. The field worker knows the difference between the informant who really enjoys abstract thought, and the one who quickly gives up the attempt with the muttered statement that this rite is done because 'it is dangerous not to do it'.[1]

Earlier anthropologists were content with giving one or two accounts of a ceremony taken from the lips of one informant. Recent work on ritual has improved in detail in that it is usually based on direct observations and the comments of specialists together with as many non-specialist informants as possible.[2] The experiments of Kluckhohn and others have shown us how far the numerical analysis of individual views can be carried if sufficient time is available and a sufficient number of ceremonies witnessed.[3] I myself only attended one chisungu, and since I was single-handed I could not record all the remarks made by the participants as well as take photographs and note the words of songs. I had to resign myself to getting salient features of the rite rather than individual variations in belief, and this is what most anthropologists probably do during their first trip, with more or less care expended in the doing.

Expressed purposes (Secondary)

Expressed purposes may also include secondary as well as primary motives. For instance people may say that their object in doing such and such acts is to give their daughter in marriage but they may also recognize that the ceremony itself gives them prestige, binds their relatives to return them economic services, or raises their credit in the community. Initiation ceremonies have

[1] It must be remembered that men tend to formulate beliefs and ethical codes in times of change; they do not commonly express them when these are unchallenged. Bemba society was going through rapid social and economic change during my visit.

[2] R. Firth, *The Work of the Gods in Tikopia*, 1940, gives very detailed records of such observations and statements.

[3] Clyde Kluckhohn, *Navaho Witchcraft*, 1944.

sometimes been reintroduced into societies where they had lapsed because they have brought chances of earning money and prestige to their promoters under modern conditions. These motives may be perfectly clearly formulated by the people concerned, although they are secondary in the sense of being contingent on the first.

Deduced purposes

But beliefs and objectives can also be deduced from indirect evidence. We may be able to deduce the importance of a symbolic act or the nature of the performer's emotional reaction to it—their interest, tension or boredom, for instance; and it is for this reason that I have recorded as carefully as possible the emotional attitudes which seem to be expressed in the ceremony I witnessed. Another method is to analyse different texts describing the rites in the hope of finding some common stress or revelation of interest. It may be possible to make some kind of statistical estimate of the recurrence of particular symbolic acts; or the repetition of statements of belief. Ceremonies which the performers absolutely refuse to leave out can reasonably be assumed to have more significance than those that are slurred over or omitted, and the preceding account gives instances of laborious work which the mistress of the chisungu ceremonies refused to shorten under any circumstances. Similarly, we can deduce that a ritual act in an African religion which is quickly abandoned in response to a European prohibition, or to the appeal of another faith such as Christianity or Mohammedanism, must be based on a less fundamental belief than one which still continues to be performed after long contact with other civilizations.

Lastly, the meaning of a vital act may perhaps be deduced by an analysis of other ceremonies performed by the same community in which an identical or similar act occurs.[1]

The anthropologists' interpretations of religion and magic are naturally based largely on sociological concepts, and they tend to emphasize the function of ritual in maintaining a particular institution, such as the family, or a reciprocal exchange system,

[1] A. R. Radcliffe-Brown's account of the meaning of particular Andaman beliefs is almost entirely based on an analysis of this kind. Cf. *The Andaman Islanders*, 1922.

such as the Kula ring. They also stress the importance of religious rites in expressing the norms of a tribe as a whole. In some cases too they have pointed out that practical results may follow from the performance of a rite which has some quite other ostensible purpose. Modern anthropologists have been less interested in the function of religious rites in relation to the individual's needs and emotions.[1]

The following types of explanations of ritual behaviour are commonly offered. First a ceremony can be described in relation to the common norms and values of a given tribe and its notions of causality. Thus a ritual in connection with a particular institution can very well be examined in relation to the ethical codes and laws governing that institution, the social group involved and the activities it carries out. For instance the different ritual acts in a funeral ceremony may be analysed in relation to the performer's dogma as to life in the after world, myths about the origin of the people concerned, the obligations binding the patrikin and matrikin of the dead man and his affinal relatives or the economic exchanges carried out between them.

The most commonly accepted view of the sociological functions of ritual is that this type of religious behaviour expresses, make public, reinforces, or teaches tribal norms. This view is epitomised in Radcliffe-Brown's statement that a society exists because it is united by common social sentiments and that these sentiments must be constantly maintained at a given intensity.[2] It follows that in the case of a given institution the anthropologist should ask how far the values and beliefs he believes to govern the activities and relations of a particular group are actually expressed or symbolized in their rites. In the case of the chisungu ceremony, for instance, we shall ask how far the relations between husband and wife, as they are enforced by law, extolled in fable, and otherwise represented as desirable by the community are also symbolized in the ceremony.

[1] This apparent lack of interest in the individual is probably due to the lack of sufficient time to study individual reactions in a single field trip. Radin, Lowie and other American anthropologists have presented material of this sort in the form of autobiographies of Indians who saw visions or went into trances, and Malinowski and Firth have always described ritual from both the social and the individual angles.

[2] Cf. A. R. Radcliffe-Brown, *The Andaman Islanders*, 1922, p. 264.

Methods of Interpretation

But anthropologists also tend to see the values of the tribe as forming some kind of system, whatever inconsistencies and contradictions there may be within the system.

Consequently they look for the expression of general norms of behaviour or beliefs about the world in any important series of religious ceremonies. It is more than likely that mortuary ritual may symbolize the performers' duty to their chief or the values they set on different economic activities as well as grief for the dead man whom they praise in their lamentations. The correspondence between the total values system of a tribe and its symbolic expression in ritual is never exact. Some basic values, that is, ideals held by the whole tribe seem to be dramatically represented; others are not. Little exact comparison of the rites and the values has ever been made, largely because anthropologists are still without a useful method of classifying tribal values in a way which would make systematic examination easy. The experiment is, nevertheless, worth making if only because it may lead them to formulate hypotheses as to the type of values and beliefs which are most frequently expressed in ritual, and those which are not. It may even make it possible, after much further work, to detect some correlations between types of social structure and types of ritual.

Similar explanations of the function of ritual are those which state, often quite categorically, that religious ceremonies exist to promote the social cohesion of the group. The emphasis here is not on any particular institution in a society or on a set of values rooted in its political, economic or domestic activities but on the importance of maintaining some feeling of unity in a group.

Such types of explanation followed closely on Durkheim's stimulating and vivid reconstruction of what he imagined a totemic ceremony to be among some of the Australian Aborigines and the function such a rite may perform in promoting group consciousness or the individual sense of becoming part of a larger whole.[1] Later observations have shown that important ceremonials are just as often occasions of group division as of union,[2]

---

[1] E. Durkheim, *Les formes élémentaires de la vie religieuse*, 1912, cf. also A. R. Radcliffe-Brown, *op. cit.* and E. E. Evans Pritchard, 'The Dance', *Africa*, vol. I, 1928.

[2] See my *Hunger and Work in a Savage Tribe*, 1932, p. 71.

and communities at such times split into clan, lineage or affinal groups or give a public display of an order of precedence. Simple membership of the group or sentiments of union are not the only ones displayed. It is in this way that structural interpretations of ritual have recently been given.[1]

For such hypotheses there is rarely any possible verification, unless a senior member of the society openly asserts that the rites promote loyalty, or unless it is found that there are two areas in one of which the ceremony is held and the other not, and that these can be compared. It is reasonable to assume that any form of joint activity makes for closer ties between members of a society who meet face to face; an important ceremony may be the occasion of the largest gathering which a man in a primitive society ever attends. However, anthropologists have shown a tendency to argue that a group experiences intensified loyalty because it has attended a ceremony, and that the ceremony exists because the group has such strong feelings that it insists on holding one—a circular argument.

Later, the emphasis on religion as an expression of group cohesion led some anthropologists to explain ritual as a symbolic representation of social tensions as well as of social harmony. The more detailed the analysis of social structure became, the more frequently were tensions seen to exist between one group and another or one social role and another.

Here the anthropologist has relied heavily on the psycho-analytical hypotheses. The hypothesis that the individual finds compensation for the frustrations or conflicts in his situation in the symbolism of dreams was early extended by psycho-analysts to the ritual field. The religious rite according to such views provides a symbolic solution for particular emotions which are either universal or else inherent in a particular social system.

Anthropologists interested in social structure—and they have been in the majority of recent years—have started to explain forms of ritual which seemed surprising or quite at variance with the social values of the tribe, as ritual expressions of hostilities which have to be repressed in daily life, or as symbolic compensations for the unpleasant roles which society may assign to an

[1] See the work of M. Fortes, M. Gluckman, and E. R. Leach.

individual or a group. Thus Bateson's ingenious analysis of the Naven ceremonies on the Iatmul islands suggests that the transvestism which occurs there can be explained in terms of the woman's desire to swagger for once as a man as a compensation for her submissive role in everyday life. Gluckman interprets a rain rite among the Zulu in which women dress up as men, carry shields, and behave obscenely and aggressively in somewhat the same way.[1]

All these conjectures cannot be proved until we have far more complete data from different areas. We do not know for instance whether the groups in question feel the tensions we impute to them, although this could probably be examined in terms of legal cases, witch-craft accusations or perhaps by means of psychological tests. Psychological interpretations are bound to be of the heads-you-win, and tails-you-lose type. If a woman behaves submissively in ritual, the explanation offered is that she is expressing the sex role that is proper to a woman in a society in which meekness in women is admired; if she swaggers the explanation is that she is reacting from this submissive role.

Lastly, ritual may have a number of practical effects which are not at all intended by the performers and of which they or the majority of them are not aware. Malinowksi points out that the series of gardening rites among the Trobriand islanders serves to organize very effectively the different stages of their agricultural work. Firth has shown that the seasonal taboos of bird snaring among the Maori are explained in religious terms but that they also give protection to the birds during the breeding season. The Bemba themselves say that they wait for the blessings of their chiefs before cutting their gardens because they believe that otherwise they would lack the goodwill of their ancestral spirits. The European observer, however, regards this ceremony as a useful device for securing that the gardens are cut at an advantageous time of the year from the point of view of weather and temperature. Such 'pragmatic' effects (to use the term as Malinowski has done so fruitfully, in his analysis of different forms of Trobriand magic) should certainly be distinguished from the

---

[1] G. Bateson, *Naven*, 1936, and M. Gluckman, 'Zulu women in hoe culture ritual', *Bantu Studies*, vol. IX, 1935.

expressed purposes of the people concerned. The latter is a system of ideas, and the former a result of social action which may not appear clearly to the anthropologist until he has examined the effects of a number of rites.

In a sense all the types of anthropological interpretations just listed can be described as pragmatic since they are based on the argument that people carry out religious rites because they fulfil some function for the individual, the society as a whole, or the groups of which it is composed; because, in short, they satisfy a need.

Lastly it is important to study ritual as a teaching device in relation to general methods of education in the society; of the public proclamation of legal obligations in ritual in relation to the other means of enforcing such duties; and to an examination of the different ritual acts as a means of giving confidence to individuals or groups.

I will advance explanations of all these different kinds in the case of the chisungu.

EXPRESSED PURPOSES OF THE CHISUNGU

Primary. When questioned directly as to why they need to dance the chisungu for their girls, most older Bemba speak with the utmost energy. It is quite clear that the rite is intended to do something, and to do something that is felt to be most necessary and important. Men as distinct from women do not know, or are not supposed to know, the subsidiary purposes of the rite, but they speak in general terms. They say that of course the rite is necessary. No one would want to marry a girl who had not had her chisungu danced. She would not know what her fellow women knew. She would not be invited to other chisungu feasts. She would just be a piece of rubbish (*cipele*); an uncultivated weed (*cangwe*); an unfired pot (*citongo*); a fool (*cipumbu*) or just 'not a woman'. They lay emphasis on the preparation of the girl for marriage and for a change of status. Men know the magic dangers to which a girl becomes subject at puberty, but it would not be proper for them to express them. Their answers, often given with considerable violence of expression, amounted often to little more than saying that the girl is initiated to prevent her remaining uninitiated.[1]

Women were prepared to be much more specific. Their answers did not refer to marriage but to the transformation of the young girl. Their replies could be divided into three types which reflect three aspects of the rite in Bemba eyes. The chisungu is danced they say, to make the girl grow (*ukumukushya*); to teach her (*ukumufunda*); and 'to make her a woman as we are'. The first object has the clarity of the typical magic intention. It is a rite designed to change the course of nature by supernatural means, and as we shall see, to test whether these changes have been brought about. The second is described as 'teaching', with the use of the word commonly now employed for teaching in European schools, although, as we shall see, this form of teaching is also a type of ritual behaviour, possibly with magic intent. The third purpose was expressed with greater vagueness and was one concerning which attitudes had to be mainly deduced.

(*a*) *The magic of growth and nubility*. What does the word *ukukushya* mean? It is the causative form of the word 'to grow'. In other words 'We do the rite to grow the girl'. It is used primarily of the jumping tests at the beginning of the rite and at two subsequent stages, that is to say the first, the seventeenth and the last days. The chisungu has of course many of the features common to rites of transition in the sense in which Van Gennep uses the term. The ritual separation of the girls was clearly marked. They slept in a separate hut and were never seen during the day unless actually participating in a ceremony. They concealed themselves very effectively, but they were also ritually hidden. They entered the initiation hut on the first day under the cover of blankets and they remained hidden in this way until the third day when they returned from the first woodland ceremony. They were covered with branches in the rite described as the hiding or fencing in of the girls. A song described them as crawling into a secret place as if through a tunnel.

---

[1] Young men would very often admit that most girls were not now 'danced' but even among educated Bemba I noticed a good deal of nostalgia for the old days when girls were 'taught'.

The Interpretation of the Ceremony

Social isolation was also marked by abstention from the usual habits of life. The girls wore old and shabby cloths tied round their waists. They were three times rebuked for tying their cloths above their breasts in the ordinary fashion of Bemba women. Their food was cooked on a separate fire. They were not allowed to wash or shave. This isolation was shared to some extent by all the actors of the chisungu. For instance, the men of the community were kept away from the important ceremonial and were rebuked for passing near the spot where the pottery emblems were made. They consistently looked the other way when the procession of women went through the village, and stood with lowered eyes when the girls were brought from the ceremony of whitening. The mothers of the girls and the *nacimbusa* should have shared the isolation of the candidates by keeping washing and shaving taboos, but airily explained their lapse by saying that they were 'nearly Christians'.

Such symbolic acts of separation occur in other forms of Bemba ritual when a change of social role has taken place, such as in the marriage ceremony proper or the rite of installation of a chief. But the characteristic element here is the number of stages the girl has to pass, and also the emphasis on the difficulty, not only of the new life, but of the tests of maturity the girl has to pass. The candidates were 'given their gardens' or made free to garden on their own. Their new fire was ritually lit and they were made free to touch the fireplace, to cook food, and to offer it to other women in the rite of the *namushimwa*. They were twice made free to eat food, once after the lighting of the *namushimwa* fire, and once by the touching of their lips with porridge and with the livers of the ritually cooked chickens on the last night of the ceremony. They were bathed, shaved, dressed in new clothes and finally brought out to receive the congratulations of the community.

These are rites of role assumption, but is there not also an element of test, or actually of ordeal, in the magic sense of the word? It is difficult to say whether the symbolic acts of separation and rejoining the community are thought to cause social maturation and can thus be ranked as magic of growth; or whether they are signs of the readiness of the candidate for such changes, or signs that the change has successfully occurred. Probably all three elements are combined in the chisungu but the symbolic jumps seemed to me to be certainly in the nature of a test or omen. The agitation of the candidates' mothers was extreme. 'What happens if the girl fails to clear the jump?' 'Nothing, but it is very good if she does. Anyhow she *must* jump it. We do not let them fail.' Such statements were made about the test of the girls' ability to catch the water insects in their mouths, or to kill the chickens by bruising their heads on the last night, and the bridegrooms' shooting at the mark on the wall.

An analysis of the song interpretations also shows the strong emphasis that is placed throughout the rite, on the duty of the girl to do difficult and unprecedented things, to climb up trees backwards or to crawl backwards for instance. The informants explained that such songs stress the difficulty of what the girl has to do. They tell her that she is to do something she has never done before and accept new demands made on her.

Van Gennep has stressed the significance of puberty ritual as the expression of a change of status. But it must not be forgotten that the Bemba women say 'we make her grow' and I believe that it will be found that many of the tests of endurance in initiation ceremonies, like 'the teasing of the girls' in the chisungu, are not only signs of ritual submission to authority and payments made for the receipt of magic protection but also are forms of ordeal or oracle magic. In other words they reflect the anxiety of parents and relatives as to whether the candidates really are grown up or socially fit for married life, as well as the recognition of the society that a change of status has occurred. It will be remembered that the mother of the girl is blamed if her daughter is shown not to have social sense or '*mano*' (page 75).

Ukukushya is also the word used for the rites designed to protect the girl from the dangers associated with the physical onset of puberty and to make it possible for her to have safe intercourse with her husband and a safe delivery of her child. Women say with lowered eyes that the chisungu is to remove the girl's fear, the fear of blood and the dangers of sex and fire which I have described so fully.

It is difficult to separate this aspect of the ceremony from the other acts that compose it since the whole chisungu is thought to contribute to this end, but the theme of the removal of danger is seen in a number of isolated songs and mimes. In one of the first songs, the danger is described as a stone that falls off the girls. The menstrual blood is represented throughout by the colour red on pottery emblems and house designs, by the red cam wood enclosed in the emblem bundles, or the light of the torch glowing red inside the model of the star (see Appendix C).

The blood is removed by whitening. One of the designs on the hut wall is known by the archaic term for whitewash. The girls themselves are painted white like the egret and they are likened to beautiful white birds. The egret is modelled as a clay *mbusa* to be given to the candidates on the last night.

Red cam wood is also used as a sign of safe return from battle. The candidates and the main actors in the ceremony were daubed with the crimson powder on four occasions—after the first jump over the faggots; on the seventh day after the first woodland ceremony; after the whitening magic; and on the last day when the symbolic lion is brought back dead to the village. The girls and their families have done something fearful and they have succeeded. They have been through danger and have escaped. The culture teaches terror of menstrual blood. The chisungu provides the means of safety. It is magic of protection which can only be secured, like other forms of magic help, by carrying out prescribed acts and by paying penalties or dues to those in possession of the secret, in this case the *nacimbusa*. It is also a series of representations or mimes depicting safety and giving a sign that safety has been reached.

The magic of fertility is also clearly another of the elements in the chisungu ritual. The whole ceremony makes the girl nubile and thus potentially fertile, but different acts are more specifically described as reproducing the sex act. They call to mind the fish which is a fertile animal and lays many eggs. One of the hut drawings also depicts a fish. The *musuku* tree is associated with fertility and is honoured in the first woodland rite. The gardening mimes are carried out at its roots. The mock bridegrooms appear with leaf horns on their heads like the witchdoctors who possess fertility magic. A snake is said to be hidden in the roof of the hut.

Expressed Purposes of the Chisungu

The ritual lighting of the girl's fire by the father's sister was described as 'begging for parenthood'. Later a branch of the *mupundu* tree, from which women gather fruit, is stuck in the roof of the initiation huts in order to make the girls equally fruitful. Two of the wall designs represent beans which are commonly symbols of fertility. One of the hut designs represents the girl's bed. In the second woodland ceremony the *mwenge*, the woman's tree, is honoured, and beer poured on its roots. One of its branches crossed with the male tree, the *mulombwa*, forms the hoop over which the girls must jump.

It is difficult to be certain how far human fertility is associated with agricultural fertility in these rites. I was never specifically told that the garden mimes were done to make the gardens yield, but merely to 'teach the girls to garden', but it would certainly be hard to distinguish very clearly between the productivity of the girls and the productivity of the seeds they sow in rites which involve the constant handling of seeds of different kinds.

To conclude I believe that the women in charge of this ceremony were convinced that they were causing supernatural changes to take place in the girls under their care, as well as marking those changes. They were changing an alarming condition to a safe one, and securing the transition from a calm but unproductive girlhood to a potentially dangerous but fertile womanhood. They were making the girls grow as well as teaching them. Hence I feel justified in speaking on the 'magic' aspects of the rite.

(*b*) *The teaching of the girls* (*ukufunda*). As we have seen, Bemba women explain that they are teaching the candidates during the chisungu ceremony. They say with great emphasis and characteristic repetition 'We teach and teach and teach the girls' and they sometimes add 'We make them clever' using the causative form of the verb 'to be intelligent and socially competent and to have a knowledge of etiquette', (*ukubacenjela*).

The educational function of puberty ritual has often been stressed by anthropologists and lectures on primitive education were formerly largely concerned with accounts of initiation schools, sometimes described as 'the only formal education' received by the primitive child. Most of the accounts of girls'

125

puberty ceremonies in Central Africa contain such phrases as 'the girls are then given *instruction* in sex and motherhood'. It is therefore important to ask ourselves at the outset the sense in which the Bemba are here using the word 'teach'.

I must admit that their emphasis on this function of the chisungu and their use of the word *ukufunda*, which they now commonly employ for European school teaching, at first misled me. Even after fairly wide comparative reading on the subject I began to imagine that the candidates had at least some direct instruction on some subject or other at some time during the ceremony. I confess to a mental picture of the girls sitting in the initiation hut and listening to talks from an old woman on what might be called in modern idiom 'marriage guidance'.

I doubt whether any such direct instruction took place during the chisungu I witnessed, or indeed in any other such rite. The time free for such teaching was very small. Added to this the girls were usually shoved away in the corner of the initiation hut and sometimes given direct orders not to look at what was going on. Their heads were, more often than not, closely wrapped under thick blankets. I never heard any part of the ceremony explained. If any useful information was handed out during the chisungu one would be inclined to think that the candidates themselves would be the last people to have a chance of acquiring it. The women said they were teaching them 'the things of womanhood' and also 'things of the gardens'. In other words, how to bear and bring up children, to cook, act as housewife, and garden, and we saw that rites representing hoeing, sowing, cooking, gathering fire-wood and the distributing of food occurred throughout the ceremony. But instruction, in the European sense, was quite unnecessary in such subjects. Bemba girls play at cooking as soon as they can stand, and they help their mothers in the house most of the day. They go with the older women to garden and also learn from them how to look for mushrooms and wild spinaches. Moreover, the more complex aspects of housekeeping such as the care of the granary and the reaping of the grain are not entrusted to the girl until some years after marriage. That is to say the chisungu rite neither gives additional knowledge or skill nor the right to use it. In the same way, Bemba girls are not ignorant of the nature of sex since many of them have been given to their husbands before puberty and some form of intercourse, usually incomplete, has taken place. They have also acted as nurses of their young brothers and sisters to an extent that is rare in most sections of our society, and they are therefore familiar with the elements of the rather simple system of child care practised in this tribe.

What then do the Bemba girls learn in their chisungu or in what sense can they be said to learn?

First of all they learn a secret language or rather, secret terms. The different *mbusa* have names supposedly, at any rate, known only to initiated women. For instance I was taken some way into the bush to be told with every precaution to ensure secrecy that 'we women' call whitewash *lota*, an archaic term, instead of *pemba*, the more common word. Girls also learn the chisungu songs. The doggerel rhymes associated with the *mbusa* (see Appendix B) are some of them widely sung, but they have a number of secret or semi-secret meanings apart from the overt one. What seems to the educationist to be the most mumbo jumbo and useless aspect of the whole affair may actually constitute one of the most prized items of information to the people concerned.

Girls are also said to learn the secret language of marriage. The Bemba language abounds in phraseology with hidden or allusive meaning. It is part and parcel of court etiquette and it is used in other special social relationships and in particular between husband and wife. 'We married people' said a male informant 'know how to say things that a young boy and girl would not understand. That is what we want a girl to learn at her chisungu'. The intimacy that surrounds the physical relation of husband and wife, described as 'the secret things within the house' seems to the European to be curious in view of the lack of other forms of intimate companionship between them, but it is evident that it is the special phraseology and the taboos of married life that a man hopes his wife will learn in the chisungu. The candidates also have to learn the rather complex sequence of the rites themselves which represents a considerable effort of memory in communities without a written language.

Nor does it matter if the girl herself does not see the whole of the ceremony which is performed over her. It is a form of education

that is recognized to be cumulative. A girl may have little intellectual understanding of what is being done at the time of her
chisungu, although she may be in a highly emotional state in
which she is likely to be suggestible to the general emphasis laid
on the importance of marriage and childbirth. Next year however
she will act as a young helper of the *nacimbusa* and so her knowledge will grow. As one old *nacimbusa* put it 'If she has seen two
ceremonies, or three, a girl will come to me and say "Tell me about
the crocodile". She remembers and then she comes and asks me
again "Tell me some more about the crocodile" and I tell her more.
But other girls have no ears. They do not ask anything. They just
say "Let it be, those are things of the chisungu" '. In other words,
clever girls begin to memorize and get more and more knowledge
of the deeper associations of the symbols and these girls probably
become specialist *banacimbusa* as they grow older. The others, no
doubt, give up when they find they cannot master the intricacies
of the ceremonial.[1]

Secondly the chisungu teaches, not the technical activities of
the wife, mother and housewife, but the socially approved attitude towards them. The women themselves see this point and, in
fact, made it to me. An intelligent *nacimbusa* will admit that the
girls know how to cook and grind but will say that after her
chisungu a young girl does her work in a different way. Such
women explain that, when young, a girl can idle in the gardens if
she likes and her mother will shrug her shoulders and say 'She is
not grown up'; but when she is married, she cannot refuse her
duties or it will be a cause of divorce. Husbands will scold a lazy
wife and this will bring shame on her family. As one woman put it:
'Before, if they were called to work they could go slowly. Now
they have to run.' In other words, the girl is told that she has to
do things with a new spirit and a new sense of responsibility. The
rite not only consecrates the woman's duties in the sense of making
them seem honourable, but it is an occasion for the public affir-
mation of the legal obligations of the marriage. There are pottery
emblems associated with most of the duties of bride and bride-

[1] The Kriges point out that a Lovedu girl is only considered properly initiated
when she has witnessed the ceremonies six times. Cf. *The Realm of a Rain Queen*,
1943.

groom in marriage. A glance at the list given in Appendix B will show that there are songs associated with the girl's duty to her husband and to her in-laws, with the correct behaviour of the mother towards her child and to the community of her fellow-women. Other songs and figurines are associated with the wife's domestic duties as a gardener or a cook. There are duties she assumed at marriage and as part of her marriage contract, and it will be remembered that during the last night of the ceremony the girl has to sing each song herself and handle the associated pottery *mbusa*. It seems likely therefore that these rites are the means by which the girl publicly accepts her new legal role. These are the obligations handed down to her. These are the *mbusa* which she is given at her ceremony and which her friends congratulate her on receiving. It must be remembered too that for the Bemba girl these marriage obligations are probably the first acts of individual responsibility she has been asked to undertake, a point to which I will return later.

There are, of course, other social obligations mimed in the chisungu ceremony, such as the proper submission of the girl to her husband; the distribution of food to the family; and the exchange of gifts. The relationship between brother and sister is depicted in the pottery image known by that name for example; there is also the squat and unattractive figure of the lazy wife. I think that these mummeries, to use the term employed by the Kriges in their description of Lovedu ceremonial, must be reckoned as rather different from the rites of role assumption mentioned above. The women were amused at seeing the images of the brother and sister but there was no insistence that the girl herself must handle these or herself sing the attached song.

It is difficult, and probably unnecessary, to draw hard and fast lines between mimetic rites designed to produce a result, and which can therefore be reckoned as magic behaviour; rites which represent behaviour associated with a social role; and rites by which the individual publicly proclaims that she is ready to accept a role which will afterwards be enforced by legal penalties. I use here the terms 'magic rites', 'representative rites' and 'rites of role assumption' because they seem to me to correspond to differences in the people's own attitude.

The Interpretation of the Ceremony

(c) *The chisungu as a rite of status change.* Uninitiated women are referred to contemptuously in Bemba society. Is there any evidence that the rites are definitely considered as a means of admitting the chisungu candidates to a new social group such as an age grade?

The ceremonies have many of the elements common to puberty ritual which is said definitely to mark the entry of a boy or girl to a new group—such as occurs, for instance, when the Sotho adolescent of either sex becomes an initiation candidate, and then a grown-up person.

As in these other ceremonies esoteric knowledge is revealed in return for payment by the candidates or their relatives in terms of endurance of suffering or discomfort—a payment in kind. The Bemba parents pay the *nacimbusa* and give her food. The girls are teased and troubled.

But here the similarities end. There is no evidence that even in former days girls who had been 'danced' were clearly distinguished in terms of clothing or ornaments from those who had not. The great *banacimbusa* wore plumed head-dresses and leopard skins but these were tributes to their individual eminence apparently, and not to any stage in their passage through a series of age grades. Linguistically, too, there is no distinct terminology describing a formal age grade. The term *mukashyana* is used for a young girl just before marriage and just after, and as we saw, the occupations of the two are very similar. Marriage does not bring an independent status in any sense of the word. Such terms as *citongo* and *cipele* are used now, at any rate, rather as terms of abuse slung about in the heat of a village quarrel than as a description of social categories. They imply a change of state from the unmarriageable to the marriageable rather than membership of a new group. They indicate possession of or absence of knowledge of marital behaviour and social etiquette. The chisungu confers the right to bear a child, but not to join an age set.

Nevertheless the girl does acquire new relationships through her chisungu and submits herself to new authorities. It goes without saying that she is in a somewhat different position with regard to her affinal relatives since the ceremony is the first of a series of rites which mark the gradual consolidation of the marriage rela-

130

tionship.[1] But the girl also assumes a position in an informal group composed of the women of the neighbourhood. The chisungu candidate of one year works the following year for the same *nacimbusa* and joins the ranks of her young helpers. The mistress of the ceremony is often the girl's father's sister, so that the head of this loosely organized cult group is also the senior woman of the patrikin. All *banacimbusa* of a district are arranged in order of age, descent and reputation, although their position is now only recognized in terms of respect and formal salutations. Associated with these women leaders of the society are younger married women of intelligence and personality, who are beginning to practise as midwives, as well as those initiated some years previously. Girls just initiated are under an obligation to help their own *nacimbusa* for one or two subsequent ceremonies, but they need not advance any further up the ladder of fame unless they want to do so. The chisungu gives them entry to the company of the leading women in the neighbourhood and makes it possible for them to rise gradually in the hierarchy of potential *nacimbusa*, although it is not compulsory for them to do so.

Within this loose neighbourhood group the older women are honoured, not as a group of equals, but, in line with Bemba ideals, as a number of persons arranged in an exact order of precedence. This hierarchy of age and fame is constantly expressed in the ceremony. 'The arm-pit is not higher than the shoulder' is the song which the company sings over and over again.[2] The chief *nacimbusa* appears in her plumed head-dress. The *mbusa* are offered again and again in order of rank precedence to the older women present. They are offered kneeling, and rolling on the back as to a chief. Dances are given 'for respect'. In fact more rites express the hierarchy of rank than any other form of symbolic behaviour in the chisungu.

It is perhaps worth noting that a hierarchy of closely related women is a much more common occurrence in a matrilineal tribe

[1] See page 44 which describes the chain of events which begins with the betrothal presents, and continues with the giving of food to the son-in-law, the first puberty rite, the chisungu, the marriage itself, and then the entering-in of the son-in-law some years later.

[2] I.e. the arm-pit was created to be beneath the shoulder, and this order can never be reversed.

with uxorilocal residence than in a patrilineal one with patrilocal residence. The pivoted relationships of a Bemba village are those based on the woman and not on the man, as we have explained.

The position of the senior women in the chisungu also reflects their activities in everyday life. The *nacimbusa* is the midwife. She attends the childbed of the girls she has 'danced'. She provides the magic which will enable them to come safely through the ordeal. She divines to find out which ancestral spirit is being born. She listens to confessions of adultery, which are often forced, if there is delay or difficulty in the birth of the baby. It depends on her to conceal or tell to the in-laws of any real or supposed bad behaviour of the girl, or any ill-omened birth. Did the girl cry out in her pains? Did she relax her efforts and 'kill' the child by collapsing from the exhausting squatting position, thought necessary during childbirth, to the floor while the child's head was about to appear? Was the baby born feet foremost? All these facts can be revealed or concealed by the *nacimbusa*.

The mistress of the ceremonies often becomes the protector (*mbosua*), or, as we might say, the god-mother of the child. In the old days she gave permission for the resumption of sex relations between husband and wife after the birth and gave advice on the many magic precautions that were needed to protect the young child. She had the right to intervene and correct. Thus the girl child delivered and guarded by the *nacimbusa* was watched by her during her growth to womanhood. She confessed her peccadilloes to the same woman at her chisungu; received admonition in her final congratulation ceremony, and remained in close relation with the *nacimbusa* and her helpers throughout her married life. It is, I think, significant that the mothers sing about giving over their girls to the *nacimbusa*. The mother is tender and indulgent, but the *nacimbusa* corrects. The mother and daughter cannot easily talk of sex matters together, but the grandmother, probably also herself a *nacimbusa*, or some non-related midwife is not limited in this way.

It is because the girl has been 'danced' and is magically changed; because she has been 'taught' and has assumed a position in a hierarchy of women and has the protection of the *nacimbusa* of her district that she is no longer a weed, a piece of rubbish or an unfired pot.

Expressed Purposes of the Chisungu

Secondary motives. Apart from such primary considerations, the Bemba, no doubt, have a number of secondary motives. As in the case of other rituals of this type the chisungu is an occasion for entertainment and the meeting of friends and relatives. These are mainly women, but men also visit the chisungu village for the purpose. As we have seen, few of the rites are solemn and a number of them provide opportunities for amusing play-acting, games and solo dancing. Women, in fact, speak of some of the rites as 'just playing'. The festive aspect of the chisungu must have been more marked in the old days when the rites took longer, the supply of food and beer was probably more ample, and the young men of the community were not away at the mines.

A number of Bemba seem consciously to realize that the chisungu is an occasion for the display of social status—the status of the parents of the bride and bridegroom and of the *nacimbusa* herself. At the ceremony I attended the exchange of food was, in Bemba eyes, on a pitiably small scale and, as we saw, Nangoshye constantly complained that she was being insulted by the mean fare cooked for her. Ceremonies in the old days seem to have involved a series of presentations of covered dishes of food (*ukutebeta*), of the kind known as 'honouring the son-in-law' that mark his reception into his bride's village before the chisungu takes place. A written account I obtained of the chisungu in the old days included four such preparations of food besides the porridge of festivity of which I have given an account.

This is a society in which the ceremonial expression of kinship obligations is important, especially in the long process of aggregating a young husband to his wife's village, so it is not unexpected that women should give importance to the chisungu as a centre of attraction for kinsmen. It is probable that much of the six months or so formerly given to the ceremony, was devoted to these ends. A successful and well-run ceremony attracts large crowds and contributes to the prestige of the *nacimbusa* and also to the village in which it is held. The dances provide an opportunity for expressing respect for status, so the *nacimbusa* employs the magic of attraction to make people come to her ceremony. Nangoshye explained that one of her objects in working so hard over the large models of snakes and other objects in the chisungu hut was to get the

133

admiration of visitors. (See page 83.) Just as the Bemba headman tries to attract people to come and live in his village and anxiously watches to see whether he is successful in building up a community, so the *nacimbusa* estimates her power by the number of women of eminence who attended throughout or who appeared on visits from time to time.

Present-day differences of income have added to the prestige aspect of the ceremony. A man of substance wants his daughter's chisungu to be talked about. Like an English father who defends the cost of a 'white wedding' by saying 'I wanted to do my best for the girl', a Bemba father will say 'Well, I don't want people to say "That is not a man of wealth! There was little beer to dance the girl in his village." ' There seems even to have been some competition for the privilege of 'owning the chisungu'—between a father and a mother's brother, for instance. It will be remembered that besides the provision of food and beer, respect can also be expressed in Bemba society by songs and feasts.[1]

A really successful chisungu is difficult to carry out under modern conditions since the absence of men and the smaller household groups result in smaller accumulations of food. No large sums of money are exchanged at the chisungu ceremony, so that chiefs and men in authority stand to gain little by a performance. I think these are the reasons why the chisungu has disappeared rather quickly. It is, moreover, organized entirely by women, and male dominance is emphasized in a modern wage-earning society.

The survival of ceremonial is apt to depend on secondary motives of this sort in some parts of Africa, such as Sierra Leone and South Africa. In both contact with missionaries has taken place over a longer period, and the people are much more sophisticated. But, in the case of the Mende, for instance, the chiefs gain a large income from the holding of the *bundu* rite for girls; this is acknowledged to be one of the reasons why it has not only not died out, but it has even increased in influence.[2] The Kriges also point out that some initiation schools in the Northern Transvaal have

[1] A man might give his wife a second marriage ceremony in her old age (the *bwinga* marriage) for respect.

[2] Kenneth Little, 'The role of the secret society in cultural specialization', *American Anthropologist*, April 1949. The privilege of holding Yao initiation ceremonies is greatly valued. (See Appendix A.)

spread among surrounding peoples for much the same reasons.[1] In such cases it might be said that the secondary motives for holding ceremonies have become stronger than the primary. Among the Bemba no such phenomenon seems to occur, and secondary motives which were originally powerful are now no longer operative.

DEDUCED ATTITUDES

Apart from the general functions of the chisungu in native eyes I have tried to deduce their attitude to different parts of the ceremony by noting the emphasis they give to them in straightforward narratives and the tension displayed by performers on different occasions and by analysing the time and energy spent. Such information does not, of course, exactly reflect the sentiments of the people concerned. Practical considerations and individual differences alter the emphasis in the case of a particular rite. One form of symbolic behaviour interests one mistress of the ceremonies, but does not attract some of her other colleagues. It would be necessary to use a questionnaire with a properly selected sample of individuals before saying confidently what 'the Bemba' think.

However, some of these clues are worth following up if only for the light they throw on the difficulties of studying ritual under field conditions.

Bemba descriptions of the chisungu given me before I had witnessed a ceremony, differ in a striking way from the account I have given. The omissions are so considerable that there is little correspondence between the sequence of events in the actual rite I witnessed and accounts given me in my first months of field-work, or even by *banacimbusa* after I had witnessed a ceremony.

Of course, the details of such rites are difficult for people to remember without recourse to a written record. It is not surprising that the most willing informants get confused and tend to confine themselves to events that are easily described or are thought likely to give the inquirer pleasure. Most of my informants were, moreover, women. Many Bemba men are experienced in classifying facts in a way convenient to the European, either because they have been to European schools or worked as

---

[1] J. D. and E. J. Krige, personal communication.

clerks or interpreters for Europeans, but most women are unused to this form of mental exercise.

It must be realized, too, that the sequence of events in a primitive ritual cannot be expected to be as regular as European religious sequences. Some ritual events logically follow each other, and no Bemba would think of reversing them; others depend on extraneous factors such as the presence of sufficient food at a given moment of time. The field-worker who is satisfied that he sees a magical connection between the order of two rites which he believes to be 'stages' of admission to this or that group, is often pulled up sharp by some matter of fact comment such as 'Of course we couldn't do it that day because X's grain failed to germinate for the beer and she couldn't get any more'.

Accounts given to me during my first months in the country resembled this one: 'Oh they take the girl out into the bush. Then she (the girl) jumps over a hoop made of branches. Then she is carried back to the village by her father's sister and her grandmother and they make payments to the *nacimbusa*. . . . (Pause.) . . . They make much beer—rich people make very much beer for their daughters. Then in the night the bridegroom comes with his bow and arrow. He shoots at a mark on the wall. The women all clap and cry "He has hit the target". Then they give the girl her *mbusa*. She is rubbed with oil and put on a mat and they throw bracelets on her lap. The *nacimbusa* takes these.' It is of some interest that this account was given me early in my visit by Nangoshye, the mistress of the actual ceremony I saw, who could very well have given me a rather complete account.

Looking through similar narratives I find that all such accounts mention jumping over the hoop of branches and the shooting ceremony on the last night. A number record the catching of the water insects in the mouth. All end with the ceremony of public congratulation at the end. Most of them refer to the teaching of the girl. None of them however, mentions the gardening mimes or the teasing of the girls. It is difficult to say whether the informants gave the selected events because they were the least secret, or because they felt they would be least likely to shock Europeans, who are believed by the Bemba to have curious and unaccountable ideas about anything to do with sex, and to be critical of aggressive behaviour such as mutilating, beating or teasing.

European accounts tended, as I have suggested, either to emphasize the obscenity of the rite or else its educational function. A missionary said 'The girl is shut up for four weeks. She must be brought food by immature girls during this time. She is given instruction in sex throughout her seclusion. Then they carry her out into the bush for further instruction. The grandmother carries her back from the bush and she has to try to catch little water insects on the surface of a pool. The girl and her bridegroom are washed in the river and both are brought out in new clothes before the village. The father-in-law gives a bow and arrow to his son-in-law and tells him to protect her from adulterers.'

The fullest account I have is one, not yet published, by the late Rev. R. MacMinn which gives many of the events I witnessed, with one addition in the form of a rite in which the man's bow and arrow was carried to the woods and placed at the root of the tree on which beer is poured. This is unlikely to be a local variation since Cisonde was a village very near to Mr. MacMinn's Mission at Lubwa, but it is a rite which strikes one as compatible with Bemba symbolic patterns and their attitude to the bow. Mr. MacMinn's account gives fuller details of the feasting and exchange of food than I recorded, but does not mention the jumps or the lion ceremonial.

To conclude, Bemba accounts given casually to an anthropologist emphasize the dramatic and public acts such as the final ritual jumps over the hoop and the bow and arrow ceremony at the end of the chisungu. They also stress the exchange of food and beer and the feasts. They omit, or minimize, the secret aspects, the lighting of the girl's fire, her purification and whitening and the pottery figures and other *mbusa* used. This is worth recording as a comment on the comparative material given in Appendix A. I have asked myself whether the Bemba chisungu is more complex than the puberty rites of neighbouring matrilineal peoples, or whether I have merely got fuller data on the Bemba. After re-reading the texts I am certain that the second is the likelier answer and that more similarities will appear between the ceremonies of these people if more eye-witness accounts became available.

To judge by the tension displayed by the performers at the chisungu I witnessed, I should say the critical moments in Bemba eyes were those I have described as magic omens or ordeals, that is to say the two jumps over the faggots and the hoop and the ritual lighting of the fire with fire-sticks which the women nearly failed to achieve. Older women also screamed and shouted at the girls as they bounced up and down on the heads of the chickens they were trying to kill. It was, indeed, the anxiety the company showed on these occasions which first led me to think that the chisungu was both a rite of passage and a magic ordeal. The last night of the ceremony with the giving of the pottery *mbusa* and the coming of the bridegroom was also a time of great emotion and the climax of a period of exhausting activities. Women egged each other on to keep up the ceremony to its wearing end with the first crow of the village cocks at dawn.

In terms of time spent, the ritual handling and presentation of the sacred emblems probably occupied more hours than any other part of the rite. The handling, preparation and presentation of the pottery emblems and the collection of the woodland and the domestic *mbusa* cost the organizers much time and energy. As I have stated there were forty-two pottery emblems, thirty-seven of them prepared specially for the Cisonde ceremony; and many other *mbusa* such as the salt, the snuff and the different roots and parts of trees. The long day's work on the pottery emblems in the hut has been described and it will be remembered that this long day's work was destroyed at the end of the very same day.

Apart from making and finding of *mbusa*, their presentation of the different women in order of rank seemed, to me at least, the most interminable part of the chisungu rite since it involved the singing of every doggerel rhyme some twenty or more times. The mimetic rites in the woods aroused interest but seemed to me more public and more subject to variation and to spontaneous interruptions of different kinds. I rarely had the feeling of the 'sacred' during these ceremonies in the woodland.[1] There was a lot of

---

[1] I am not using this term in a Durkheimian sense but rather to describe reverent, serious, quiet behaviour conforming to ritual rules.

joking and talking and although there were admonitions by the *nacimbusa* to work harder, to be more serious, and to dance more strenuously (see p. 73), it was plain that these were not spontaneous emotions.

The teasing of the girls was apparently considered to be a duty rather than a pleasurable excitement.

There remains the question of the significance of the ceremony to Bemba in terms of its survival in times of change. The chisungu was forbidden by missionaries some thirty to fifty years before I saw a performance in 1931. It is a conspicuous affair since it consists so largely of drumming and dancing and it is not a rite which can be performed in secret within a hut. It is run by women alone and does not have the backing of the chiefs who have supported initiation ceremonies quite tenaciously in some parts of Africa. Present-day economic factors such as shortage of food and the absence of men at the mines, also militate against the persistence of such a rite. In these conditions it is worth asking which part of the chisungu has actually survived.

The rites were everywhere shortened in 1931 and 1933 when I was in the country. In many places they were not performed at all. In these cases the puberty ritual proper, that is to say the bringing of the girl to the fire after her first period, was retained alone. Although the chisungu itself was not organized, yet there was a combination of the first *ukusolwela*, rite (see p. 54) and the seclusion of the girl in a special hut for some days in villages near the motor road leading from Broken Hill to Kasama and also in the mine compounds at Luanshya and Ndola, all of them areas of maximum contact. This would seem to bear out the conclusions to which the analysis of Bemba comments lead, namely that it is the magic rites of protection that the people consider the most essential part of the chisungu. It also supports Schapera's hypothesis that magic rites tend to survive in contact with Europeanism, while religious ceremonies associated with moral values or prayers to ancestral spirits tend to be abandoned.

The following table gives some attempt at a numerical analysis of the morals taught by means of the chisungu songs and *mbusa*. It will be referred to again.

TABLE I

	Pottery figures	Pottery floor models	Wall designs	Songs	Total
Chisunga rules Protection of fire	2			8	10
Social obligations of husband and wife.	14	1		4	19
Obligations to in-laws	3				3
Domestic duties	2			8	10
Agricultural duties	3	1		3	7
Maternal duties	4			3	7
Obligations be-tween mother and daughter				3	3
Sex and fertility	4	2	1	5	12
Chief's power	3	1		3	7
General ethical rules	2	1		6	9

THE CHISUNGU IN RELATION TO TRIBAL DOGMA AND VALUES

The relation of the chisungu to the marriage institution of the Bemba has been clear from the start. It expresses marriage morality—the girl's submission to her husband and his duty to provide for her, and the domestic, agricultural and sexual obligations of both. It provides for the public acceptance of these

The Chisungu in Relation to Tribal Dogma and Values

duties, most of which are represented in mime. It gives magic protection to the parties concerned.

How far does the ceremony express other tribal beliefs and values? The following diagrams attempt to show the relation of certain characteristic features of Bemba culture, as it is described in Part I, to the chisungu and to other ceremonies which go to form the ritual pattern of this tribe.

The most important of these ritual series are three in number, if importance is judged, as I think it should be, by the length and complexity of the rites and the time and interest shown in them. The first of these ritual series is the ceremonial surrounding chieftainship—the long and arduous rites of royal burial, the almost equally protracted and complicated ceremonies for the installation of a great chief, and those for the building of his new village and his sacred relic huts. The second is the series of economic rites carried out at the clearing of the bush, the firing of the piled branches on the cleared site, the sowing of the seeds, and the harvesting and first fruits—and in the old days those concerned with war. The third comprises the chisungu ceremonies themselves.

The ritual pattern in all these ceremonies is based on an essentially homogenous body of beliefs—that is to say the dogma which links authority with the exercise of supernatural power based on access to ancestral spirits by those who have correctly handled sex and fire. In order to secure blessings in war, for tree-cutting, sowing, first-fruits, the filling of the granaries and for good weather, human fertility, harmonious relations in the village or a successful reign for the paramount chief, those in authority must have ceremonial intercourse with their head wives and then light new fire.[1] The same must be done when a new role is assumed, when, for example, a chief is installed or a girl made nubile, or a couple married. Such people are separated from the rest of the community and restored to it after an act of ceremonial intercourse —the lighting of new fire, the touching of the lips of the aspirants to the new role with a particle of food cooked on the new fire,[2] and their presentation to the community for congratulation and

[1] The economic rites are described fully in my *Land, Labour and Diet in N. Rhodesia*, 1939.

[2] *Ukubalishya* or *ukubapa kakabe.*

141

	Special features	*Dogma*
Environment and activities	Shifting cultivation with annual food shortage.	*Security* through chief's supernatural powers; kept potent by sex-fire taboos. *Security* through magic of food production, storage and division. *Security* through conduct pleasing to ancestors.
	Hunting and fishing.	As above.
	Domestic activities.	Women only can cook and must do so on a 'pure' fire.
	Absence of storable wealth.	*Security* through social ties with those who will share work and food.
	High infant and maternal mortality.	*Security* through sex-fire taboos, protective magic, conduct pleasing to ancestors.
Social structure (a) Authority system.	Hierarchical order of govt: (Paramount, chiefs, headmen). Authority based on descent and seniority among men and women.	Observance of hierarchy brings supernatural blessing. Chiefs and ancestors help their inferiors if treated properly. Respect to senior women brings help in childbirth.
(b) Descent system.	*Matrilineal descent* and succession. (Conflict between father and mother's brother.)	Belief that children produced from women's blood; activated only by semen and ancestral spirit. Belief that father's sister can cause sterility by cursing.

Expression in chisungu rites	*Expression in other rites*
Mimetic rites giving girl her fire and marriage pot, and initiating sex-fire taboos. Mimetic rites representing gardening duties; ritual cooking of seeds and distribution.	*Chief's accession* ceremonies give him entry to ancestral shrines. *Chief's marriage* gives him marriage pot. *Rites of protection* from impure fires, unregulated sex, death. *Agricultural rites.* Sowing, first fruits, tree-cutting.
Mime of fish traps. Mime of hunting in wood. Mime of bow and arrow ceremony.	*Chiefs* or headmen bless fish poisoning. Ritual round chief's bow.
Mimes of domestic activities and protection of fire.	
Mime of feasting of son-in-law, and ritual food division.	Rites of blessing granaries; magic expansion of granaries.
Girl initiated into sex-fire ritual; fertility rites	Protective magic for infants and those in childbirth. Chief's blessings. Ancestral rites.
Songs and *mbusa* about chiefs. Headman spits ancestral blessings on girls. Constant miming of respect to elders in food and other offerings. *Mbusa,* the things handed down from the ancestors.	Hierarchical order of chiefs' rites (Paramount followed by chiefs, headmen). Seniority expressed in ritual precedence.
Brother and sister figure modelled. Mothers hand on child-bearing to children. (River ceremony.) Father's sister makes the girl's new fire.	Shrines to apical ancestress, of royal line. Shrines to maternal ancestors. Functions of clans in court ritual. Functions of reciprocal clans.

	Special Features	*Dogma*
(c) Marriage and family.	Husband and wife mystically related. Husband and wife's obligations.	Belief that man and woman mystically related in marriage. Sex in marriage potent and a source of blessings or danger. First intercourse dangerous.
	Marriage. Uxorilocal becoming virilocal. Husband gradually incorporated in wife's group. Tensions of early years.	
(d) Village grouping	Village composed of relatives headman has persuaded to join him. Frequent changes in composition.	Village blessed by headman's ancestors; made 'hot' or 'cold' by his sex activities; protected from dissension by magic.
(e) Age grouping	Seniority in all activities based on age. Women's grouping in family and village by age.	Ancestors bless those who respect seniority.
Some salient values.	Fertility very highly valued.	Fertility secured through blessings of ancestors and chiefs and senior relatives, especially father's sister. Fertility also secured through magic and protection against witchcraft. Successful childbirth through keeping marriage rites.
	Desire to build up village, following, subjects.	The blessing of ancestors brings a large community. Magic rites can also produce it.

Expression in chisungu rites	Expression in other rites
Girl protected from dangers of first intercourse: taught way of safety by seniors; given her marriage pot; taught to hide things of house. Miming of husband's duties by mock bridegrooms. Pottery images of husband's and wife's duties.	Ceremonies surround chief's relation with his head wife. Chief's marriage rites.
Miming of stages of incorporation of husband bridegroom. Honouring of husband. Washing his hands.	
Headman blesses girls before and after ceremony; girl given fire.	Ordeals to determine success of new village site; blessings of ancestral spirits through headman: ritual initiation of headman's fire; building of ancestral shrines; magic protection against illness.
Constant miming of women's seniority by age; Girls humiliated by older women in return for initiation; Girls make obeisance to every householder in village.	Ancestors called on in order of seniority: first fruits tasted in order of seniority.
Numerous fertility symbols: Bridegroom honoured for virility and represented as magician; rite of 'begging for parenthood'; girl handed on parenthood by her mother.	Chiefs pray for fertility of land and women at all ceremonies.
Miming of food division and cooking. Magic of attracting guests.	Headman's prayers for increase of village and magic rites for this purpose.

admonition, as in the ceremony of *ukushikula* after marriage or the installation of a new chief or chieftainess. The same words are used for all these constituent ritual acts, and it would be difficult for a passer-by to distinguish one rite from another.

This fact surely accounts for the importance of the chisungu rite in Bemba culture. It is the occasion on which the girl is given her fire and her marriage pot and made responsible for their care and their use. On her handling of the hearth depends her husband's power of access to his ancestral spirits or, if she be married to a headman or chief, the blessings which are available for gardens, bush and village, political life and warfare. A glance at the chart will show that except for individual magic rites, there are no ceremonies in the last column which do not, in the last resource, depend on the chisungu or on the abbreviated forms of puberty ceremony now carried out instead. The supernatural powers of the Citimukulu and his brother chiefs are directly pivoted on the chisungu and its magic and didactic acts; this purely feminine rite is therefore essential to the welfare of the whole tribe.[1]

The chisungu can also be considered of importance to the maintenance of tribal traditions, because of its direct emphasis on 'things handed down'. The *mbusa* are referred to specifically in this way and this is said to be their value. The central act of an economic rite is a prayer and supplication to the ancestors when the officiant asks for what is wanted, blessings on the seeds for instance, or peace. He asks for them from beings who will not always grant these requests. The words are uttered spontaneously and the sentences have no very fixed form. They mention individual ancestors by name, vary the terms of address, and add a number of immediate and special requests as well as the more usual demands for blessings and fertility. For instance a headman offering the first fruits to the ancestor was heard to add at the end of his discourse a fervent appeal that I might not miss when I went out shooting, as I had on the previous day.

The defined elements here are the time and method of approach to the ancestors and the status and position of the officiant. With

[1] This suggests a hypothesis for comparative research. If my interpretation of the importance of the chisungu is correct a similar emphasis on instruction and care in handling fire will be found wherever the chief's supernatural power is thought to be closely linked to it. This question will be discussed.

these conditions fixed there is a wide range of possible wants that can be voiced, meeting the need of the moment or of the group or the person concerned. These are rites of supplication in which the Bemba voice their needs and try to persuade themselves that they will be fulfilled.

In the chisungu however the women do not voice new desires, but always those that have existed in the past. The rites consist of an intricate succession of acts the value of which lies in more or less exact repetition. The *mbusa* must be made in the same way and the pottery models on the floor cannot be altered. These are rites which represent and proclaim the established rather than ones which enable the performers to meet new needs. The mimes and emblems of these initiation rites form a charter for the transfer of roles that have to be constantly assumed in each generation. They do not grant the men or women who perform them any help in the present troubles of Bemba married life, such as the prolonged absence of men from the tribal areas or the growing divorce rate. There is no element in them of supplication or prayer. It is for this reason that the chisungu must be reckoned as a rite of maintenance of tribal traditions.

To turn again to the chart it will be seen that all the major rituals of the Bemba reflect the importance they attach to fertility and the supply of food. The chisungu is more closely concerned with fertility than rites of supplication performed by chiefs, yet I never heard a prayer uttered by a chief which did not contain a special appeal to the ancestors for parenthood (*bufyashi*). The cycle of agricultural ceremonies is one of the most important tasks the chiefs are responsible for. The links between the three sets of rites are here close.

It is not easy to account for the tremendous emphasis on fertility and the care of children in Bemba culture. The desire is likely to be strong in all societies where social structure is largely based on descent and groups can only be enlarged by the birth of new children. There are, however, many African tribes with similar social structures in which the emphasis on fertility does not seem to be ritualized in this pronounced way. But it must be remembered that in Bemba culture the lack of any permanent form of possessions makes rights over labour—here rights over the labour of the younger generation—of particular importance. There may also be a correlation between fertility rites and matrilineal descent and in fact such a correlation seems to hold good in Central Africa (see Appendix A). Bemba believe that the child is entirely formed from the physical contribution of the mother and not the father, and similar beliefs may hold in the other matrilineal tribes in the area. It is moreover common to find in primitive society that the woman is regarded as solely responsible for the failure of a couple to produce children. Impotence in man is recognized but not sterility. In patrilineal Bantu societies it is common practice for the man's agnatic kinsmen to provide bride-wealth for him to secure him a wife. If she proves barren the cattle or other objects are commonly returned or another girl provided from the same lineage group. In a matrilineal society of the Bemba type the situation is rather different. The children of a marriage belong legally to the girl's family and it is to their gain if she produces children. This fact may account for the great care and attention given to fertility rites for girls among such people. The correlation of matrilineal descent with an emphasis on fertility is a hypothesis which will have to be tested more carefully in other areas. It would, of course be possible to relate the high infantile mortality rate that exists among the Bemba to their desire for children and their anxiety over them. This is in fact what many Bemba do. I have for instance been told in answer to a challenging question of mine about the protective rites performed for children. 'Well! Just look what a lot of our children die'. However, high infantile mortality rates are too common in Bantu society for this to be more than a contributory cause to the desire for fertility.

The salient features of Bemba social structure are also reflected in this ritual. The characteristic attitudes to authority in this very hierarchical society are expressed in ceremonies by which chiefs are created and maintained in their supernatural powers, and in those economic and other ceremonies performed by the chiefs themselves. The chisungu is not specially concerned with political life although some of the pottery emblems 'teach' the girl to honour the chiefs.

However, the hierarchy based on age, which is also characteristic of every type of structured relationship among the Bemba, is one of those which is frequently symbolized in the chisungu by the offering of food in order of age; by acts of obeisance to seniors; by the singing over and over again of the song about the immutability of precedence based on age, which runs 'The arm-pit cannot be higher than the shoulder'. The girl's proper conduct is expressed in the phrase 'be submissive, or make yourself soft and pliant before your elders' (*ukunakila kubakalamba*).

There is in fact a greater expression of the principle of precedence by age in the chisungu than in the chiefly rites themselves. This may be due to the fact that all rites of role assumption naturally give importance to age since it is those who have already assumed the senior role who can hand it on to the juniors. It is also true that Bemba girls are not removed from their own family to be put under the control of their mothers-in-law as in a patrilineal society, but they are placed under the authority of different older women in their own and other villages. Some of these are related to the girls and some are not. It must be remembered too that the chisungu is a public ceremony given over to teaching while most of the chiefly rites are done in secret and people merely assume that they have been correctly carried out.

Turning now to the social groups based on descent, it is worth noting that there is very little ritual expression of clan or lineage unity in the chisungu in spite of the fact that it deals with marriage and procreation. The principle of matrilineal descent is very strongly held here in spite of the domestic authority the father manages to win, which is greater than that reported from other matrilineal peoples in the area such as the Yao. The dogma as to the nature of biological descent was never questioned during my visit or the belief that the woman was responsible for the production of the child.[1] Exogamy rules within the clan are carefully kept, and clan greetings used. Yet although in some Bantu societies clan and lineage precedence is expressed in first-fruit ceremonies and members of different clans sit apart in clearly marked groups at tribal rites, in Lubemba there is no ritual ex-

[1] I quote in my article on the Bemba in *African Political Systems* edited by E. E. Evans-Pritchard and M. Fortes, 1939, (p. 97) an amazed comment made by a patrilineal Ngoni about Bemba beliefs on the subject: 'If I have a bag and put money in it, the money belongs to me. But the Bemba say a man puts semen into a woman and yet the children belong to the woman, not to the man.'

pression of this principle of social grouping beyond the precedence given at the court to the descendants of certain clans who accompanied the first Citimukulu to the present territory, and some ritual duties based on clan membership. In the chisungu however, it is the family which is emphasized and not the lineage. It must be recalled that the Bemba boy provides his own small token payments at marriage and does service for his father-in-law. His maternal relatives do not often help him and they are not economically interested in the success of the marriage as are bride's relatives among the patrilineal Southern Bantu. The boy himself is making an individual contract with all his wife's relatives. The girl's father and mother and the father's sister are the main actors in the ceremony and the father is the potential head of the extended family which will be based on uxorilocal residence.

Further, the clan and lineage have no political functions as corporate groups except in the case of the royal dynasty. It might therefore be concluded that ceremonies for expressing corporate feeling are not necessary. It might be equally well concluded that the ceremonies connected with chiefs' succession do in fact portray the principles of matrilineal descent and that the chisungu emphasizes the girl's duty to bear children for her maternal relatives. These suggestions should be tested in other matrilineal societies.

It seems clear that the maintenance of a stable family group is a difficult matter among the Bemba. There is the desire of the girl to stay with her own people which is opposed to that of the boy who wishes to return to his, and there are no economic links to bind them to one village rather than another. This type of contract may account for the chisungu ritual which stresses the link between husband and wife; the supernatural sanctions against adultery; and the constant admonishment of the girl to submit to her husband, to give him honour and also to give honour and food to her in-laws. The series of presentations of food to the son-in-law might also be listed as part of the whole process of winning the young bridegroom and persuading him to stay in his wife's village.

To conclude, Bemba chieftainship rites express a number of beliefs that are common to the chisungu such as the sex-fire-blood association and the link between political authority and the access to ancestors. They combine to stress the importance of fertility, children, food, respect for authority based on descent and age, and the need to build up village communities. With these common beliefs and values each series of ritual acts has its own emphasis. The ceremonies run by men include the care of chiefly relic shrines and the passing on of ancestral spirits to the chief; those run by women involve the care of the chisungu emblems and the passing of the nubile status to the girl.

The reiteration of the same message in a series of different ceremonies is perhaps only to be expected in view of the tendency of all elaborate ritual to develop multiple purposes. If we classify the activities or social relationships round which religion and magic centre the connection between the chisungu and the whole ritual pattern of the Bemba will become even clearer.

Religious and magic ceremonies tend to be associated with:

(*a*) *Natural environment*, e.g. Worship or personification of sun, moon, stars; shrines at unusual objects (waterfalls, mountains, rocks); personification of wild animals or plants; magic properties associated with animals or plants. (Chisungu ceremonies distinguish between bush and village and use bush magic.)

(*b*) *Economic activities*. Agricultural, hunting, fishing, pastoral, care of the granary, etc., ceremonies. Rites of supplication to supernatural powers or magic acts—Sacralization of particular domestic animals or plants—Ethical norms. (Chisungu represents agricultural and domestic activities and crops grown by women; magic rites related to agriculture and ethical norms.)

(*c*) *Biological processes*. Sacralization of biological processes of birth, sex, food, health, ill-health, death. (Chisungu is a puberty, nubility and fertility rite with religious and magic aspects, and expounds ethical rules.)

Social structure

(i) *Maturation rites of assumption*. Maturation rites for assumption of age status or entry to age grades; rites of role assumption, e.g. installation of chiefs; initiation of diviners; assumption of roles of husband and wife: Ethical behaviours expected of role holders.

(Chisungu is a rite of social maturation and role assumption;

employs magic of growth and tests of social maturation; and expounds the ethics expected of married women.)

(ii) *Social relationships*. Contracting social relationships, e.g. marriage, adoption, clan membership, legitimacy rites, reconciliation ceremonies; expressing relationships, e.g. ritual expression of duties of father, mother's brother or other kinsmen; ending relations, e.g. ritual expulsion from clan, removal of death from widower.

Magic of social relationships, e.g. Success magic; beauty or popularity magic; witchcraft and sorcery; Ethics of social relations.

(Chisungu contracts marriage relationships; expresses rights of father, mother and father's sister; expresses the relationship of brother and sister; expounds the ethical rules of kinship.)

(iii) *Social groups*. Rites of maintaining or expressing group structure, or expressing corporate obligations, e.g. Clan ceremonies, ancestor worship, chiefly ceremonies; representation of precedence;

Ethics of citizenship. (Chisungu expresses precedence based in age and authority in the women's group.)

(iv) *Ultimate beliefs and values*. In the sense of dogma as to the afterworld, transmigration of souls, beliefs as to union with supernatural, e.g. aspects of mortuary ritual and ancestor worship; trances, dreams, asceticism, mysticism. (Chisungu shows no traces.)

The chisungu is a form of puberty ritual, so, as suggested in the Introduction, it inevitably has a double focus since it is made to represent the attainment of sexual and social maturity alike. But it has many other aspects as well and is linked with nearly every occasion or relationship which is sacralized in Bemba society, as the chart shows.

The chisungu uses certain ritual devices and not others in this list of religious and magic activities.

Even such a summary classification of ritual practices as is given here, shows, firstly, they are used to control what is uncontrollable by rational means (the rain that will not fall, the crops that yield poorly, the husband who will not love his wife, the new chief who may or may not have the personal authority necessary to command) and that control is secured according to the people's belief either by supplication, the exact use of magic formulae or good behaviour. Secondly, they are used to maintain and perpetuate systems of social relationship and the structure of groups. They act as charters to maintain the power of those who already exercise it and express the moral rules on which the social structure depends. Lastly, they may provide the individual with spiritual experiences and represent the tribal philosophy or view of the world.

The chisungu, as I have explained, makes little use of supplication to or worship of supernatural beings, but great use of the exact performance of ritual acts and elaborate symbolism and of magic formulae and substances. The way in which these mechanisms are used will be discussed later.

UNCONSCIOUS TENSIONS AND CONFLICTS

I have already referred to some recent attempts to interpret ritual in terms of emotional conflicts, whether conscious or unconscious (cf. pp. 118–9). Some of the tensions connected with puberty can be said to be universal, since they are inherent in the ways in which human beings grow, reproduce themselves, and rear the children born to them. Examples of some of these common emotional attitudes are mentioned in the introduction to this book.

Psycho-analysts will also notice many universal symbols in the chisungu ceremony. The serpent and other animal symbols are of wide distribution. So are the mimetic representations of journeys through dark and difficult places to reach knowledge and safety. Such imagery commonly occurs in dreams. The frequent oral handling of the *mbusa* and other objects in the chisungu may also be significant from a psycho-analytical point of view. However, since no study of the symbolism in Bemba dreams or other revelations of their unconscious fantasies has ever been made this is merely a presumption.

Anthropologists, as distinct from psycho-analysts, tend to be more interested in the emotional conflicts produced by the characteristic features of a particular social structure than in universal human attitudes. One characteristic feature of this sort is a system of reckoning descent through the matrilineal rather than the patrilineal line, which may give rise to conflict between the mother's brother and the father; or an emphasis on primogeniture, strong enough to provoke unconscious resentment in the younger sons of a family. Bateson and Gluckman have suggested that conflicts of this sort find in ritual an expression which they cannot secure in daily life.

Anthropologists tend to use such explanations in the case of ritual which cannot easily be interpreted in any other way, either because it is at variance with some other part of the same ceremony, or because it seems to fit poorly with the idiom of the tribe in question. 'Why do Zulu women dress up as men in a rite designed to produce rain?' asked Gluckman in a recent broadcast. Because (he announces) Zulu women react against the lowly status they have as wives in the kraals of their husband's relatives. They find compensation in ritual by aping the behaviour of men. In a 'rite of reversal' in which they assume men's clothes, herd cattle like men, and carry men's arms, they throw off their subjection and acquire the necessary feeling of confidence that they will be able to produce rain for the tribe.[1]

There are many incongruities in the chisungu. I have been quite unable to interpret some of them. There is a contradiction, to European ways of thinking, between the concentration of fears around the beginning of married life and the open pleasure in sex relations which Bemba express. Puberty is eagerly looked forward to by the girls. They and their parents watch the growth of their breasts with interest and excitement and openly discuss the approach of womanhood. Girls are enthusiastic about the prospect of marriage and are taught that sex relations are pleasant and that it is their duty to give pleasure to their husbands. They do not seem to fear the first act of intercourse or to apprehend that it will be painful. It will be recalled that a young bride reaches this stage very gradually since she is given to her husband many

---

[1] I have probably gone further than Gluckman intended in this sentence, and I have also made his treatment of ritual sound much more crude than it actually is by selecting only one aspect of his interpretations for mention.

months before puberty and forms of partial intercourse are practised before she is fully grown. Yet, in spite of this, intercourse is thought to be dangerous. Moreover, it is the act within the marriage bond that is feared, not the act outside it.

The taboos surrounding marriage may be accounted for superficially in terms of Bemba belief, as I have already tried to show. Since it is through marriage that a man is able to get into touch with his ancestral spirits, the relationship is, for that reason, considered dangerous; dangerous because it is a source of power. Taboos of the Bemba type may exist in other tribes where access to ancestral spirits can only be made after an act of intercourse in legal wedlock followed by purification. Data on this point are not available from other areas at present.

It is difficult to believe that the Bemba associate guilt with sex in marriage, even though they speak of married couples as being hot, or with 'bad things on their bodies', if they have not been purified in the approved way. It is at least possible that sex is only considered shameful in association with a man's ancestors who are, in this society, his maternal uncles and grandfather. In daily life a Bemba behaves with reticence and shyness before his mother's brother since he may one day inherit the latter's wife together with his name, his status and his bow.[1] There may thus be an extension to the spirit world of attitudes to living relatives, which would explain the resolute attempt to keep a 'hot' person away from the spirit shrines.

The taboos may also reflect the anxieties associated with marriage in Bemba society, for it is, after all, a frail link on which to depend for an approach to supernatural power. Margaret Read has pointed out that among the Nyasaland Ngoni, who are patrilineal with strong patrilineages, and who practise marriage by bride-wealth, girls are protected before marriage and the ceremony involves a test of virginity. After marriage there are few, if any, taboos on handling fire. Among the neighbouring Cewa who are,

---

[1] It is possible that the castration complex takes a different form in matrilineal societies in which a young man succeeds to the role of his maternal uncle and not his father. The reluctance to associate sex with an approach to the ancestors may be connected with it. Malinowski made suggestions along these lines in 1927 in *Sex and Repression in Savage Society* but little serious comparative work has been done on these lines since then, so far as I know.

like the Bemba, matrilineal with weak matrilineages, and who have divided authority over the family and marriage by service and token transfer, there is little emphasis on premarital chastity. Marriage involves a test of the virility of the bridegroom, not of the virginity of his bride. After marriage however, the taboos surrounding the sex act are put in motion and the anxiety they engender remains constant throughout married life. The Ngoni bridegroom is certain of his rights in his wife once the cattle have been found for the bride-wealth. His lineage acquires permanent control over her reproductive functions; if he dies, he will be replaced by another lineage member. The Cewa man, on the other hand, contracts a marriage more easily and more at his own inclination; he gives his own labour for his bride, not the cattle of his patrilineage. But he never acquires full power over his children or full, let alone permanent, control over his wife.[1]

Gluckman suggests that there is a correlation between strong patrilineages and stable marriage.[2] There may also be an association between the strength of the lineage, the presence or absence of bridewealth, and anxieties expressed as taboos surrounding sex in marriage. Further work on this subject will have to be done before we can speak with certainty or even probability.

However strong the fears of the Bemba are, the way of escape from them is easy. The correct observance of ritual rules and reliance on the elders—the elders who preside over the chisungu and other ceremonies, and the chiefs who bless and curse—is sufficient. Bemba society is surely a 'shame' rather than a 'guilt' society, to use Ruth Benedict's terms.[3]

It is curious that the Bemba, whose marriages are trial marriages in their early stages, should express such a strong belief in the mystic links uniting husband and wife in the chisungu ceremony. Bemba men or women can leave their partners fairly easily, for there are no complicated marriage payments to be returned as there would be among the patrilineal Bantu. Yet the Bemba are

---

[1] Cf. M. Read, 'The moral code of the Ngoni and their former military state', *Africa*, vol. XI, 1938.

[2] M. Gluckman, 'Kinship and marriage among the Lozi of Northern Rhodesia and the Zulu of Natal', in *African Systems of Kinship and Marriage*, ed. A. R. Radcliffe-Brown, 1950.

[3] Ruth Benedict, *The Chrysanthemum and the Sword*, 1946.

firmly convinced that the conduct of each partner to a marriage has a magical effect on the health of the other, and even on that of a third party who commits adultery with one or the other.

If a man dies, his spirit is thought to linger round the body of his widow, and to be a potential danger to anyone subsequently marrying her. The same is true of a widower on the death of his wife. It seems clear that the clan of the man or woman is involved, since, unless the wife is inherited, a substitute from the dead partner's clan is required to sleep with the surviving partner in order to fetch his or her spirit back to the clan.

One could interpret this requirement by saying that the spirit of a dead Bemba is thought to haunt the living if the departed man or woman has been defrauded of his or her rights. If this interpretation is correct, it can be assumed that a man who sleeps with the widow before the necessary ceremony of 'taking off the death' has taken place is regarded as defrauding the dead man of the marital rights he had acquired. The clan brother who sleeps with the widow to take off the death which lingers on or around her presumably acts as the social equivalent of the dead man and not on behalf of the clan as a whole; the matrilineal clan or lineage does not normally act as a corporate group with regard to the marriage of one of its male members, although the woman's lineage, in the person of her mother's brother, does assume such a position of control.

Should it be objected that the initial rights of husbands over wives in Bemba society are much less substantial than those of husbands in the patrilineal bride-wealth tribes, this must be admitted; yet in Bemba society, perhaps just because of the lack of durable property in which status can be expressed, there is a tremendous insistence upon points of precedence and honour, and fights over what seem to us to be trivial claims and dues. So the apparent contradiction between the strength of the mystic links between spouses and the weakness of the economic ties between them is not so surprising a paradox in terms of Bemba culture as it would be in our own. Moreover however uncertain a husband's rights as father may be, his sexual rights over his wife are never questioned. It is these which are at issue in the ceremony of 'taking off the death'. These interpretations, however, are guesswork;

much more comparative information is needed before adequate ones can be given.

Another apparent paradox is the contrast between the position of the bridegroom in daily life, and the role in which he is depicted in the chisungu. In village affairs he must be submissive and quiet, as befits a stranger. He works under the orders of his in-laws and only gradually wins his position as head of his own family. In the chisungu he appears as a roaring lion, a lion-killer, a crocodile, a hunter, a warrior and a chief. The bridegroom in a matrilineal society of the Bemba type is honoured as a *genitor*, not as a *pater*. The bride belongs to her own matrilineage and the bridegroom is allowed access to her to make her fertile. He is welcomed in the village as a procreator, and honoured as such.[1] The bride's family is indebted to the bridegroom for 'the gift of a child'. In the chisungu rite it is the bridegroom's sister who 'begs for parenthood'. The virility of the bridegroom is emphasized throughout the rite, and the marriage ceremony which follows is a test of his procreative powers; he must give a sign of his potency by throwing a burning brand out of the house on his marriage night. The chastity of the girl is not praised either in the chisungu or the marriage ceremonies. It is sociologically irrelevant in societies of this type.

We might expect to find some kind of association between this kind of matrilineal organization and ritual stresses on fertility, such as tests of the virility of the man or a ritual marking of the first conception. I think evidence for it exists. Among the Fort Jameson Cewa the virility of the man is tested by a fire-lighting ordeal in the bush. If the fire lights, the man is known to be potent. The Nyanja give ritual stress to the conception of the first, sometimes the second, child of a union. The Yao sacralize puberty. Yao puberty rites lead to a marriage ceremony, and marriage ceremonies are followed by a celebration of the birth of the first child of the union. An obsolete Yao rite apparently honoured the virility of the man after his wife had been found to be pregnant. It seems possible that the Bemba ceremony of 'taking the child' is a

[1] Yao informants told Clyde Mitchell that a son-in-law was just like a rooster who comes into the yard to fertilize the hens but never owns them. Bemba fathers have more extensive powers than Yao fathers but they are depicted in the same light in proverbs and folk-tales.

similar solemnization of the fertility of a union. (See Appendix A.)

If a Bemba husband fails to give his wife a child, his marriage comes to an end. If he makes her pregnant, but she dies in childbirth, he will be held responsible by the heads of her matrilineage and by her father and mother. He is said to have 'killed' their child.[1] On the other hand, if he succeeds in the hazardous enterprise of Bemba marriage, he 'founds a house' and acquires not only status but rights of approach to his own matrilineal ancestors.

The honouring of the son-in-law in the chisungu also enacts the desire of the womenfolk to attract a young man to make his home in their village. There may be more in the chisungu mimes than this. It is at least possible that the women had an unconscious sense of guilt about robbing fathers of their children, children who are so much wanted and which only men can give. Bemba girls are brought up in a male-dominated society and are taught to kneel to men and to put them first. Their fathers are respected autocrats in the home, but are dethroned as their children grow up and realize that ultimate power lies with their mothers' brothers. The women court men to give them children, but they do not allow them the full rights of a sociological father or *pater*. They deny him ultimate power over his children; perhaps they compensate him by giving him exaggerated respect in the chisungu as the procreating male.[2]

Sex hostility is not apparent in the chisungu. There are songs which can be interpreted as mocking at men but I did not hear them sung, and they do not seem to be an integral part of the ceremony. The women certainly stress their complete command over matters concerning childbirth. The mother of the girl, her father's sister, and the mother of the boy unite in this respect: this sex grouping cuts across those based on lines of descent. The secrecy of the chisungu may be women's compensation for their seclusion from other aspects of tribal life. But there is nothing to

[1] When a Princess was safely delivered of a child in the old days, the friends of her lover did the dance for a lion-killer returned from the hunt and shouted 'He is saved! He is saved!'

[2] D. Schneider reminds me that according to psycho-analytical theory the penis of the man is equated with his child. He suggests that the Bemba father is robbed of his child but compensated by the symbolic representation of his virility in the chisungu.

match the ritual hostility between the sexes shown in some other initiation or marriage rites.[1]

Traces of hostility are revealed in the man's attitude to the chisungu. At least one Bemba man told me that unless the rites were performed 'our wives will hate us and give us no respect'. I have also heard remarks from women which seem to show that they are anxious lest they alienate the husbands attracted to the matrilineage. For instance, girls are instructed not to cry out in childbirth 'because it is a thing of shame. These are the secret things of women. Because the man will hear and will say "It is I who gave her that belly. I am ashamed because other women don't cry out like that".'

To conclude, Bemba evidence supports the suggestion that there is a connection between matriliny and girls' initiation ceremonies which emphasize the importance of fertility. In any society in which it is believed that women provide all the physical substance from which the foetus is formed, this would be natural; it is the case in Bemba society. Moreover, the connection between matriliny and girls' initiation ceremonies has been observed in a number of other African communities.[2]

I have suggested that there are also other possible associations, between matriliny characterized by absence of marriage payment, for instance, and instability of marriage with anxieties and taboos centring round the beginning of married life. A further association is suggested between matriliny combined with uxorilocal marriage, and initial inferiority of the young husband combined with compensating honours given him in the rituals of marriage or initiation. I have also suggested, very tentatively indeed, that in this particular matrilineal society there may be a connection between the lack of open hostility between the sexes and an unconscious feeling of guilt at robbing the man of his children, which is expressed in fears on the part of the women that the men will leave them, and on the part of the men that their wives will not respect them unless taught to do so by the chisungu.

[1] Cf. M. Gluckman, 'The role of the sexes in the Wiko circumcision ceremonies', in *Social Structure* edited by M. Fortes, 1949, and P. Mayer, 'Privileged obstruction of marriage rites among the Gusii', in a paper read to the Royal Anthropological Institute, 1950.
[2] See Appendix A for a further discussion on this point.

The end of the second woodland ceremony. Preparing the hoop of crossed male and female saplings for the girls to jump. The *mxenge* or female sapling has sprung into the air and will have to be sunk in the ground again

The lion model down which the girls blow to make a roaring sound,
together with the helmet (*Mulume wa ngala*. Song 42)

The model of the lion together with the snake model

Unconscious Tensions and Conflicts

Such suggestions cannot be dignified by the name of hypotheses. They are no more than likely guesses. It remains for the sociologist to follow them up in similar societies, and for the psycho-analyst to interpret them in terms both of universal symbolism and the analysis of Bemba dreams and other expressions of unconscious fantasies or conflicts.

PRAGMATIC EFFECTS

The intentions, conscious or unconscious, of the performers of a rite must be carefully distinguished from the actual effects they may produce, either on the state of mind of individuals, or on the working of particular institutions. The Trobriand islanders practise love magic in the firm belief that the saying of certain words or the use of certain herbs makes a man invincibly attractive to a woman, or a woman to a man. The magic itself does not produce this effect, of course, but the fact is that lovers who believe themselves to be irresistible act in such a way that they actually prove to be so. All types of ritual can be similarly regarded as social mechanisms which produce certain results in the individual or the group, quite apart from the manifest or latent content of the performer's beliefs. It is as a social mechanism that the ritual of different cultures shows such similarities. Symbols differ widely, so do beliefs, and there is an almost bewildering variety of ceremonial sequences, but as methods of social action ritual types are not in reality very numerous, and they will be found to conform to certain general rules.

From this point of view we can distinguish in the chisungu a number of ritual devices that are very widespread, and which here produce effects on the individual girl, on her kindred, and on the institution of marriage, and in the maintenance of Bemba values. The first of these may be described as the device of the 'marked stage' which seems to me typical of all rites of role assumption. For whatever conscious or unconscious reasons, the Bemba girl and her family approach the time of puberty with apprehension and anxiety. The series of ceremonial acts of her chisungu may be regarded as giving her the assurance that she is fit to assume her

161

new role and providing an acceptable proof that she has successfully reached a new stage in life. She has been gradually made free
to eat the different foods of the tribe and to prepare them, and the
different ceremonial acts have shown everybody that this process is
complete. The bride is made indubitably clean. She has the right
weapons to protect her from the magical dangers of her new life.

If the marked stage is a ritual device which is common to all
rites of role assumption and status change, the device of the
ordeal or omen is probably more widely associated with such rites
than has been assumed. The chisungu is a test in the eyes of the
performers. Whatever her doubts or fears the girl has jumped the
faggots successfully; she has caught the *njelele* insect and killed
the chickens. The teen-ager in our own society has no such tan-
gible proof that she is actually a 'grown-up' and can safely and
successfully behave like one.

The device of the public pronouncement is similarly a common
ritual act in most ceremonies of role assumption. We saw that the
Bemba girl on the last night of her chisungu was obliged to handle
each model and to sing each song herself, and I have suggested
that it is impossible to decide whether such mimetic acts should
be considered as magic rites intended to make a new relationship,
or as legal acts involving the girl in a public assumption of her new
duties. It is noticeable that in the analysis of rites given on page
140, by far the greater number of the pottery *mbusa* are those
referring to the obligations of husband and wife; these are the
mbusa which the initiation candidates themselves have to handle,
while singing the accompanying songs. From the girl's point of
view such speculations are perhaps irrelevant. All such public
pronouncements must be regarded as means by which the girl gains
confidence that she is now able to act on her own. This is probably
the first time the girl has been asked to announce her individual
responsibility in any way, after a life very free of individual undertaking or responsibility in the midst of an extended family.

I stress the devices which seem to me to contribute to the
individual security of the girl because rites of passage have been
considered since the days of Van Gennep almost entirely as a means
of creating or representing group ties. This aspect is of course of
great importance to the sociologist, but it should not be studied to

the exclusion of the functions the rite performs for the individual, the role aspirant, as I have called her here.

Another device which is prominent in the chisungu is of course the mechanism of the sacred emblem and its associated formula. This ritual pattern is also very common in ceremonies intended for the passing on of roles or of systems of values. In the chisungu a series of related ideas are associated with certain symbols, the pottery figurines, and with fixed forms of words, the doggerel rhymes that are sung. This is a very interesting mechanism and one that is of very wide use in Bantu Africa as Cory and others have shown.[1] First it is evident that the designs and the pottery emblems form a sort of *aide-mémoire*. Women started to hum the songs when they saw the *mbusa*, as I observed myself when watching the making of the pottery figurines. Mrs. Culwick was told specifically by a Bena woman that the models were useful to make women remember the songs.

It became clear to me also in the course of Bemba village life that the figurines not only act as mnemonics for the songs but that they also come to represent moral attitudes and obligations and to represent them in a quotable form. I have heard a line of such a rhyme shouted by a girl's mother to an idle bride as a form of rebuke. On an occasion when a young married woman was tempted to go off to a beer-drink and leave her baby unguarded in the hut behind, an older woman suddenly shouted to her the song associated with the house *mbusa* (cf. Appendix B, No. 51). This song calls to mind the moral tale of the mother who leaves her baby alone in the house so that it falls into the fire and gets burnt. The girl in question looked irritated and impatient, and then shrugged her shoulders, gave up her project and went inside her house. In such circumstances the chisungu rhymes enable the Bemba to give formal expression to public morality. In other words the seemingly meaningless doggerel becomes a weapon. Bemba women recognize this as is shown from the comment made on the crocodile model. 'The girl will remember "that is what they taught me by the crocodile".'

[1] Cf. H. Cory, 'Figurines used in the initiation ceremonies of the Nguu of Tanganyika', *Africa*, vol. XIV, 1943–4. Such figurines also occur among the Bena. Cf. A. T. and G. C. Culwick, *Ubena of the Rivers*, 1944.

Another interesting feature of the emblem mechanism is that it provides a fixed form, a model and a song with the possibility of multiple meanings in this case. It is in the nature of symbols, whether they occur in dreams, speech or action, to become the centre of a cluster of different associations. The efficacy of ritual as a social mechanism depends on this very phenomenon of central and peripheral meanings and on their allusive and evocative powers. It makes possible interpretations that vary with the age, the knowledge and even the temperament of individual performers. The essential fact about the *mbusa* is not their exact meaning but the fact that they are what they are—'things handed down'— Hence they act as signs that things will go on as they have gone on, and that powers given to mankind before will be given to them again. They are used as the basis of rites of charter maintenance.[1] I have pointed out that one of the striking aspects of the chisungu I witnessed was the insistence that the designs should be modelled exactly, even though the work involved hours of tedious labour. This was so even in the case of the pottery snakes and other symbols made in clay on the floor of the initiation hut, which were destroyed on the evening of the day on which they were made. This insistence on exact detail in, for instance, the spacing of the beans and pumpkin seeds that decorated the emblems, was combined with a variety of explanations of the symbols used. The interpretation of the songs given in the appendices show that there is in every case at least one double meaning for each symbol. The hoe represents the woman's gardening duties but it also represents the husband who makes his wife fertile. The miming dances round the *musuku* tree are done 'to honour the *musuku*', the women's tree, and women said that if they failed to do these actions there would be no parenthood. But there was also a reference to the woman's duty to get firewood now that she was married. Another set of ideas centred round the blessing of the girls' emblems that were tied to the tree and handled with the women's mouths. 'We bless them with our spittle.' Here a variety of meanings is loosely associated: the tree that bears much fruit and hence symbolizes fertility, the tree that provides wood used for firewood, the honouring of the tree with spittle by which the

[1] I give the term charter the meaning that Malinowski did.

ancestors' blessings are conveyed. Another example is that of the tortoise who breaks the habits of a lifetime, not only by climbing trees but by climbing them backwards as the girls are asked to do. The mime represents the unusual thing, the woman who is ready to do her husband's work if he is away and other difficult or almost impossible tasks. She is also to be like the tortoise who puts his head under his shell, in that she is to keep silent about her relations with her husband. But she is also taught that she is not to be like the tortoise who puts his head out looking for food when he is in other people's houses, but keeps his head inhospitably in when he is in his own house—in other words does not tell his guests he has supplies of food. (Appendix B, No. 50.) Such interpretations show how the same symbol can at one and the same time represent the thing that must be done, and the thing that must not be done.

As in dream life the symbols of the chisungu evoke a variety of linked associations, verbal and other. The salt, the firewood, or the curious figurines stand for certain emotional associations common to the whole community, but they may also acquire special meanings in the light of that particular ceremony, or even in terms of individual experience. The 'secret' meanings of the *mbusa* were, as we saw, gradually learnt by the more intelligent women through a series of subsequent repetitions, questions, answers and guesses. But the more obvious interpretations of a representative rite could change with the times. For instance, the miming of the bridegroom as an old man with horns on his head was described by older women as a representation of a witch doctor who has charms for the fertility of women; but a young girl explained the matter in practical terms as showing that it is 'sensible to marry an old man nowadays since he will not go away to the mines and leave you stranded'.

All symbolic objects make it possible to combine fixity of form with multiple meanings, of which some are standardized and some highly individual. Long and complex ritual of the chisungu type inevitably represents a cluster of ideas, understood, half-understood or merely felt. Mimetic rites or the use of designs or figurines are an admirable mechanism for conveying such associated notions, and moral concepts.

A legal contract of marriage defines the behaviour expected of husband and wife very exactly, but a marriage ceremony evokes patterns of desirable conduct and stirs up familiar and approved attitudes which cannot be exactly described. Such emotional attitudes may be as essential to the maintenance of the institution of marriage as the legally attested contract, and it is doubtful whether they can be expressed or transferred to people of different temperaments and circumstances so well by means other than symbolism. Compare for instance in our society the efficacy, as a social mechanism, of the marriage contract, and of a marriage ceremony. The first must surely be specific to be effective. It must apply exactly, or more or less exactly to the marriage of a particular couple. The contract must be framed in words which cannot possibly be misunderstood. Exactitude is so important that experts in marriage law and legal terminology are paid to draw up the terms of the agreement. The ritual, on the other hand, owes its virtue to the fact that it conveys fundamental and common attitudes, while it allows for a penumbra of individual interpretations and sentiments which may become just as firmly attached to the same set of symbols. It does not particularly matter how many meanings and shades of meaning a particular mime or emblem has, although it is necessary that a certain body of common attitudes should be conveyed to the young couple and their relatives and these should be associated easily with the symbolic emblems. A chisungu design or a song may vary from year to year, but it is important that the performers should believe that the dance, or song, or design, is the same as it always was.

I have, so far, stressed the pragmatic effects of the chisungu on the Bemba individual. It also has a number of effects on tribal institutions and structure, and some of these have been described. As a ritual device this puberty ceremonial can be considered as a mechanism of the cult group type. Complex symbolism does not survive, in a society without written literature, unless an individual or a social group is responsible for keeping it alive and handing it on. Such individuals acquire authority and are able to exercise discipline in the sphere with which the rite is associated.[1]

---

[1] Malinowski's routine method of analysing a rite was to sort the data under the following headings: ritual behaviour, dogma, ethical rules, charters (which he assumed, incorrectly, generally to be myths), and personnel.

Pragmatic Effects

In Lubemba the chisungu puts power into the hands of the *nacimbusa*, who is an authority outside the girl's own family although in some cases she is the sister of the girl's father. She is not a member of the bride's own matrilineage. A mother cannot 'dance' her own daughter even though she is a *nacimbusa* of repute, in this initiation ceremony which enforces the rules of marriage and maternity.

The ritual mechanisms used in the chisungu may be further elucidated by continued comparison of this cycle of rites with the chiefly ceremonies already referred to. The difference between the two is striking. It is not only that the ancestral ceremonies consist of prayers while the chisungu consists of meticulously performed magic rites, and mimes, but that the personnel of the two ceremonies is selected in quite dissimilar ways. Those who approach ancestors—the chiefs, priests and headmen—do so by virtue of descent. The ritual is handed on by hereditary succession in the case of headmen, who use quite simple prayers to the ancestors. In the case of big chiefs, who are the focus of very complex ritual, the ceremonies are in the hands of ritual specialists, also chosen on the basis of descent (*bakabilo*). Thus the long rites for the burial of a Citimukulu, the installation of his successor and the building of his new village are controlled by hereditary buriers and keepers of the king's shrines, or by clan authorities with special ritual functions at the court. The chisungu is mainly carried out by commoners with no special relation to the chief and his court, although its occurrence will be reported to the ruler, as is any other important event in his territory. The *banacimbusa* are individuals who have won their way to their position instead of inheriting it. The officiants at the nubility rites are selected on the basis of age, personality and, to a certain extent, location, rather than of lineage, clan or descent from a royal line.

There is a marked difference too in the way the rites are performed. The headman tends to pray to his ancestors at dawn or dusk when the village is quiet and no one is passing to and fro. It does not matter whether other worshippers are present. The rites of great chiefs are secret and no unauthorized people can be present when the Citimukulu prays before his relic shrine. Death used to be the penalty for the man who entered a shrine without

167

due permission. The common people hope and believe that the rites have been performed for them; they do not think that they themselves have a part to play as worshippers. There are secret elements in the nubility rites, but they are mysteries of interpretation and linguistic usage rather than ceremonies carried on behind barred doors. The main features of a chisungu on the other hand are its crowds and its thronging dancers. Again the ancestral ceremonies are performed in a reverent and quiet way. Nothing could be in greater contrast than the spirit of the chisungu with its noisy dancing and singing, its extravagant burlesque and its crowded scenes. The chisungu proclaims and teaches and requires a big concourse for its effect: it repeats, reaffirms and hands on by emblem and mime. The ancestral prayers are supplications to spirits who can give and withhold. The approach to them is difficult and can only be made by men in authority who have made themselves ritually pure. If Bemba believe in chiefs at all, they believe that they are worshipping chiefs acting as intermediaries for them, because that is their concept of kingship. They do not need to watch the rite of supplication itself.

I have tried to find explanations for an elaborate set of rites. They were ceremonies performed by people of a culture that was strange to me and in a language which I did not understand thoroughly enough for an adequate study of verbal symbols. The task has been one which no anthropologist could hope to achieve completely, but it extended my knowledge of Bemba institutions and values and set me, and I hope others, problems for comparative study in other matrilineal tribes. It has given me a conception of the great variety of different purposes which men seek to achieve by ritual behaviour.

I have interpreted the functions of the chisungu ritual from a number of points of view. I have taken it as given that some of the emotions associated with growing up in human society are universal, although they are expressed in a variety of different ritual forms. I have shown that the rites perform a particular function for Bemba society, for the different groups of which it is composed, such as the matrilineages and the extended family, and also for the individual actors in the ceremony—the girls chivvied here and there under their covering blankets, the anxious mothers waiting for them to jump over the faggots, and the commanding organizers of the rites. Some of my explanations are based on sociological assumptions and some on psychological ones. I have not been able to draw neat boundaries between the two.

The emotional and intellectual needs of individuals, as they are conditioned by the society in which they are brought up, seem to me a proper study for social anthropologists, as proper as the analysis of institutionalized roles, social relationships or social groups on which so much emphasis has been laid recently. The one cannot be studied without the other. If the observations made here under the title of 'pragmatic effects' mean anything, they point to the number and variety of emotional attitudes which can be expressed by symbolic behaviour and the multiple, and often changing, functions of such rites. Single explanations of ritual behaviour, however satisfying to the observer, seem to me to deny the nature of symbolism itself and its use in human society to express the accepted and approved as well as the hidden and denied, the rules of society and the occasional revolt against them, the common interests of the whole community and the conflicting interests of different parts of it. The use of symbols in ritual secures some kind of emotional compromise which satisfies the majority of the individuals who compose a society and which supports its major institutions.

APPENDIX A

The Distribution of Chisungu
Ceremonies in Central Africa[1]

I t is impossible to map the distribution of girls' initiation
ceremonies in Central Africa completely, since there are so
many areas for which we have no information. Nevertheless
they seem to be widely practised. A number of tribes in Northern
Rhodesia, Nyasaland, the Congo and Angola hold puberty rites
for girls which are called by the same term as that used by the
Bemba—chisungu. Other tribes hold ceremonies which seem to be
very similar in that they are individual rites organized on a family
basis and related to the institution of marriage, and that they consist of the seclusion of the candidates, mimes, singing and dancing,
and they exclude any physical mutilation such as clitoridectomy,
which is practised among some of the Eastern and Southern
Bantu. These ceremonies are however called by different names. In
yet a third group of peoples, mainly Nyasaland, and Tanganyika,
girls' initiation schools are held, either instead of individual ceremonies, or concurrently with them. In some tribes these schools
occur side by side with circumcision schools for boys, and in
the case of the Yao, a final ceremony is held jointly for boys and
girls.

The group of tribes which practise chisungu rites is a large one.
It can be divided as follows:

Northern Rhodesian peoples

(*a*) In North-Eastern Rhodesia among the Bisa-Lala-Lamba
tribes which are culturally and linguistically akin to the Bemba;[2]
the Kaonde of North-Western Rhodesia and Kazembe's Lunda

---

[1] I am indebted to Mary Douglas (Tew), W. H. Whitely and Violaine Junod
for collecting much of the material used in this note. Numbered references are
given to the bibliography. [2] No. 64.

170

who are also closely related;[1] and among the Bemba living in the Belgian Congo.[2]

(*b*) Among the Nsenga on the left bank of the Luanga river, originally an offshoot of the Lala, Drourega mentions a rite by this name in a work which appeared in 1927;[3] it also exists among the neighbouring Ambo of the Petauke district.[4]

(*c*) The Alungu, a tribe of Tanganyika origin living to the north of the Bemba, practise the chisungu.[5]

(*d*) The Ila, living on the Kafue river in North-Western Rhodesia, have a girls' initiation rite called chisungu, but actually not very similar to the Bemba rite, which was described by Smith and Dale in 1920.[6]

Congo Peoples

In the Belgian Congo, chisungu ceremonies are mentioned by Devers among the Lunda in the South Katanga area,[7] while Lambo describes such ceremonies among the Congo group of Lala.[8] Marchal speaks of a *kisungu* rite among the Shila on the western bank of the Luapula.[9]

Portuguese Angola peoples

The evidence from Angola is somewhat confused. Milheiros writing of the Lunda and Luena of the Kaianda region, uses the term *Nkanga* for girls' puberty rites,[10] while White speaks of *Kanga* ceremonies among the Luchazi, who lie across the Northern-Rhodesia-Angola border, and among the Chokwe. Van Buggenhout however uses chisungu for girls' puberty rites throughout the area, that is to say those of the Lunda, Chokwe and Luena of Angola.[11]

All these tribes are of Congo origin and mostly of Lunda stock. The Bemba say they are an off-shoot of the Luba, and Coxhead believes that the ancestors of the Bisa, the Bemba and Kazembe's Lunda arrived in North-east Rhodesia in the middle of the eighteenth century. Verhulpen and others consider that these tribes all broke off from the Lunda kingdom established between the Bushmaie and Lubilishi rivers during its period of expansion in

[1] No. 42, No. 53, p. 88.   [2] No. 14, No. 59.   [3] No. 19.
[4] No. 64, p. 63.   [5] No. 8, p. 39.   [6] No. 54.
[7] No. 16.   [8] No. 37.   [9] No. 39.
[10] No. 43.   [11] No. 4.

the seventeenth century, and this seems the most likely explanation.[1] The Kaonde also claim Luba origin. The Lunda and related peoples of the south-west Katanga area in the Congo are described as descendants of seventeenth-century emigrants from the North Lunda area before it became Luba-ised, while those in North-Western Rhodesia, now described as Lovale, are composed of Lunda and Luena, who settled in the fifteenth century, and Chokwe, Luchazi and Mbunde who emigrated from Angola 50 years ago.[2] According to McCulloch's summary, Lunda offshoots also entered Northern Angola and the Western part of the Belgian Congo in the late sixteenth century and early seventeenth century, where they settled as conquerors among the local Bantu inhabitants and became the ancestors of the present Luena, Luchazi and Chokwe.[3]

It is probable that chisungu ceremonies are much more widely distributed among these Lunda or Lunda-derived tribes in Angola, the Congo and Northern Rhodesia, than our present information indicates.

All these tribes are agricultural rather than pastoral. They all follow matrilineal descent and succession. Some practise temporary and some permanent uxorilocal marriage, and some virilocal marriage or mixed type unions. Marriage payments tend to be low; instead, the husband serves his father-in-law according to the Bemba pattern. Where marriage payments rise, as in the Angola group, there is a tendency towards virilocal residence.[4] Ancestor worship is pronounced, and this cult is associated with chieftainship, although kingdoms with 'divine' kings and centralized governments of the Bemba type are not now common in this group. The information does not tell us whether blood-sex-fire taboos are strong.

Among the Bisa, Lamba, Lala and Kaonde peoples, the group most akin to the Bemba, marriage is initially matrilocal with marriage by service and token payments. Chieftainship is associated

[1] See M. McCulloch, No. 40, pp. 9–13 and A. I. Richards, No. 48, Chap. I for discussions on these points.
[2] No. 40, p. 89 analyses the evidence for the Angola area.
[3] No. 40, p. 57.
[4] Vide A. I. Richards, No. 51 for a discussion on the degree of variation in marriage practices which are inevitable in matrilineal and matrilocal societies.

with ancestor worship. The Bisa have a number of chiefs, as have the Lala, and it seems that the recognition of a Paramount Chief of the Lamba was a post-European phenomenon. The Mwinilunga Lunda have a paramount chief of acknowledged authority in the Kazembe, but the Kaonde were divided into small autonomous chiefdoms.[1]

Apart from the Lamba, the chisungu ceremony in these tribes seems to be less closely associated with marriage than among the Bemba. Among the Lala of the Congo there is little insistence that the rites should precede marriage, and sometimes they take place two or three years after it.[2] The Kaonde celebrate the rite two or three years before puberty. Melland regards this chisungu as a puberty rite advanced before the girl's first period for fear she should become pregnant before her chisungu has been danced.[3] There is no specific mention of the use of pottery figurines in the ceremony, nor of virility tests.

The Lamba ceremonies are more fully described than the others in this group. Salient elements in the rites are the bringing of the girl to the base of an *umwenje* tree followed by a long period of seclusion during which the girl must be covered with blankets when she emerges for any purpose from the initiation hut.[4]

The initiation ceremonies of Bemba peoples in the Congo territory lying roughly between L. Tanganyika and L. Mweru seem to resemble those of the Bemba in North-eastern Rhodesia in outline. Verbeke speaks of a preliminary *kukobeka* or engagement rite followed by the chisungu, or '*shisungu*', when dolls of both sexes and various vases are shown 'to the young couple and there is a final ordeal of arrow throwing carried out by the bridegroom'.[5] Delhaize describes a somewhat similar ceremony with an interesting rite called *kulasila kisungu*, which he translates as 'to chase the hymen', when the bridegroom pretends to shoot the girl with a bow and arrow. The marriage rite called *buina* which follows, in the case of the first two wives of a man, involves giving an arrow by the father to the bride—a common symbolic act throughout this area.[6]

To the east, the Nsenga, an offshoot of the Lala, on the left

---

[1] No. 64, pp. 56, 62, 68.   [2] No. 37, p. 255.   [3] No. 42, pp. 76–80.
[4] No. 18, Chap. IX.   [5] No. 59, pp. 57–59.   [6] No. 14, pp. 173–227.

bank of the Luangwa river, formerly held an individual chisungu
rite for a girl at the end of a three or four month period of seclusion
following her first period. There were three parts to this ceremony
—a dance held by 'medicine women', and a dance by the candidate herself on designs traced on the ground in low relief, with the
last of these on a crocodile design. The girl was then given presents.
Lastly there was a night-long dance by naked men and women to
which the term chisungu was given.[1] Parts of this ceremony, and
in particular the mention of designs in low relief and the symbol
of the crocodile, seem to be similar to the Bemba chisungu, but
the data are not full enough for further comparison to be made. The
Ambo chisungu described by Stefaniszyn makes special mention of
the importance of the taboos of 'fire and salt' at this time.[2]

The Lungu to the north of the Bemba are a matrilineal people
who came to their present home from Tanganyika, but may have
come originally from the Congo. They apparently practise
uxorilocal marriage. Their chisungu ceremony has features which
resemble those of the Bemba. The bridegroom has to put a spear
through the roof of his bride's mother's hut. Then his supporters
face the hut with bows and arrows while the girl's parents and
relatives stand outside the hut door. They take the arrows and it
is explained that these are to kill adulterers. The rite concludes
with a test of the virility of the man, who shouts out 'I have eaten
the chisungu of my bride' if the marriage has been consummated.[3]

The southern Lunda and Ndembo of the Congo reckon descent
matrilineally, and marriage is initially uxorilocal. Here again the
son-in-law makes slight marriage payments, but gives service for
his bride.[4] Among the Angola Lunda descent was matrilineal but
marriage payments were made and marriage has become virilocal.
Ancestor worship is practised in both the Congo and Angola.
Chiefs exist, but the people are mainly divided into small chiefdoms and princedoms. Large kingdoms like that of the Bemba and
the Kazembe's Lunda are not reported. Beliefs as to blood, fire and
sex are not described.

In the chisungu described by Devers in the district of Mutsha-
toha, on the railway west of Jadotville, the girl is made to lie on

[1] No. 19.   [2] No. 64, p. 52.   [3] No. 8, pp. 39–41.   [4] Nos. 16 and 17.

the ground in front of a *mbudi* tree, and then secluded in the bush. On her return she is daubed with red ochre and oil and stands in the centre of the village while the people dance round her during the day and following night.[1] The ceremony resembles closely that described by Buggenhout and Wens for the Lunda of Angola, a rite which he believes to be of wide distribution. Here again, the essential act of the chisungu is the bringing of the marriageable girl to the foot of the *mbudi* tree. Her mother lays her naked between two blankets with her face to the tree, and then calls the men and women of the village and sometimes of neighbouring villages. Dancing goes on till nightfall when the men retire. The girl is taken to a special hut for seclusion for two or three months, and the women dance round the hut each night until there is a final feast and dance. The relation of these South Lunda ceremonies to their marriage institutions is not clear, but these chisungu are evidently nubility rites since the girl is either betrothed before the ceremony, or her husband is chosen immediately after it. There is no mention of pottery figurines or of virility tests.

From the sketchy data we have, the common features of the ceremonies among the Bemba, Bisa, Lala, Lamba, Kaonde, Alungu, Nsenga, Ambo and the Southern Lunda are the individual nature of the puberty rite, the seclusion of the girl, the mimes and the dancing. Some common symbolism exists among the Bemba, Bisa, Lamba, Lala and Kaonde and the Alungu. The ceremony at the foot of the *mbudi* tree in the Congo and the Angola chisungu rites, and the *Umwenje* tree among the Lamba, and the designs in low relief of the crocodile among the Nsenga, also seem to be common features. Nowhere are the ceremonies so complex as among the Bemba unless we are to assume that the data we have are very inadequate indeed.

The Ila, who were also listed above as practising a chisungu, belong to a different ethnic group. Their origin is obscure and they have been frequently raided by Lunda, Luba, Lozi and Kaonde and split up by internal fighting. They have a curious descent system, since succession is patrilineal, but a man belongs to his mother's clan. Marriage is contracted with the payment of a high bride-wealth in cattle, and residence is patrilocal. Ancestor

---

[1] Nos. 16 and 17.

worship is highly developed. There are numerous chiefs, and a centralized government was never achieved.

Here there are boys' circumcision schools and similar schools for girls in the Nanzela district. The chisungu rite consists of the seclusion of the girl for two or three months after her first period, in a special hut, round which the women dance each evening. The whole ceremony is called the *kuzaluka* while the term chisungu is reserved for the great feast and dance which takes place at the end of the rite, when cattle are distributed among family and clan relatives. If the girl is not betrothed before the chisungu her husband will then be chosen for her.[1]

The *Ngoma* ceremonies of the plateau Tonga who are neighbours of the Ila, are very similar to the chisungu of the latter tribe, although differently named. The Tonga are matrilineal with no fixed rule of residence at marriage, although Dr. Colson's figures showed a slightly higher rate of virilocal residence.[2] Ancestor worship is practised but there is no institution of chieftainship.

The details of the puberty ceremony of the two tribes are rather similar although the social organization differs so markedly. In both areas the girl is urged to sit in the dark during her seclusion and to play on musical instruments. Her body is rubbed with red clay. The girl is covered with blankets whenever she leaves the hut. Among the Tonga this period of seclusion is known as *kuvundike*, the term used for the covering of tobacco with leaves to make it ferment. After this come the ceremony of emergence from the hut, the ritual bathing of the girl and a feast of chickens, goats and cattle. Women mimic the birth of the girl and do a dance which represents the cattle killed for the occasion.[3] The neighbouring Sala appear to have similar rites.[4]

Among the peoples who practise individual puberty rites for girls, but who do not use the term chisungu, the most important are the matrilineal tribes of Nyasaland and its border districts in Tanganyika and Northern Rhodesia. The tribal admixture in Nyasaland is a complex one owing to the constant movements of people that have taken place there. There were two major migra-

---

[1] No. 54, Vol. II, pp. 28–34.   [2] No. 7, p. 49.
[3] E. Colson, unpublished MSS.   [4] No. 3.

Children go to the fields with their mother when very young

Girls learn to grind the millet and cook at a very early age

tions. One from the south consisted of Zulu off-shoots who crossed the Zambesi river in 1835, and proceeded north as the conquering 'Ngoni' to settle in a number of separate districts to the west and east of Lake Nyasa: one from the Mozambique area consisted of Yao, Makua, Lomwe and Makonde. The Yao entered Masasi and the neighbouring districts in Tanganyika in the 1850's and later moved north into Nyasaland where there are now four Yao settlements, and also to the east of the Lake in Tanganyika. The Makua-Lomwe and Makonde now inhabit the district south of Lake Nyasa.

Besides these major movements of peoples, years of slave-raiding scattered the less war-like tribes then living in Nyasaland and brought Arab influence into the country. Some of the Yao, who themselves became slave-raiders, adopted Islamism and so did some of the Cewa.

From the point of view of this note therefore we have to deal with matrilineal peoples of different origins, the Congo group and those of the Portuguese East African coast. Some of them became Moslems and some did not.[1] The presence of conquering patrilineal Ngoni has altered the matrilineal emphasis in some areas. The first group of matrilineal peoples to settle was the Cewa, Nyanja and Nsenga, who resemble the Bemba-Bisa-Lala-Lamba group in culture, but have a tradition of having arrived much earlier from Lubaland. These are described by Tew as the Maravi group (i) and they now inhabit the region south-west of the Lake and extend into the Luwanga province of Northern Rhodesia.

The second matrilineal group is formed by the Tumbuka-Kamanga peoples of the north-eastern shore of Lake Nyasa, and the Winamwanga and the Wiwa. Little is known of this complex of tribes, but Tew concludes that their 'ethnic sub-stratum consisted of people closely related to their Maravi neighbours to the south'.[2]

The third matrilineal group is formed by the Mozambique tribes already referred to, that is to say the Yao, the Makua-Lomwe and the Makonde.

---

[1] No. 58. See Introduction from which I have taken this classification of the Lake Nyasa region peoples.
[2] *Ibid.*, p. ix.

177

Appendix A

All these matrilineal tribes are agricultural, although some of the Yao now keep cattle. Succession is matrilineal and residence commonly uxorilocal. Marriage payments vary but are, or were, of the Bemba token-payment kind, in most areas. The political units are of the petty chiefdom type. Yao and Maravi chiefs had ritual powers and made approach to ancestral spirits, but kings with centralized government of the Bemba or Mwinilunga Lunda type do not occur. There are suggestions that fire taboos exist among the Yao, and the Maravi, with special taboos on eating salt.

The characteristic features of girls' puberty ceremonies, as distinct from those of the Bemba, is the presence of double or triple rites with a strong emphasis on the ritual of pregnancy as well as on that of puberty. Boys' ceremonies occur and are elaborate among the Yao, Makua and Makonde. Circumcision is practised in boys' initiation schools and is said by Livingstone to have been introduced to the Yao by Arabs.[1] The right to hold ceremonies is highly prized in this group and is usually the prerogative of chiefs. Among the Maravi people a masked dancing corporation, the *Vinyau*, takes an important part in the initiation ceremonies of boys and girls.

Among the Maravi peoples, the Cewa carried out initiation rites for girls which bear some resemblance to those of the Bemba. Girls were usually married very young here, and generally before they reached puberty. Hodgson's account of the ceremonies of the Cewa of the Dowa district of Nyasaland, written in 1933, is probably the fullest.[2] He speaks of a simple puberty rite which takes place at the girl's first period, followed by the full ceremony which was postponed till after the second month and always coincided with the slack season after harvest. The girl, or girls, are dragged out of the initiation hut by the female instructors to the sound of a musical instrument imitating the voice of the jackal (*fisi*). Throughout the ceremony the *vinyau* dancers in masks representing various animals such as the hare, elephant, antelope or vulture, and costumes of wicker and grass, perform after each meal and sometimes tease and beat the girl. On the first day she is taken into the bush, taught secret songs, made to climb a tree and stripped naked and then carried to the village with

[1] Quoted by M. Tew. No. 58, p. 19.   [2] No. 29, pp. 131–6.

178

flour on her head on an older woman's back. On the second day the girl is covered with flour and chased through the bush being reminded of her past sins. On the third day the masked animal dancers predominate; the girl is reclothed and presented to her relatives and four men dance dressed as women with bananas as false breasts. On the fifth day the girl gets a new name, and husband and wife are presented in humility to the rest of the community.

The Cewa girl was supposed to be deflowered by a man other than her husband at the end of her first period and this man was styled the *fisi* or jackal. If the girl reached the time of her main *cinamwali* without being married then a second *fisi* had to be chosen to sleep with her after the rite, and he might not afterwards become her husband. Cullen Young suggests that there was a test of the virginity of the girl before the final dance in the great *cinamwali*,[1] although this would be unusual in the case of these matrilineal peoples. A third ceremony, a pregnancy rite, was evidently held after the girl had been pregnant for three or four months.

J. M. Winterbottom, in an account of girls' puberty rites among the Cewa of the South-western area of the Fort Jameson District of Northern Rhodesia, speaks of the whole *cinamwali* beginning with 'the little initiation' at puberty, and continuing till 'the great initiation' when the girl has become pregnant, as being all one rite. The first ceremony at puberty proper initiates the salt and fire taboos which are important in Cewa belief. The main ceremony, which is a nubility rite, involves dancing on pictures in low relief in a small circle of mud. A crocodile and a snake are the most important of these designs and the comparison between these and the pottery floor designs of the Bemba is evidently close. A virility test is important here also. If the bridegroom fails to light fire by twirling the firestick in its notched groove once, then he is considered to be impotent. The girl is also asked on the morning after her marriage night if her husband has proved virile, and he is mocked by the villagers if he has not. Another man is then called 'to eat the *cinamwali*'. A pregnancy rite takes place here as among the other groups of Cewa cited.[2]

[1] No. 11.   [2] No. 63.

Appendix A

Marwick, writing in 1947, described a contracted and much simpler form of the *cinamwali* limited to the time of the girl's first period. The *vinyau* dance is now prohibited in some areas.[1]

The matrilineal Nyanja seem also to have a series of rites for girls similar to those of the Cewa, and ending in the celebration of the birth of a first, or sometimes a second child. The main ceremony is a nubility rite in which pictures are drawn on the ground with ashes or flour set in a small circle of mud, and on these the women dance. Werner describes the men dancing in grotesque masks of wood and cloth at these rites, and uses the term *zinyau*, presumably the same as *vinyau*, for these dancers. She speaks of a procession round the village by women carrying 'certain mysteries' among the lake-side Nyanja. These details bring to mind much of the Bemba chisungu ceremonial and the mysteries may well be pottery figurines.[2]

The Tumbuka-Kamanga group, which also includes the Henga and the lake-shore Tonga, are matrilineal, with marriage by service instead of by payments, and uxorilocal residence. Only by heavy payments could the bridegroom win the right of taking his bride home to live with him in his own village.[3] In areas where the people have become patrilineal owing to Ngoni influence this position is changed. Chiefs and centralized government are again absent from this area. Petty chiefs are responsible for acts of ancestor worship.

Among the Tumbuka puberty rites for boys were simple and individual; the youth was given medicine and 'some tests of manhood'.[4] The girl was usually betrothed before puberty and when this event occurred she was 'housed' or secluded for a week to three months. After this period there was a dance, teasing and punishment of the girl for her former peccadilloes, an examination for virginity and finally a washing rite and, in some districts, a covering of the girl with ashes or flour to show she has become clean.[5] As among other tribes in this group it was dangerous for the girl to become pregnant before the final dance known as the *usamba*. Wiwa and Winamwanga rites are somewhat similar.[6]

---

[1] M. G. Marwick, personal communication, 1947.
[2] No. 61, pp.127–8.   [3] No. 58, p. 58.
[4] *Ibid.*, p. 63.   [5] No. 11; No. 20, p. 151.
[6] No. 5, p. 38.

Distribution of Chisungu Ceremonies in Central Africa

For the tribes of Mozambique origin we have the fullest material on the different Yao groups. These are matrilineal people with a strong avunculate. Residence is mainly uxorilocal and the 'ideal' group consists of a man and his married sisters, with their husbands and children. Ancestor worship was formerly practised but many Yao are now Moslems. The political units were petty chiefdoms in which the rulers had at least some ritual functions.

Both boys' and girls' initiation schools existed and were elaborate. The annual initiation ceremonies (*unyago*) are among the Yao of Lindidisi are described by Heckel as 'the most important part of the culture of the Yaos.'[1]

The term *unyago* is used, according to Stannus, for the boys' ceremony, *lupanda*, the girls' *ciputu*, and the *litiwo* rite at the first conception of the girl. There follows a naming ceremony for the new child. Thus the rites conform to the serial pattern characteristic of this group. The links between the male and female rites seem however to have been unusually close and the final acts of both took place jointly at the *lupanda* lodge of the boys.[2]

Boys' initiation schools could only be held under the order of a chief or important headman and the right to hold such a ceremony was jealously disputed. Girls' schools could be organized by heads of villages.[3]

The boys' *lupanda* is a rite of circumcision. It is held very early in the boys' life, that is to say at 7 to 8 years. The symbolism resembles that of the Bemba chisungu in that pottery representations of animals are drawn in low relief on the ground and mimes of agricultural activities take place as well as of hunting, crafts, and other activities. The zebra, hyena, sable, elephant and other animals are also mimed.[4] Stannus, writing about the Machinga Yao, mentions seventeen animal images and the figures of a drunken woman and a woman dead in childbirth. Such models sound very much like those used among the Bemba.[5]

The girls' *ciputu* took place before puberty and parallels closely that of the boys. Clitoridectomy used to be practised among

---

[1] No. 28, p. 19.   [2] No. 55, p. 296.
[3] No. 58, p. 19. She quotes here from H. L. Duff, *Nyasaland under the Foreign Office*, 1903, p. 312. Mair says that the right to hold girls' ceremonies among the Dedza Yao was inherited from the original holder, who received the power from a chief. (No. 38.)   [4] No. 47.   [5] No. 56.

Moslems but was discontinued in 1903.[1] The *ciputu* consists of a month's seclusion in the girls' dormitory, with singing and dancing. Interesting elements were an attack on the village by women dressed as men followed by a mock trial and the release of prisoners. Animals made of wicker were manipulated by the men to frighten the girls. Mimes of the girls' work in agriculture, cooking and housebuilding were frequent. At the end of the ceremony a roof was carried over the heads of a group of girls as a symbol of their position as the pillars of the house (cf. the Bemba song given on p. 199).[2] Ritual defloration of the girls took place in the old days. The final ceremony of the girls was held jointly with the boys at the *lupanda* lodge.[3]

A pregnancy rite, the *litiwo*, was held when the young bride first quickened with child. In singing, dancing and feasting the virility of the man was honoured: Heckel, writing of the Yao of Lindidisi, talks of 'an initiation of first birth' when the husband is praised highly in song and hymns. A naming ceremony for the baby took place when it was six months old in this area.[4]

Stannus mentions ceremonies now extinct, called *kulukwi*, and says that these were held in the case of wives who had not conceived since their *ciputu* rite.[5] Their husbands were put through various tests of manhood including the splitting of a notched stick with an axe. Mitchell working among the Yao in 1949 did not see this rite.

Weule, writing in 1909, says the initiation ceremonies of the Makua were more elaborate than those of the Yao.[6] For the Makonde, their southern neighbours, we have a full description by Lyndon Harries.[7] The girls' rites have some parallels with those of the Bemba. The candidates, who are usually ten to fourteen years old, sit in a row in front of the *ciputu* house with a bow, which is afterwards carried in a dance procession round the village and is said to represent vaginal distension. Games on the subsequent day include teasing the girls and the representation of male activities. The hunting of a gazelle means the man's hunt for a partner and a woman is afterwards trapped in a hunting net. On

---

[1] No. 55, p. 296. [2] No. 61, p. 126. [3] No. 56, p. 234; No. 38.
[4] No. 23, pp.24–26. [5] No. 56. [6] No. 58, p. 26.
[7] No. 27, pp. 24–6.

the second night the vaginal extension practised by so many of the tribes in this area, including the Bemba, is initiated ceremonially. Later the mothers of the girls get new fire from a brand taken from the *ciputu* fire, and carried round the village. A month's semi-seclusion follows in which the secret of the songs is revealed in return for the fees paid to the instructress. On emerging from the hut there are more mimes in which a man hunting for game with a bow is again depicted. Later a log of a tree which represents a phallus is brought into the house. There are a number of further symbols including instruction on the care with which the father's property must be handled as distinct from the mother's.

Further research will probably show that rites of the chisungu type are much more widely distributed in Central Africa than appears from these scattered references. I would also expect to find far more common features in the ceremonies than have been referred to here, if more direct observations had been available, for it will be recalled that the accounts of the Bemba chisungu given from hearsay evidence differed considerably from my own observations of the rite and were limited to outline descriptions of one or two of the more dramatic incidents.

From the material presented here it is only possible to pick out certain common features in the chisungu, or chisungu-like ceremonies mentioned. First, the emphasis in all these ceremonies is on the magical danger associated with the girls' first period, and on the first act of intercourse after this event. Ritual defloration, or rather intercourse with a man other than the husband on the first occasion after puberty, took place among the Cewa, and formerly among the Yao, while among the Bemba it was limited to the case of the wife of a chief. The information is not full enough to enable us to tell whether the taboos surrounding sex, blood and fire are as pronounced among the other tribes mentioned as they are in the case of the Bemba. The material Margaret Read gives us on the Cewa suggests that this may be so in their case, as do the references to menstrual and fire taboos among the Yao and other Mozambique tribes. The taboos are specifically mentioned by Doke in the case of the Lamba.

The ceremonies are everywhere considered to be a preface to marriage and there is a general fear of the birth of a child to a girl who has not received the magic protection given her by the chisungu rite. For this reason the ceremony tends to be advanced earlier and earlier in some tribes and takes place some years before puberty among the Kaonde, the Yao, Cewa and Makonde. For this reason, too, there is a wide incidence of double rites of protection for the girl, one designed to save her from the immediate dangers of menstruation and the other to make possible safe marriage.

There is a universal stress on the importance of fertility in marriage, and this is marked not only by nubility ritual but also by pregnancy rites of different kinds. The Cewa have a simple puberty rite followed by a ceremony performed after a month or two, as well as the *vinyau* dance, which is, to all appearances, closely associated with fertility. The Nyanja perform a second rite after the first or second child of a union has been conceived, while the Yao sacralize puberty leading to marriage, and follow this with a rite that takes place when the first child of a union is born. It seems possible that the Bemba rite of 'taking the child' is a celebration of a fertile union of this sort.

The virility of the man is also both tested and honoured ritually. The Bemba chisungu ceremony emphasizes it, and the succeeding marriage rites are tests of the virility of the man, not of the chastity of the woman. The Yao rite of celebrating the virility of the man after the girl is pregnant is another case in point. Among the Fort Jameson Cewa the virility of the man is tested by a fire-lighting ordeal in the bush. If the fire lights the man is known to be potent. The Alungu rite had similar features. I have discussed elsewhere my reasons for suggesting that virility tests of this kind are more common in matrilineal societies than patrilineal.

The ritual mechanisms seem to show at least some similarities throughout the Northern Rhodesian and Nyasaland group. The use of a special initiation hut for the singing and dancing is common, although it is not stated whether designs are painted on the walls of the hut as in the Bemba chisungu. The presentation of pottery emblems is not commonly mentioned, although it is reported among the Nsenga where the women dance on pottery models of crocodiles and other designs made on the ground. The Nyanja make similar models. Among the Cewa animal representations are made by the *vinyau* society; agricultural mimes are performed in the case of Yao boys' and girls' rites, and miming is generally common in the ceremonies.

One similarity of form noted in these abbreviated accounts is in the rites in which the girls are brought to the base of a named forest tree; this occurs among the Bemba, the Lamba, the Lunda of Angola and those of Jadotville. A log of a tree is brought into the hut among the Makonde, and another special feature is the search for pots of beer which occurs among the Bemba and the Nyanja.

The ceremony of shooting an arrow at a mark which takes place on the last night of the Bemba chisungu, and the giving of an arrow to the bridegroom at the Bemba wedding is paralleled among the Alungu, and in the Tumbuka-Kamanga country where an arrow is shot at a tree. Makonde ceremonies also use the bow as an important symbol. The bow appears to represent the stretching of the vagina in some cases; the bow and arrow are also used to represent the hunting or searching for the bride; the possession of the arrow seems to symbolize the husband's possession of the bride.

Since most of the tribes recorded are of Lunda origin, it is not surprising that there are similarities in the symbols used in the rites.

It is not possible to answer all the questions I asked as to the possible connections between chisungu rites on the one hand and matrilineal structure, marriage by service and uxorilocal residence on the other; nor those between chisungu as practised by the Bemba and the existence of ritual chiefs who can approach the ancestral spirits only after intercourse in marriage and ritual purification. The evidence on which to test these hypotheses is simply not available.

Suffice it to say that the correlation between girls' individual puberty rites and matrilineal organization is very marked in Central Africa, and that both the glorification of the role of the nubile girl and the praise of the man from another clan who gives her fertility, are consonant with the beliefs on which matrilineal organization rests in this area.[1] Boys' ceremonies exist side by side

---

[1] The only patrilineal tribe which I remember in this area which has individual puberty rites for girls and none for boys is the Nyakusa. Cf. G. H. Wilson, No. 65, p. 238.

with girls' among the peoples of Mozambique origin as they do on the coast from which the Yao, Makua and Makonde come, but the girls' rites are not mere replicas of the boys' but are definitely a series of nubility ceremonies starting with puberty and ending with the celebration of pregnancy and childbirth. The coincidence between matriliny and agricultural activities which was postulated by some of the earlier evolutionary writers, such as Bachofen and Schmidt, exists here in actual fact.

This correlation has probably little bearing on the chisungu, except that in this area the introduction of stock has usually been followed by the giving of cattle as a marriage payment for the bride and hence the bridegroom's acquisition of rights over his children, and his achievement of the equally important right of virilocal residence. Where the high marriage payments are made, as in Angola or in parts of Nyasaland, the Bemba matrilineal, uxorilocal marriage by service pattern, which I have tried to associate with girls' fertility ceremonies, tends to disappear.

I cannot test the validity of the correlation I tried to suggest between the importance of the Bemba chisungu and an ancestral cult mainly carried out by chiefs. The evidence is not full enough on this point. Nevertheless it is worth pointing out that the Bemba are the only people in this group with ritual kingship and a centralized government developed into key institutions of the whole tribal structure, and the Bemba ceremonies are more complex than those of any of the other tribes mentioned. The rites among Kazembe's Lunda may be found to be as complex, but on the present evidence, the Bemba are the only other tribe in the group which has, or had, a 'divine' king, chiefs with ritual powers, matrilineal descent and uxorilocal marriage. From the evidence at present available the ceremonies that come next in order of complexity are those of the Yao. Here there is no 'divine king' or centralized organization, but the strength of the matrilineage and the emphasis on matrilineal descent as a basis of residence seems to be stronger than in the other tribes in the area, judging from Mitchell's evidence. The other questions I have asked throughout this book must await their answers when the field evidence is fuller.

APPENDIX B

Songs Sung During the Ceremony

T he following are the songs transcribed during the ceremony witnessed. They represent little more than half of the songs actually sung and less than that proportion of the chisungu songs known by the average *nacimbusa*. The songs are given with literal translation together with the different interpretations offered. These latter are given in some detail as they show the variety of traditional meanings associated with ceremonial songs of this kind. The whole appendix illustrates the point made on p. 164 that the fixity of a form of words or a design allows multiple interpretations without losing the value associated with a 'thing handed down'. The differences in interpretation are either absolute as in the case of song No. 10 or else they are variations in crudity as between the explanations given by the uneducated *nacimbusa* or the educated Bemba. I am indebted to Mr. I. A. Nkonde for a complete set of interpretations of the latter type and for help with some of the translations, and also to Mr. Paul Mushindo and Mr. Kasonde.

No. 1. *Entering in.* This is the song sung when the girls are first brought into the chisungu hut (p. 64) crawling on all fours under blankets:

Tuingile shyani?	How are we going in?
Tuingile mipempe;	We are going in as through a tunnel into a dark place;
Nga bakolwe.	We are going in like monkeys.

Interpretation. Mipempe are the grass reeds built to form a narrow passage into the interior of a fishing weir. Hence it conveys the idea of a passage into a secret place, i.e. the secrets of the

187

mbusa. It is also a passage concealed from the outside world as the girls are concealed from the eyes of the rest of the community under the blankets. Monkeys are represented throughout the chisungu as being enterprising in thefts, usually for the sake of the family.

The immediate interpretation given was that the song meant the hiding of the girls from the village; and that the crawling was meant to make them look ridiculous. I. A. Nkonde gives:

'How shall we go into the ceremony? Shall we enter like monkeys that crawl in in stealth? Thus we show we are forsaking the normal way of life. But we have to go through dark and difficult places before we get wisdom.'

Kasonde says:

'How shall we enter in? We shall enter exposing our buttocks like monkeys.

We are free in the house.

There is nothing secret to us.'

No. 2. Setting the Fish Traps. Sung while making imitation fish traps out of leaves (p. 65):

Ubwamba bwali bwandi!	Here is my fishing weir!
Ndetabataba no mono.	I am bustling about to set a fish trap in it.

Interpretation. Ubwamba is a fishing dyke built in mud across a backwater. The *mono* is the conical fish trap set in it. *Bwamba* also means nakedness and hence is used as an euphemism for the sex organs. The leaf cups with which the women pretend to catch each others' fingers apparently represent the fish-traps and also the vagina of the woman. Fish appear as symbols of fertility throughout the ceremony and the women mention this in immediate explanation of the relation to the words of the song, i.e. 'The mother says,"The girl was my responsibility, but I cannot teach her everything. I have tried to do so up to now but I have failed and therefore now I have to entrust her to the *nacimbusa* to carry out the ceremony for her. If she refuses it means there is no hope for my girl".'

No. 3. The Chisungu falls off. Sung after the girls have made their first jump over a faggot bundle and are carried back to the village (p. 66):

Twakula icibwe	We have dragged a big stone down from the hills (twice)
Twakula icibwe	
Twaleta!	We have brought it in!
Cipapa cambale ico mulila	It is the skin of the leopard which makes you cry
Twakulakula!	We have dragged it and dragged it!
Twaleta!	We have brought it in!

Interpretation. The heavy stone is the weight of the chisungu, the dangerous difficult condition from which the girl is to be freed. (Cf. the expression 'the chisungu falls'—chisungu *cawa*). *Mbale* is an old term for leopard—the animal which cannot change its spots and which represents the hard new life. The leopard skin was also associated with the function of the *nacimbusa* who wore such a skin in the old days. The women explain the song as one of rejoicing that the chisungu has fallen off. Nkonde phrases it: 'We are dragging something of a problem; we have brought it in. The heavy stone is the difficulties the girls have to go through before they are called mature women.' Kasonde says: 'The *mbale* skin you have been crying for, we are dragging and dragging it in to you. We are at last bringing you the beautiful girl you have been waiting for.' Thus there are ideas as to the difficulty of the new life, the secrets to be revealed and the realizing of an object long waited for expressed in this song. The leopard represents the hardships the girls will have to face in future.

No. 4. Behold the husband as a lion. Sung after the return to the initiation hut after the first jump:

Iseni mutambe!	Come and look!
Tutwale uko bacibashyale	Let us take them for the purpose for which they were made,
Cinkolobondo.	To the *cinkolobondo.*
Napelwa na mulume ua nkalamo,	I have been given to my lion husband,
Iseni mutambe!	Come and look!

Interpretation. The *cinkolobondo* is the mortar or grinding trough. It is also, according to Nkonde, the tree of life. A *nacim-busa* interpreted: 'They have given the girl to the *nacimbusa*. It is the father who is the lion.' Others said that the husband was the lion. Nkonde writes: 'Behold we are bringing the girls to the place of life (the *cinkolobondo* tree).' I think also to the occupations of married life, i.e., to the mortar or grinding trough. He added 'I am given to the husband. He is no coward. He is as strong as a lion; so come and see what kind of a person my husband is!' Kasonde says: 'I am destroyed or smashed up by this male lion.'

No. 5. Teasing the girl. Sung during the teasing of the girls:

Tumutemyetemye,	Let us shake her, shake her,
Mulwani uauma	The enemy has made himself hard
Mwansa Kabinga!	Mwansa Kabinga!

Interpretation. Mwansa Kabinga is a legendary character who occurs in Bemba songs. The women attempted no explanation. Nkonde writes 'Let us shake them and trouble them, for during their girlhood they behaved as though they did not know they would be liable to punishment during the chisungu ceremony, if they were rude to their elders. So now let us take revenge on them. This teaches them to bear difficulties.'

No. 6. Honouring the nacimbusa. Sung by a young man doing a dance of respect to the *nacimbusa* (p. 68):

Cindamo nindwala!	I dance here but I am ill;
Nai mwana ua cimbwi	I am the child of the hyena;
Namucelela shiŋanga.	I have greeted the magician.

Nkonde writes: 'I cannot dance because my girls are ill. But I am hard like the hyena's child and I shall do my duty. We therefore bow our heads and greet the *nacimbusa* who has made it possible for our daughters to be initiated.' Kasonde says: 'The girl was hard and difficult to deal with and must be disciplined.'

No. 7. The wild pig. Sung at the root of the *musuku* during the first woodland ceremony to the action of scratching up seeds (p. 70):

Munjili,	You wild pig,
Sebe mpolo!	Hoe up the rough grass!

Songs Sung During the Ceremony

Interpretation. Mpolo is wild grass. The pig gets up early to look for food and the girl is to do the same after she is married. Pigs root up food in rough ground and hence the girl must be prepared to work hard to get food for the family. Nkonde's version is 'Young girls, seek wisdom now you have entered into womanhood. The provision of food is now in your hands and you have to feed those about you and bring up the children in the manner we have taught you'.

No. 8. The guinea-fowl. Also sung at the root of the *musuku* tree to the action of churning up the ground:

We makanga,	You guinea-fowl,
So lindo!	Come here and wait!

Interpretation. The guinea-fowl scratchs the soil to find food, as the pig does. There is a similar emphasis on the need for looking for things instead of expecting them to lie on the surface. The guinea-fowl is also a sex symbol and appears in one of the wall-designs and as a large pottery emblem in the hut. Women said the song was to teach the girl industry. Nkonde writes: 'You are like a guinea-fowl. You have to look for things yourself. The whole world is in your hand. It is your duty to make the best of it.'

No. 9. The little garden. Also sung at the root of the *musuku* tree to the action of sowing seeds and scraping them up with the hands (p. 71):

Akabala,	The little garden,
Balala.	The garden of the ground-nuts.

Interpretation. This is a typical example of meaning by inference rather than in the actual word content. Women explained 'When the rain falls you hoe ground-nuts'; or 'It is to teach the girls how to garden'. Nkonde writes: 'You do not use the word garden for land that has not been dug. You cannot expect to get ground-nuts, or anything else, where you have never worked. The blood comes from a cut which means that nothing on this earth can be got without labour.'

No. 10. The tortoise starts to climb. A song sung while the girls are made to climb legs foremost up the *musuku* tree (p. 71):

191

Appendix B

Fulwe tanina;	The tortoise does not climb;
Lelo anina ku mukolobondo.	But today it is climbing the *mukolobondo* tree.

Interpretation. The tortoise does not naturally climb trees. If he climbed he would be breaking away from old habits as the girls will have to do, now that they are married. He is climbing up backwards. The *mukolobondo* tree is one with a very smooth bark which is very difficult to climb, but its fruit is very sweet.

Kasonde contributes: 'If you say you do not know how to do these impossible things, how can you keep house? How can you live? All right, we shall teach you today to do such things whether you like it or not.' Other informants specified in what way the girl was to do the unusual or impossible, i.e. by getting the firewood if needed, although that is reckoned as a man's job. One *nacimbusa* contributed the idea of reticence as expressed by this song. If the husband commits adultery, the wife must say nothing about it, but just ignore it, however difficult. Nkonde, as usual more in accord with European ideas of morality, added: 'You say you never do a thing but when the testing time comes your resolve breaks down and you do a thing against your habit, like the tortoise, who suddenly started to climb a tree.' Another interpretation is that given for song 50 of the tortoise which sticks out its head when visiting, i.e. asks for food, and puts it in when at home, i.e., conceals food.

No. 11. The monkeys climb. The girls pretend to bite at a maize cob with their mouths (p. 72). They sing:

Kolwe kulya kwakwe,	The monkey eats everything,
Kwa mutali shya;	It put us in difficulties;
Eya nine ku mukolobondo.	That's why he climbs the mukolobondo.
No. 12. Kolwe ita nyina.	The monkey calls its mother.

Interpretation. The monkey is here represented as foraging for food. He is also, like the tortoise, climbing the smooth bark of the *mukolobondo* tree. Explanations given by the women were concrete, i.e., that the girls should imitate monkeys because they eat everything on trees and they forage for food for the family as the

192

Songs Sung During the Ceremony

good housewife should. Kasonde added: 'We must eat in order to live and therefore we must be prepared to face difficulties some-times.'

No. 13. The order of precedence. The song is repeated constantly when giving offerings of *mbusa* to the elders in order of precedence. (Pp. 72–3.):

Kuapa takacila kubea　　The arm-pit is not higher than the shoulder.

Interpretation. As it is impossible to reverse the arm-pit and the shoulder, so it is impossible for the younger ever to reach higher status than the older.

No. 14. Honouring with the mouth. This was the song sung con-stantly when objects were picked up with the mouth instead of the hand and were offered in order of precedence.

Tolela nando,　　Let me pick it up,
Tolela na mulimo,　　Let me pick it up with my mouth.
Mbusa yandi.　　My *mbusa.*

I have no interpretation beyond the obvious one.

No. 15. Forward and backward. This was the song sung when the girls crawled four steps forward and four backward. (p. 74.)

Konta kanandi　　Mark one step after another!
Konta!　　Mark it!
Tatubwelela pa numa.　　Let us not turn back.

Interpretation. Two contradictory interpretations were given. One said that the girls must go back if they have made a mistake and must put it right, and another that the girls have entered a new world and must not turn back.

No. 16. The Hunt on the roof. When looking for presents on the roof of the hut the women sang: (p. 75)

Mumfwayile akasoka mu mu-tenge.　　You look for a little snake for me on the roof.

Interpretation. The snake is the hidden thing. (See also p. 87.)

193

Appendix B

No. 17. *The bridegroom's gift.* When looking for *mbusa* in the covered baskets the women sang:

Wakunkupukwila;	You have uncovered it,
Mwalye nsomo lye.	You have eaten the whole *nsomo.*

Interpretation. The *nsomo* was the bridegroom's gift. It refers to the gifts of food given ceremonially to the bridegroom during the different stages of the marriage ceremony. These dishes have small gifts placed on top and the food must be distributed and not eaten.

No. 18. *The girls' invitation.* The girls distribute the cooked food to their fellows and sing:

Fisabo fyesu fyapwa;	The food from our gardens is finished up;
Pokeni bamayo.	Help yourselves, mothers.

Interpretation. This is the song that goes with the rite that makes the girl free to garden. The women said: 'Now we have danced the child as a gardener. She must start to cultivate herself now.'

No. 19. *Begging for fire.* This is an important song sung as the women rubbed the fire-sticks in a frenzied effort to produce sparks (p. 76):

Twaisa kulonda mulilo	We have come to beg for fire.
Nkalamo twapapata.	Lion, we beg it of you.

No. 20. They also sang:

Shikishiki!	Scratch! Scratch! (The operating of the fire-sticks)
Uafyala banga?	How many children have you borne?

Interpretation. The sticks are rubbed on the back of the girl's father's sister who can give or withhold parenthood. The girl is told that she owes fire to the older woman whose hands ache from the rubbing. She must take over now. She must take her turn at the bearing of children now. The lion is the bridegroom, the chief, or the male principle throughout the ceremony. The bridegroom is begged for fire. The whole rite is called 'begging for parenthood'. Nkonde added that the girl is taught not to forget to keep the fire taboos.

No. 21. Further teasing songs:

Fitula panse,	Things from outside the house,
Te fikansa.	Cause no arguments.

Interpretation. The girl is not to sit chatting with friends who might urge her to criticize her husband.

Many similar songs have been omitted.

No. 22. Take the girl to the crocodile. When showing the pottery *mbusa* to the girls, the women sing:

Mutwale umwana,	You take the girl,
Kuli ŋwena.	To the crocodile.

Interpretation. The crocodile is the royal totem and represents authority and tradition, either exerted by the chief or the husband. Nkonde suggests that if the girl does not go through the ceremony, she will not be loyal.

No. 23. The nacimbusa adorned. The *nacimbusa* was honoured by the song:

Bana cinyampinyampi,	The children of Cinyampinyampi
Cimbusa cikulu conda na ngala.	The great *mbusa* brought them forth with her nails

Interpretation. The children of Cinyampinyampi (a legendary figure) are brought forth by the great *nacimbusa,* the mid-wife. *Ngala* also means the plumed head-dress worn by the *nacimbusa* in the chief's court and the song refers to her honour there.

No. 24. The stool. The women play at chasing each other off a stool. They sing:

Mwikala pa cipuna	Don't sit on the stool.

Interpretation. This is a reference to the Bemba custom of chasing away each official burier of the chief after he has fulfilled his great office. Nkonde saw in it an instruction to young girls not to sit in the presence of their elders.

No. 25. The bat song. The women sang:

Kasusu tole nda,	Little bat pick the louse,
Leke icungulo cise	Wait for the evening to come.
Tubike muleya pambali,	We will put amorous play aside
Ubwangalilo bucili ku mtuima	While we remember things in our hearts.

Interpretation. This was said to represent the woman who goes out to hunt for lovers in the dark, which a girl should never do. She raises her skirts to expose herself, like the wings of a bat. Nkonde said that the evening is the time for play, but the housework must be done before chatting with friends.

No. 26. The hawk song. The women sang:

Mpungu yalela;	The hawk has cried out;
Akuangala.	It is in play.

Interpretation. The hawk pounces down on food without ceremony. The girl must never do this.

No. 27. Imitating our mothers. When the girls swung to and fro above a pool of water in the whitening ceremony, the women sang:

Kucilingana Lesa,	Following the ways of God
Tupashyana mayo	We imitate our mother.

Interpretation. This was explained as an imitation of an act of birth and also as teaching the girls to bathe in the river during menstruation. Nkonde added: 'It is our duty to follow God and to pass on knowledge as we had it passed on to us. We make you a mother as your mothers were to you.'

No. 28. The spotted lion. On returning from the whitening ceremony the girls sang:

Twaile sobela nkalamo yamabala.	We tracked a lion in our gardens and reported it.
Cibinda talaba.	The hunter has not forgotten.

Interpretation. Nkonde hazarded that the ceremony is like the spots of the lion which never change or are forgotten. You have been the victim and therefore, do not forget the instructions.

No. 29. The evil spirits:

Ndelila ku ciwa kuli mayo.	I am crying to my mother because of evil spirits.

No. 30. The groping bridegroom. On the last night the mock bridegrooms come in as blind men feeling along the walls of the hut with their hands. They sing:

Ndepalampanta kafifi,	I am groping about in the dark,
Nalwala.	I am ill.

Interpretation. The bridegrooms pretend not to see the *mbusa* of the girls. They are ashamed to come to the hut where the work has gone on. An educated Bemba wrote: 'I am outwitted. I cannot see what I am doing. I am ready for mishap.'

No. 31. The Nacimbusa triumphs. The *nacimbusa* comes in in triumph and pretends to sleep on the mat the bridegroom gives her. They sing:

Yansakasengele,	Spread the mat,
Tulale yansa.	So that we may sleep.
Banacimbusa basose,	The *banacimbusa* say,
Mwatufimba.	You have wrapped us in cloth.

Interpretation. The bridegroom pays the *nacimbusa* with a mat to hand over the secret things to the bride. The *nacimbusa* tells the bride she must accept her husband. The instructions must be given so that they are understood.

No. 32. The lion skin. The *nacimbusa* appears in the *ngala* headdress and sings:

Lupapu nkalamo ngaisa	The skin of the lion is worn
Kwa Mwamba	At the court of Mwamba.

Interpretation. The *nacimbusa* is honoured as the messenger of a great chief. The skin of a lion used to be worn by the messenger of Mwamba in the old days.

No. 33. The bridegrooms bring firewood. The bridegrooms bring firewood strapped to the backs of their young sisters. They sing (p. 106):

Kuteba taulabwela,	You have not come back from fetching firewood,
Kalombo we mushya,	Kalombo you slave,
Uko wile kuteba.	From where you went to look for the faggots.

No Interpretation.

No. 34. *The shooting of the mark.* The bridegrooms come with bows and arrows and shoot at a mark in the wall. They sing:

Nalonshya inama yandi,	I have tracked my game;
Taibula mwine ualasa.	I have speared one.

No. 35. *The man is the peak of the house.*

Cikulu mwaume muyanda;	The man is the peak of the house;
Efyo tuumfwe.	That is what we have understood.
Na banakashi abapikula cisumbe.	It is women who make the pinnacle on top of the roof.

Interpretation. The chisungu is the apex of the hut roof—a complicated part of the roof to make. The man is the mainstay and support of the house. He has to solve the most difficult problems. The man is the head of the house. Women understand how to plait the roof framework. The woman knits together the home.

No. 36. *Greeting the dawn.* The drunken crowd of women run round the village to greet the dawn. They sing:

Mukolobwe!	Mr. Cock!
Nga waya,	When you have gone,
Iseni tuangale.	Let us come out and play.

Interpretation. Kasonde said: 'Now that the cock has crowed let us play,' i.e. at man and wife.

No. 37. *The lion song.* Another chisungu song sung on the last morning was:

Songs Sung During the Ceremony

Ualele cisungu,	You have slept with the chisungu child,
Ualele nkalamo.	You have slept with the lion.

Interpretation. It is dangerous to sleep with a girl after puberty. It is like the danger of the lion. The young man is warned not to sleep with his bride without the right precautions.

II

The songs that follow are those which are sung when the girl is presented with her pottery figurines.[1] The majority of the songs are given here, but omissions have been made when the meaning of the song is very obscure.

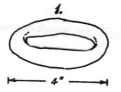

Fig. 1. *The bracelet*

No. 38. *The bracelet* (*likosa*) Fig. 1. This is a model of a bracelet. It is put over the wrist of the girl, or else swung in her hand. The following words are sung:

Kampele mulume,	It was given me by my husband,
Akakaŋanda.	The little house.
Mayo tambene!	Mother look at it!

Interpretation. It is the husband's duty to clothe his wife and the bracelet represents this obligation. The betrothal present (*nsalamo*) is also usually a bracelet. The initiate is ritually clothed with bracelets made of grass at the end of the chisungu when she is ceremonially bathed in the river (p. 109). Hence the girl calls her mother to look at what her husband has given her, i.e. the bracelet,

[1] The collection I made for the museums of the Universities of Johannesburg and Cape Town differ slightly from that seen at Cisonde village. The former have been described by Schofield. Op. cit.

and thus she hints that the time has come for her to be given to her husband. The song can apparently also be translated as 'Go and give me to my husband'.

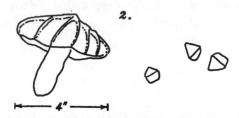

Fig. 2. The necklet beads (2 forms—one representing the whole conus shell and one the triangular discs made from it to be used as beads of a necklace).

No. 39. The necklet bead (*mpande*) (Fig. 2). Two forms are used in the chisungu ceremonies—the whole conus shell as shown in the drawing or a triangular section such as the Bemba regularly wear as neck ornaments. There are many historical associations with such shells. They are, for instance, placed on the body of the dead paramount chief when he is buried.

In the chisungu the model of the bead, strung on bark string, was swung to and fro by the mistress of the ceremony while the company sang:

Mpande yandi,	My mpande bead,
Yapona kwi sano.	It has fallen in the chief's court.

Interpretation. There was considerable unanimity in explanation here. Informants all agreed that the *mpande* represented the wife. If the husband has wronged his wife so that she runs back to her own family, then he has lost his head. To get his wife back he must approach his relatives-in-law with great circumspection and must bring presents as he would if he had let something fall in a chief's courtyard. This is a typical example of the allusive use of a couple of doggerel lines to refer to a marriage obligation. The *mpande* shell is also used as a vagina symbol in some parts of Africa. This meaning was not specifically mentioned to me by Bemba informants.

Songs Sung During the Ceremony

No. 40. *The star* (*ntanda*) (Fig. 3). This is a big pot with a narrow mouth and perforated sides. A lighted taper is put inside so

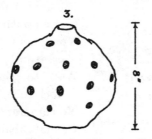

*Fig. 3. The Star (with perforations so that a lighted
taper will burn inside).*

that it shines out to represent star-light. A pottery lid is then fitted on top and the initiated girl must balance it on her head, if possible with the torch remaining alight inside. The company sings:

Ulekashye ntanda bushiku;	You gaze at the stars at night;
Ulantuka ukashika.	You revile me obscenely.

Interpretation. Here there seems to be a complicated double meaning, and probably more than two. Women answered questions about this figurine with shame and hesitation. They said that the light which shone through was the blood inside the woman, which it is so terrible to display. *Ukashika* is to be grave, weighty but also to become red. The most horrible curse a man can use is to swear by the menstruation of his wife. It is a thing which a woman can hardly bring herself to whisper in explanation. The surface meaning is, however, given cheerfully. However badly a husband swears at his wife, she must not answer back. This is a typical example of words with a readily repeatable meaning and concealed associations known as 'things underneath' (*fintu fya panshi*).

No. 41. *The little spoon* (*kakombo*) (Fig. 4). The initiate stands opposite the 'bridegroom' on the last night of the ceremony.[1] She pretends to pour water on 'his' hands with the model of the spoon

---

[1] Represented by his sister.

and to rub the floor beneath as though she were muddying it over. All sing:

Cibale! Cibale!	Cibale! Cibale!
Kasambe mulume,	Go and wash your husband,
We cinangwa!	You ignorant (uninitiated) creature!
Na panshi ulala (or utota),	And to the ground make obeisance,
We cinangwa!	You ignorant creature!
Cibale! Cibale!	Cibale! Cibale!

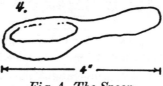

Fig. 4. The Spoon.

Interpretation. Here the meaning was clear and the actions representative. The girl here imitates in song her part in the ceremony of purification after intercourse. She takes water from her little marriage pot and pours it on her husband's hands. The initiated girl knows how important it is to do this but not the girl who is a weed, or an uncultivated plant, because she has not been danced. Cibale is a legendary figure.

Fig. 5. The man with the plumed head dress worn on the 'bridegroom's' head.

No. 42. The man with the plumed head-dress (waume ua ngala) (Fig. 5). This helmet-like model was worn by the female representative of the bridegroom, who balanced it on her head while the girl was washing her hands as above. They sing:

Mwansa Cembe!	Mwansa Cembe! (twice)
Mwansa Cembe!	
Mulume wa ngala waisa.	The husband with the plumed head-dress has come.

Interpretation. Mwansa Cembe is a legendary figure in whom no one seemed to show much interest. The song itself was sung with great excitement (see p. 86). The husband comes wearing the plumed head-dress which was given by the chief to brave warriors. He comes in triumph. The girl kneels to him. 'It is to show honour to the husband. The girl must praise him.'

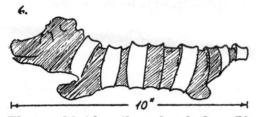

Fig. 6. The crocodile (the tail was here broken off in firing).

No. 43. The crocodile (ŋweno) (Fig. 6). The girl holds the crocodile figurine in her hand and the company sing:

Luyamba,	Crocodile,
Uikata ku matete.	You have caught in the rushes.
Nani shyaleka ku matete?	Who has been left in the rushes?
Luyamba.	Crocodile!

Interpretation. The crocodile, for which *luyamba* is an archaic term, is the emblem of the royal clan. There seem to be varied, or else obscure, meanings attached to this *mbusa*. One woman said it was given the girl 'to honour the chief'; another that it was to teach her not to dally by the river at night. An educated man said that the song meant that the husband is a member of the royal crocodile clan, i.e. a chief, since he provides everything for the home and is the protector. The rushes are the offences which a woman may commit by breaking the marriage vow on revealing the secrets of the home. The young woman must look out for the husband who may be waiting like a crocodile to seize her.

No. 44. The garden mound (mputa) (Fig. 7. See also p. 97). This figurine was balanced on the girl's head while the company sang:

Mwibala,	Through the garden,
Teti mupite muntu,	No man must pass,
Nga apita ni muka mwaume.	If it is the wife of the man who has passed.

Interpretation. Here again, we have multiple meanings and, to the European at least, great obscurity. The model is a representation of the round garden mounds which it is specifically the woman's duty to cultivate. One informant said glibly, 'No one

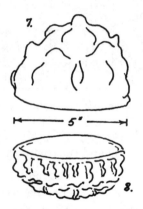

Fig. 7. The garden mound.
Fig. 8. The garden.
Both used in the second woodland ceremony.

must take a woman's garden.' But the *mputa* represents a cultivated and owned place, e.g. a chief's garden in which it is tabooed to have sex intercourse. 'The married woman is like a garden through which a man should not pass when he knows the girl is someone else's wife. If others respect his wife, he should do the same to theirs.'

No. 45. The gardens (Amabala) (Fig. 8. See also p. 96). This is one of the *mbusa* carried out into the bush for one of the ceremonies (p. 92). The women dance round it after a rite centring round the offering of the different seeds of the tribe to the elders in order of rank.

Interpretation. I have no song and no satisfactory interpretation. Women said the *mbusa* was shown to the girl to teach her to garden.

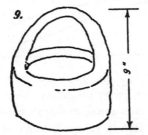

Fig. 9. The Clan. (The basket which is swung in a girl's hand, while the man's family is the crown worn on her head.)

No. 46. The clan (mukoa) (Fig. 9). This is a model of a basket with a handle. The girl swings it by one hand while she balances on her head a pot shaped like a helmet, as shown in Fig. 5. The company sing:

Cupo asenda pa mutwe;	She carries her marriage on her head;
Uaseshya mukoa.	Her clan is dangling in her hand.

Interpretation. There seemed to be no difficulty about this *mbusa.* Informants told me at once that since the girl was married she had to put her in-laws in a place of honour above the members of her clan, i.e. on her head; the clan relatives must be swung below in the girl's hand.

No. 47. The hoe (lukasu) (Fig. 10). The girls pretend to be hoeing a garden. They sing:

Nimpa kalonde.	Give me my little hoe (archaic).
Ndea ku mabala.	I go to the gardens.
Kabala kalala.	The little gardens of the ground-nuts.

or

Nimpa kalonde.	Give me my little hoe,
Nsebaule kongwe.	So that I can make ready the hymen.
Mulume wamona.	You have seen your husband.

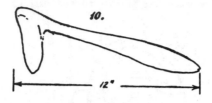

Fig. 10. *The Hoe.*

Interpretation. Here is a good example of different layers of meaning. First the initiate is to work hard at hoeing. Another rational explanation was that the girl was to be taught how to hoe when pregnant without hurting herself. Then a woman said, with a gesture and a wink, the girl would be hoed up by her husband as the ground is. The second of the two rhymes has a frankly sexual meaning—the girl wants to be given to her husband.

No. 11. *The egret (nkoba) (the white bird associated with the magic of whitening or cleansing).*

No. 48. *The egret (nkoba)* (Fig. 11). The company sings:

We kakoba! We koni!	You little egret! You bird!
Shimwalaba mpemba.	Do not forget the whitewash.

or

Nkoba yandi yapwa,	My digging stick is finished;
Yalobela mwibala.	It is lost in the garden.

Songs Sung During the Ceremony

Interpretation. There is a play on words here. *Nkoba* is the white bird to which the girl is likened during the ceremony of the whitening magic. The *nkoba* is also a small digging stick used as a rake.

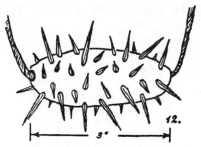

Fig. 12. The porcupine (worn round the girl's neck to prick her if she did wrong before her initiation).

No. 49. The porcupine (chinungi) (Fig. 12). This is a small rod of clay stuck with spines and threaded with string. It is put round the neck of the girl like a necklace and she has to swing it to and fro so that the spines prick her on the breast and neck. They sing.

Cinungi posa matamba,	Porcupine throw the waves (spines)
Kulya twalilwa na mubemba.	We are benighted by the lake.

Interpretation. It was supposed that the girl who had deceived her bridegroom was hurt by the spines, and that this showed her what her husband would do to her when she was married. Nkonde comments: 'Wrongs are never hidden. They come to light one day.'

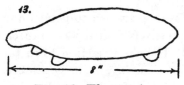

Fig. 13. The tortoise.

No. 50. The tortoise (fulwe) (Fig. 13). The women jog up and down and mime a tortoise putting its head in and out. They sing:

Fulwe pa fyakwe,	The tortoise when it is at home,
Aingishya mukoshi;	Puts in its head;
Mu cifwambaka.	Into its shell.

207

Appendix B

Interpretation. You know the kind of woman who is reticent about food in her own house for fear she may have to distribute it; that is to say she puts her head under her shell. But when she is in other people's houses she puts out her head and looks into this pot and that so that she may get offered food. The girl must be hospitable.

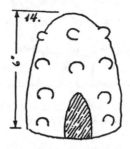

Fig. 14. *The house (used with a miniature door of reeds which pulls in and out).*

No. 51. *The house (ŋanda)* (Fig. 14). This is an ingenious model. It has a loose door made of reeds which pulls in and out on a string while the accompanying song is sung:

Mwana alelila,	The child is crying,
Nshisalile uko alele,	I did not see where it lay.
Tandabula.	The door is swinging.

Interpretation. This song seemed to point an important moral. Women told me impressively that it was to teach the girl how to look after her baby. The child referred to in the song is crying because the door is left swinging, i.e. it is open because the mother has gone to a beer-drink and left her baby alone. (*Kutandabula* also means to chatter.)

No. 52. *The mortar (kabende)* (Fig. 15). The initiate is given a pestle and made to imitate the pounding of grain and to sing:

Kabende kandi,	My little mortar,
Kamekelo.	I will show it off.

208

Fig. 15. *The mortar.*

Interpretation. The woman is to pound grain quickly for her husband and not slowly as she did when she was a girl.

No. 53. *The nursing mother (Coshi wa ŋoma)* (Fig. 16). The mother is pregnant and is shown carrying four babies at the same time, one at her breast and three at her back. This model was thought exceedingly funny by the Cisonde women. They sang:

Mayo alembepa!	My mother deceived me!
Coshi wa ŋoma!	Coshi ua yoma!
Kanshi uambepafye;	So you just deceived me;
Naimita umusuku.	I have become pregnant again.

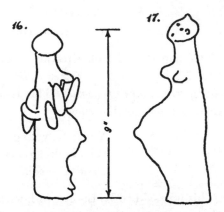

Fig. 16. *The nursing mother (Coshi wa ŋoma).*
Fig. 17. *The pregnant woman.*

Interpretation. Coshi wa ŋoma was a midwife of legendary fame and is merely addressed in this song. The girl complains because her mother told her to wean her first child too soon so that it died;

209

or alternatively told her that she would take the first child if her daughter had a second one. But she was tricking her and now the girl has two babies to look after. The moral stressed is the duty of refusing intercourse with the husband before the baby is weaned, i.e. at the second or third year. This is the common Bemba practice.

No. 54. The pregnant woman (mwanakashi) (Fig. 17). The song is:

Kasuba kawa;	The sun has set;
Kasuba kaeli aya.	The sun has already gone.
Nshiku shyafula;	The days are fulfilled;
Kanshindama musuku ila.	Let me go and honour the *musuku* tree.

Interpretation. The *musuku* tree bears fruit and stands for fertility. The pregnant woman is also wrapped in its bark. Nangoshye explained the song by saying, 'the days are over; my time has come to give birth.'

No. 55. The man who is a fool. This is a model of a low helmet-shaped pot which the candidate puts on her head singing:

Mwe mwaume,	You man,
Shiwawela-e!	You are a fool!
Ntunta mutima.	You have no courage.

Interpretation. The man should look after his wife but he does not do so.

No. 56. The young man walking smartly. This is a figure of a jaunty young man all dressed up. The song is:

We kalumendo!	You little young man!
Shicenda mukola!	Who walks so smartly!
Baisa.	They have come.

Interpretation. This was said to be the son-in-law who has gone to get hoes for the marriage; or alternatively, in modern idiom, who has gone to work for the Europeans. One informant said that the song implied that the dressed-up man idling about the village does not always get the bride he wants; another that the girl has insisted on marrying the smart young man but he has gone away and left her.

No. 57. The man without arms. Cilume ca ciboa (Fig. 18). This is the man with an enormous male organ but no arms. He lazes about the house finding fault with his wife, but he does not do any work or sit with his fellows making nets or baskets in the men's shelter. The husband who 'just sits' seems to be comparable to the *cipuba*, the girl who takes no pride in her domestic duties and knows nothing (p. 88).

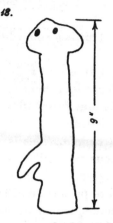

*No.*18. *The lazy man who has no arms to work.*

No. 58. The lion (mundu) (See pp. 106, 129). This is the largest and most elaborate of the *mbusa*. One of the projections at the side is hollow so that a roaring noise is made by blowing down it. It is used on the last day of the ceremony to imitate the roaring of the lion which is likened to the husband.

No. 59. The pipe (pipee). The women pretend to smoke like Europeans do.

The girl is told she is not to smoke all day and to neglect her duties.

No. 60. Sonsa nkalamo. This is a model like a tree with clay projections on it. The song tells the woman to run in answer to a summons or to be obedient to her husband, according to men informants. Women, on the other hand, say that it tells the husband to honour the wife!

No. 61. The hearthstones (amafwasa). The girl stands on this initiation hearthstone and pretends to balance a pot on it.

Some informants said the girl was to be taught cooking; and others that the hearthstones represented the settled married life.

No. 62. The pot (mutondo). The girl is to carry water and look after the house.

No. 63. The cardinal bird (kabangula). This is a small white bird with red spots on it. It represents the *nacimbusa*, since it has a red crest like the plumes of the *nacimbusa* in old days.

No. 64. The hyena (cimbwi). The girl is told not to steal like the hyena.

No. 65. Cibone Musuba. This is a conical-shaped model covered with small projections.

It is said to represent a tree and it is also the name of the beautiful head-wife of a legendary chief. The husband is to look upon his wife as the most beautiful of all women just as the chief preferred his head-wife to all others.

No. 66. The centipede (congolo). This is an animal about six inches long like an enormous caterpillar, which appears with the rains. The *congolo* has many legs.

The song warns the girl to perform purification after twins; or, according to another account, she is warned not to have intercourse too frequently or she will have twins—multiple births like the many legs of the caterpillar.

Regional Bibliography

(In Appendix A references are made by number to this bibliography)

1. Baumann, H. 'Die Mannbarkeitsfeiern bei den Tsokwe und ihren Nachbarn.' (*Baessler-Archiv*, Vol. XV, 1932)
2. Brelsford, V. 'Some reflections on Bemba Geometric Art.' (*Bantu Studies*, Vol. XI, 1937)
3. Brelsford, V. 'History and Customs of the Basala.' (*J.R.A.I.*, Vol. LXV, 1935)
4. Buggenhout, H. van and Wens, A. 'Coutumes d'initiation: le Kisungu.' (*Bull. Jur. Indig.*, Vol. I, 1933)
5. Chisholm, J. A. 'Manners and Customs of the Winamwanga and Wiwa Tribes.' (*J.A.S.*, Vol. IX, 1910)
6. Colson, E. 'The Plateau Tonga of Northern Rhodesia.' (Colson and Gluckman (eds.) *Seven Tribes of British Central Africa*, 1951)
7. Colson, E. 'Residence and Village Stability among the Plateau Tonga.' (*Human Problems in British Central Africa*, Vol. XII, 1951)
8. Coxhead, J. C. C. 'The Native Tribes of North-eastern Rhodesia, their Laws and Customs.' (*R.A.I. Occasional paper, No.* 5, 1914)
9. Cullen Young, T. *Notes on the Customs and Folklore of the Tumbuka-Kamanga peoples*, 1931
10. Cullen Young, T. 'Tribal Intermixture in Nyasaland.' (*J.R.A.I.*, Vol. LXIII, 1933)
11. Cullen Young, T. 'Habits and Customs of the olden days among the Tumbuka-Kamanga peoples.' (*Bantu Studies*, Vol. X, 1936)
12. Cullen Young, T. and Hastings Banda (Eds.). *Our African Way of Life* by John Kambalame, E. P. Chidzalo and J. W. M. Chadangalara, 1946.

13. De Cleene, N. 'La Famille dans L'Organisation social des Mayombe.' (*Africa*, Vol. X, 1937)
14. A. Delhaize. 'Ethnographie Congolaise chez les Wabemba.' (*Bull. Soc. R. B. Geogr*, Vol. XXXII, 1908)
15. Dellille, A. 'Besnijdenis bij de Alunda's en Aluena's in de Streek ten Zuiden van Belgisch Kongo.' (*Anthropos*, Vol. XXV, 1930)
16. Devers, R. 'La rite d'initiation "*Kizungu*" dans le Sud de la Lulua.' (*Bull. Jur. Indig*, Vol. II, 1934)
17. Devers, R. 'Fiançailles et Mariage chez les Ndembo.' (*Bull. Jur. Indig*, Vol. I, 1933)
18. Doke, C. M. *The Lambas of Northern Rhodesia*. (1931)
19. Drourega, M. 'Initiation of a girl of the Asenga tribe.' (*Anthropos*, Vol. XXII, 1927)
20. Fraser, D. *Winning a Primitive People*. (1914)
21. Garbutt, H. W. 'Native Customs in Nyasa and the Yao.' (*Man*, Vol. XII, 1912)
22. Gluckman, M. 'The role of the sexes in the Wiko circumcision ceremonies.' (In *Social Structure: Essays presented to A. R. Radcliffe-Brown*, ed. M. Fortes, 1949)
23. Gluckman, M. and Colson, E. (Eds.). *Seven Tribes of British Central Africa*. (1951)
24. Gouldsbury. C. and Sheane, H. *The Great Plateau of Northern Rhodesia*. (1911)
25. Hambly, W. D. *The Ovimbundu of Angola*. (Field Museum of Natural History, Publications 329. Anthropological Series, Vol. XXI, 1934)
26. Hambly, W. D. 'Tribal initiation of boys in Angola.' (*American Anthropologist*, Vol. XXXVII, 1935)
27. Harries, Lyndon. *The initiation rites of the Mkonde tribe*. (Rhodes-Livingstone Institute, Communication No. 3, 1944)
28. Heckel, B. 'The Yao Tribe, their Culture and Education.' (University of London Institute of Education, *Studies and Reports*. No. IV, 1935)
29. Hodgson, A. G. O. 'Notes on the Achewa and Angoni of Dowa District, Nyasaland.' (*J.R.A.I.*, Vol. LXIII, 1933)
30. Holdredge, C. P. and Young, D. K. 'Circumcision rites among the Ba-Jok.' (*American Anthropologist*, Vol. XXIX, 1927)

Regional Bibliography

31. Horn, H. 'A Holiday in N.W. Rhodesia.' (*Zambezi Mission Record*, VI, No. 85, 1919)
32. Jaspan, M. A. *The Ila-Tonga Peoples of North-Western Rhodesia.* (International African Institute Ethnographic Survey, West Central Africa Part IV, 1953)
33. Jaspert, F. und W. *Die Volkstämme Mittel-Angolas.* (1930)
34. Johnson, W. P. *Nyasa, the Great Water.* (1922)
35. Johnston, H. H. *British Central Africa.* (1897)
36. Labreque, E. 'Le Mariage chez les Babemba.' (*Africa*, Vol. IV, 1931)
37. Lambo, L. 'Étude sur les Balala.' (*Bull. Jur. Indig*, Nos. 8–10, 1946)
38. Mair, Lucy. 'A Yao Girl's Initiation.' (*Man*, Vol. LI, 1951)
39. Marchal, R. 'La famille chez les Bashila.' (*Bull. Jur. Indig*, Vol. 5, 1935)
40. McCulloch, Merran. *The Southern Lunda and Related Peoples.* (International African Institute Ethnographic Survey, West Central Africa Part I, 1951)
41. McCulloch, Merran. *The Ovimbundu of Angola.* (International African Institute Ethnographic Survey, *West Central Africa Part II*, 1952)
42. Melland, F. H. *In Witch-bound Africa.* (1923)
43. Milheiros, M. 'Lundas e Luenas: Posto de Gaianda.' (*Mensario Administrativo* 15 and 16, 1948)
44. Read, Margaret. 'Moral Code of the Ngoni and their former Military State.' (*Africa*, Vol. XI, 1938)
45. Richards, A. I. 'Mother-Right among the Central Bantu.' (In *Essays Presented to C. G. Seligman*, 1934)
46. Richards, A. I. 'Preliminary Notes on the Babemba of North-Eastern Rhodesia.' (*Bantu Studies*, Vol. IX, 1935)
47. Richards, A. I. 'Reciprocal Clan Relationships among the Bemba of North-Eastern Rhodesia.' (*Man*, Vol. XXXVII, 1937)
48. Richards, A. I. *Land, Labour and Diet in Northern Rhodesia.* (1939)
49. Richards, A. I. 'The Political System of the Bemba of North-Eastern Rhodesia.' (in *African Political Systems* ed. Fortes and Evans-Pritchard, 1940)

50. Richards, A. I. *Bemba Marriage and Present Economic Conditions.* (Rhodes-Livingstone Institute Paper No. 4, 1940)
51. Richards, A. I. 'Some Types of Family Structure among the Central Bantu.' (in *African Systems of Kinship and Marriage*, ed. Radcliffe-Brown and Forde, 1950)
52. Sanderson, M. 'Ceremonial purification of the Yao.' (*Man*, Vol. XXII, 1922)
53. Slaski, J. (with Whiteley, W.). Peoples of the Luapula valley (in *Bemba and related peoples of Northern Rhodesia*, International African Institute Ethnographic Survey, East Central Africa Part II, 1951)
54. Smith, E. W. and Dale, A. *The Ila-Speaking Peoples of Northern Rhodesia* (1920)
55. Stannus, H. S. 'Notes on Some Tribes of British Central Africa.' (*J.R.A.I.*, Vol. XL, 1910)
56. Stannus, H. S. 'The Wa-Yao of Nyasaland.' (*Harvard African Studies* No. III, 1922)
57. Stannus, H. S. and Davey, J. B. 'Initiation ceremonies for boys among the Yao of Nyasaland.' (*J. R.A.I.*, Vol. XLIII, 1913)
58. Tew, Mary. *Peoples of the Lake Nyasa Region.* (International African Institute Ethnographic Survey, East Central Africa Part I, 1950)
59. Verbeke, A. 'Le mariage chez les Tribus d'origine Babemba.' (*Bull. Jur. Indig*, Vol. I, 1933)
60. Weeks, J. H. 'Notes on the Bangala of the Upper Congo River.' (*J.R.A.I.*, Vol. XXXIX, 1909)
61. Werner, A. *The Native Races of the British Empire—The Natives of Central Africa*, (1906)
62. White, C. M. N. Unpublished MSS., 1947
63. Winterbottom, J. M. Unpublished communication from Rhodes-Livingstone Institute.
64. Whiteley, W. and Slaski, J. *Bemba and related peoples of Northern Rhodesia*, with a contribution on the Ambo by B. Stefaniszyn, S. J. (International African Institute Ethnographic Survey, East Central Africa Part II, 1951)
65. Wilson, G. H. 'Introduction to Nyakusa Society.' (*Bantu Studies*, Vol. X, 1936)

Index

Index

Index

Health (cont'd)
  Infant mortality, 28, 34, 142, 148, 159
  Magic of, 29
  Malaria, 28
  Pulmonary complaints, 28, 34
  Rites for, 143, 151
Henga, 180
Hunting, 26, 73–4, 106–7, 119, 142–3
Husband
  in Chisungu, 43–4, 54, 58, 106–7, 144–5
  Duties of, 75, 83, 102–4, 140, 144–5
  Honoured as procreator, 102, 158, 159
  Integration into family of, 40–2, 133, 144, 158
  Mock-bridegrooms; *see* Chisungu, Ceremony witnessed
  Rights of, 102, 103, 157–8
  Symbols of, 78, 81, 95, 102, 103, 189–90, 194–5, 210, 211
  Virility of, 46, 100, 145, 156, 158, 159, 164
  See also Mimes, Respect

Ila, 17, 171, 175–6
Initiation; *see* Chisungu, Puberty

Kamba, 54
Kaonde, 17, 40, 170, 172, 173, 175, 184
Kawonde, 175, 185
Kinship Relations
  Brother-sister, 20, 38, 40, 49, 58, 82–3, 129, 143, 152
  Father-daughter, 41, 49, 56
  Father-mother's brother, 42, 142, 152, 154
  Father's sister, 29, 34, 40, 44, 46, 56, 58, 62, 77–8, 85–6, 125, 131, 142–5, 150, 151, 167
  Grandmother, 49, 98, 108, 132
  Mother's brother, 38, 39–42, 44, 46, 81–2, 152, 155, 159
  Sister-sister, 39, 41, 42, 49
  Son-father, 20
  Son-in-law, 40, 41–2, 43–7, 133, 140, 143, 150, 159
  See also Father, Husband, Mother, Wife
Kluckhohn, C., 114
Krige, J. D. and E. T., 128, 129, 134, 135
Kuper, H., 113

Lala, 40, 170–3, 175, 177
Lamba, 17, 40, 170, 172–3, 175, 177, 183, 185
Language, 14, 55, 81, 127, 130
Leach, E. R., 118

Lion
  Cursing by, 29
  -killer's dance, 66, 96–7
  See also Chisungu, Symbols
Little, K., 134
Lomwa, 177
Lovale, 172
Lovedu, 52, 53, 60, 128, 129
Lozi, 175
Luba, 171, 172, 175
Luchazi, 171, 172
Luena, 171, 172
Lunda, 170–3, 175, 178, 185–6
Lungu, 171, 174–5, 184–5

Macminn, R., 137
Magic
  Activating agencies, 28–30
  of Attraction, 83–4, 133, 145
  Beauty, 19, 90, 109, 124, 152
  Distinguished from religion, 112, 139
  Economic, 119, 142–3, 151
  General functions of, 151
  Granary, 143
  Growth, 98, 121–5, 152
  Hospitality, 145
  Love, 19, 161
  Nubility, 121–5
  Ordeal, 20, 37, 66, 70–4, 97–8, 122–4, 130, 136, 138, 145, 158, 162
  Protective, 27, 52, 53, 124, 139, 141, 142–5, 148
  See also Blood, Chisungu, Ceremony witnessed, Fertility, Fire, Mistress of Ceremonies, Sex, Supernatural Agencies
Makonde, 177, 178, 182–6
Makua, 177, 178, 182, 186
Malinowski, B., 112, 116, 119, 155, 164
Maori, 119
Maravi Group, 177, 178
Marriage
  Ceremony, 43–7, 52–3, 110, 145, 166
  Disruption of, 40–3, 49, 50, 83, 128, 147, 150, 156
  Father's power over, 49
  First intercourse in, 38, 45–6, 53, 54–5, 144–5, 154–5
  Head-wife's position, 32, 36, 40, 49, 103, 141, 145
  Legal emphasis on, 128, 165–6
  Modern changes in, 83, 147
  Mother's brother's power over, 40, 44
  Payments at, in cash or service, 40, 42, 43–4, 150, 156
  -pot, 31–2, 46, 78, 110, 143, 145, 146
  Preferential, 42, 106
  Remarriage, 34, 49
  Rites, 33, 43–7, 52–5, 110, 144, 166
  Rule of residence in, 40–3, 44, 46–7, 144, 150

Index

Index